THE GENESIS OF
THE BROTHERS KARAMAZOV

THE GENESIS OF
THE BROTHERS KARAMAZOV

THE AESTHETICS, IDEOLOGY, AND
PSYCHOLOGY OF TEXT MAKING

ROBERT L. BELKNAP

NORTHWESTERN UNIVERSITY PRESS
STUDIES OF THE HARRIMAN INSTITUTE
1990

Northwestern University Press
Evanston, Illinois 60201

Printed in the United States of America

Library of Congress Cataloging-in-Publication Data

Belknap, Robert L.
    The genesis of The Brothers Karamazov : the aesthetics, ideology, and
psychology of text making / Robert L. Belknap.
        p.   cm. — (Series in Russian literature and theory)   (Studies of the
Harriman Institute)
    Includes bibliographical references.
    ISBN 0-8101-0845-3. — ISBN 0-8101-0846-1 (pbk.)
    1. Dostoyevsky, Fyodor, 1821–1881. Brat 'ia Karamozovy.
I. Title   II. Series.   III. Series: Studies of the Harriman Institute.
PG3325.B73B38   1990
891.73'3—dc20   90-7227
                                                                                          CIP

CONTENTS

PREFACE

Being social animals, authors always write as part of a collective. I thank the entire community whose work is embedded in this book. My family, my colleagues, and my students at Columbia have given moral and intellectual support for years, and a number of editors and others have enabled me to try out versions of these chapters in their pages or at conferences or lectures. The *Ulbandus Review, Dostoevsky Studies,* William Todd's *Literature and Society in Nineteenth Century Russia,* and the *American Contributions* to the Fifth, Sixth, and Seventh International Congresses of Slavists all printed materials incorporated in this book, usually with changes suggested by colleagues from around the world. I am grateful to the earlier publishers for the chance to use their materials in this new version. The Harriman Institute at Columbia University has included this book in its series of studies. Founded as the Russian Institute in 1946, the W. Averell Harriman Institute for Advanced Study of the Soviet Union is the oldest research institution of its kind in the United States. The book series Studies of the Harriman Institute, begun in 1953, helps bring to a wider audience some of the work conducted under its auspices by professors, degree candidates, and visiting fellows. The faculty of the institute, without necessarily agreeing with the conclusions reached in these books, believes their publication will contribute to both scholarship and a greater understanding of the Soviet Union. A list of the studies appears at the back of this book.

The Harriman Institute and other Columbia programs have supported parts of my research, and the Kennan Institute gave me an invaluable chance to work at the Woodrow Wilson Center, using the Library of Congress and the other resources of Washington. The Rockefeller Foundation gave me a month at the Bellagio Center, the ideal place for final editing and rewriting. In addition, research for this book was supported in part by a grant from the International Research and Exchange Board (IREX), with funds provided by the National Endowment for the Humanities and the United States Information Agency. None of these organizations is responsible for the views expressed.

Ruth Melville did a wonderful editing job for the Northwestern University Press, and finally, Deborah Martinsen, Robin Miller, Saul Morson, the late Rose Raskin, and an anonymous reader for the Harriman Institute series read the text with generous care, entered into fruitful dialogue with it, suggested much of what is of value in it, and caught errors, obscurities, and infelicities. For those that remain, I can claim full authorial credit.

Robert L. Belknap
Columbia University
New York, 1989

CHAPTER
ONE

INTRODUCTORY

I
THIS BOOK STUDIES THE WAYS IN WHICH DOSTOEVSKY TRANSFORMED THE MATERIALS HE INCORPORATED INTO *THE BROTHERS KARAMAZOV.*

Several years ago, I wrote a book about the structure of *The Brothers Karamazov*, the way the parts of the novel were organized to form an effective whole. Now, like Plato's geometers, I have progressed from that study of fixed relationships to a study of the moving patterns and patterns of motion that recur as the text emerges; as the Romans expressed it, I have moved from the study of the *dispositio* to that of the *inventio*. By *inventio*, the Romans meant "discovery" more than "invention," and this book rests on the sense that major literature is rarely if ever invented out of nothing. Rather, its authors discover its elements in the existing writing and other materials they copy, imitate, quote, use, parody, or react to in other ways. In this sense, Dostoevsky's novels are not the work of one mysterious genius but his collaboration with hundreds of writers, some living, some long dead, some great, some deservedly forgotten, in a common enterprise of which their work and his are inseparable parts. Although all literature is participatory in this way, the results need not be uniform. Even if Dostoevsky had read exactly the same things as Boborykin, he would have processed these materials so differently that his works would remain distinctively Dostoevskian. This book attempts to describe the ways Dostoevsky processed the materials he incorporated in his novels.

Many of Dostoevsky's sources are lost forever, and much of his experience can only be guessed at on the basis of accounts in letters, newspapers, memoirs, or other documents whose own literary nature clouds our perception of what he did and saw. Two parts of his experience, however, can be reproduced quite well. These are his reading and his writing; I shall rely heavily on these bodies of experience, not because they exclude others, but because they are the most nearly knowable. With some authors, such reliance would produce not only a partial but a distorted picture; but Dostoevsky focused so much of his life upon the literary world that his reading and writing contain not only a substantial but also a representative sample of the experience he incorporated into a novel.

Two rich traditions of essentially positivist scholarship have made Dostoevsky accessible to this kind of study. The first has sought in his experience, including his reading, the stimuli and prototypes for many of the events, ideas, and characters in his writing. The second has worked out the creative history of his various works, the hard facts in his workbooks, letters, and other materials that show the way he went about writing the novels. Between these two ample bodies of established fact, the creative intellect, which has not been explored so fully, assimilated the sources and articulated the plans and drafts. Scholars have already proved that Dostoevsky often used minor literature, bad literature, journalism, and letters as sources for his novels. If I could completely describe the way he transmuted such dross into gold, I could theoretically assemble a few thousand pages of nineteenth-century materials; program a computer to make the proper selections, transformations, and arrays; and crank out a new Dostoevsky novel. In practice, my goals are even less modest. I want to describe the laws that govern the relationship between what goes into and what comes out of an eminently creative mind.

II
SOME SERIOUS READERS OBJECT TO SUCH STUDIES.

Two generations ago, much of our most rigorous literary scholarship followed the tradition of German positivist *Quellenforschung* or that of French *explication de texte*, whose sense of literary allusion and context emerged from classical philology. In recent years, our liveliest literary scholars in America have again been asserting that strong poets engage in "triumphant wrestling with the greatest of the dead,"[1] or that "semiosis-producing ungrammatical constants result from intertexuality."[2] In the first of these statements, Harold Bloom is certainly wrestling with his own critical inheritance; and in the second, Michael Riffaterre is alluding to many of the meanings explicit in his inherited tradition of philological intertextualities. In the generation between the outbursts of genetic scholarship, many of the finest literary minds ignored or repudiated the traditions that had earlier been so fertile.

In the twenties, as today, certain readers treated such studies as an intrusion into the sancta of the muses. Even Freud, who loved to excavate arcana, gave eloquent expression to the taboo I propose to violate: "Unfortunately, before the problem of the creative artist, analysis must strike its arms."[3] Freud uses his military metaphor here with the bluff regret of an old scientist who would have liked to challenge all nature, but his humble acceptance of limitation might just possibly be one of those disguises that Stanley Edgar Hyman thinks Freud learned from that older housebreaker Sherlock Holmes.[4] Certainly such handsome protestations of humility did not deflect Freud and many of his followers from the penetralia of the creative mind. Yet his disclaimer does reflect one crucial fact about most Freudian investigations of the creative intellect. They try to see through the layers of complexity to certain basic driving forces and generating patterns that are not numerous enough to distinguish an important artist from others in whom the same simplicities exist.

This commonsense argument against reductionism in studying important works confronts a more basic and more fashionable position today: there are no important works because importance, and even meaning, inhere in readers or in a critical consensus, and not in authors, or even in texts—except perhaps the texts that make this argument. This denial rests on the truism that we mortals necessarily evaluate or interpret within a psychological, social, and critical milieu and are biased by it. In responding to this obvious human condition by refusing to seek any quality or meaning within texts, such critics resemble the zealots in Lucretius who commit suicide upon realizing that they are not immortal. Rather than studying many readers of one text, this book will study one reader of very many texts, Fedor Dostoevsky. If one accepts distortion as a part of the human condition and not a new discovery, Dostoevsky's particular ways of distorting may offer probes into the working of a creative mind. Such a postnihilist approach has not yet become fashionable, but it may prove to be one of the critically energetic alternatives to solipsism or epistemological despair when those doctrines come to seem old-fashioned again.

I realize, of course, that I continually risk self-delusion. My efforts to give names to the transformations of Dostoevsky's sources will sometimes lead to the terminology developed by psychologists not so much for the creative process as for the work done in dreaming or remembering. In using such words as displacement, condensation, overdetermination, mechanism, or conservation law in these pages,

I must beware the fate of those whose similes take over their discussions of the creative process. Plato compares geometrical insight to a sudden recollection; in fact, he even suggests that it is a recollection.[5] A more self-conscious mathematician like Henri Poincaré compares it rather to the work of a second, unconscious self, while others compare it to a dream or visitation by an outside being, and some convert this analogy into their operative explanation. But all these metaphors and similes are old-fashioned ways of saying that much of the creative process takes place without the author's attention or intention, a point that many authors, including Dostoevsky, have made without metaphor.

Most authorities divide the creative process into three stages: preparation, inspiration, and elaboration—and have little objection to discussing the first and the last of these three. Authors and biographers have written a great deal about preparation. It may take the form of outside stimuli, like the adulation Tolstoi and Dickens thrived on, or the attacks Flaubert seemed to need, or the security Trollope needed, or the competition Balzac courted. It may take the form of training, whether in the family, like John Stuart Mill's; or in school, like Thomas Wolfe's; or in the journals, like Chekhov's; or in the theater, like Shakespeare's, or in any of the other places where artists shape themselves. It may take the form of rituals to woo the muses or prepare the mind, like Pushkin's working in the autumn, or Houseman's in the afternoon, or Schiller's keeping apples rotting in the drawer, Maupassant's taking ether, or others' gambling or buying a yacht to put themselves under an urgent deadline to produce a profitable book. In general, it is hard to conceive of a preparation so outlandish that it has not worked for some creative artist or other. I will discuss Dostoevsky's known preparations later.

At a certain point, according to the usual formulations, the preparation is complete, and the creative imagination or the muse takes over, often unexpectedly, often in sleep, often after a dark night of the soul when such inspiration seems to have departed forever. We know a good deal about the exhilaration and the sense of fulfillment that tend to accompany this moment, and we have often been told that the moment may be as fleeting as that epileptic instant in which Muhammad toured Paradise, but most scholarly and most autobiographical accounts abide by the taboo against analysis of what they acknowledge to be the center of the subject at hand.

The third stage is traditionally the hardest to define. Poets have long since abandoned Horace's precise prescription of a ten-year reworking for poems, and Mozart and Samuel Johnson could complete their elaboration, if any, before setting pen to paper. Pushkin described the way his heroine decided to get married without consulting him, and Tolstoi displayed surprise at his hero's death. Dostoevsky himself apologized to his editor about a delay in submitting the eighth book of *The Brothers Karamazov:* "All through the 8th book there suddenly appeared many altogether new characters, and at least in passing, each had to be sketched as fully as possible, and therefore this book turned out bigger than I had originally indicated." Such polished or postponed intervention of the muses casts doubt upon the nature of this last stage of creation. The Mozartean anecdotes would suggest a kind of inspiration that embodies editing, and the Dostoevskian ones would suggest a kind of editing that embodies inspiration, or at least discovery.

This book treats inspiration more as transformation than as generation out of nothing and seeks to describe the rules governing that creative transformation. The search for such rules is not new. Livingston Lowes's *Road to Xanadu* begins with an attack on the idea that Coleridge's exalted creative state was discontinuous with his years of study. Lowes tracks virtually every phrase in *Kubla Khan* to one or another passage in Coleridge's beautifully documented reading and speculates on the ways "hooked atoms" link together to form this extraordinary poem. Dostoevsky scholars have considered the creative process in ways I will discuss later, but all such studies face one ultimate objection, which Allen Tate expressed with the unanswerability of the subjective: "I have myself found it applicable to the work of poets I don't like."[6]

III

AN UNDERSTANDING OF NOVISIMILITUDE JUSTIFIES SOURCE STUDIES.

Tate was one of the major poets and major critics in the period when source studies were least popular, and his reaction deserves attention. It centers, I think, on the importance of originality. To explain how inspiration became sacrosanct, too holy for study, I should like to anatomize and perhaps mythologize the worship of originality, beginning with the kind of raw literary experience great works produce in good readers. At certain moments in literary history critics try to tell their readers about such impressions. In response to reading Tolstoi and Dostoevsky, George Steiner wrote:

> Great works of art pass through us like storm-winds, flinging open the doors of perception, pressing upon the architecture of our beliefs with their transforming powers. We seek to record their impact,

to put our shaken house in its new order through some primary instinct of communion. We seek to convey to others the quality and force of our experience. We would persuade them to lay themselves open to it.[7]

In the past few decades, this kind of impressionistic criticism, unlike impressionist painting, has lost its preeminence in the marketplace and much of its intellectual respectability, as Steiner acknowledged when he subtitled his book "an essay in the old criticism." Some call it the "gee whiz" school of literary criticism, partly because the proper impact of a major text finds expression in words that can be faked undetectably and that wear out embarrassingly fast in the history of criticism, to be replaced by others: great, powerful, impressive, rich, serious, cool, or awesome. At moments like the present, when this essentially autobiographical approach falls out of favor, those critics, good and bad, who cannot ignore affect seek disguises for their impressionism.

The three chief displacements of affect all contain claims about the origins of a text. These claims belong to the classical, the realistic, and the romantic aesthetics, but these three traditions are not so much episodes in intellectual history as immortal ways of looking at the created world. Dostoevsky made all three claims, and the critics in Homer were already using them. The classical critic calls a text divine in origin if it hits him hard, and the classical poet, seeking as poets so often do to put favorable words in critics' mouths, constructs the illusion of divine intervention in his own creative process. Thus Dostoevsky claims that Homer may have been sent to humanity by God, Lucretius called his master Epicurus a god,[8] and Hesiod claimed divine intervention in his own work. In writing his autobiographical critique, Hesiod may well have believed a dream about the muses to be a visitation, while Lucretius certainly did not believe a real god would visit earth. In all such cases, however, the ultimate evidence for divine inspiration is the impact on the reader, and the statement that a work is inspired displaces the statement "Gee whiz!" I know of no poet or critic who ever said, "Apollo inspired this work of art, but it must have been an off day."

The second displacement of affect has a literal meaning in metaphysics and is intimately connected with the realistic aesthetic. It can be summed up in two words: "How true!" Homer understood this displacement. When poetry had forced Odysseus, the coolest killer of his time, to weep and hide his tears, he expressed his emotion in a double piece of pseudogenetic criticism, saying "How divine!" like a classicist and "How true!" like a realist: "Demodokos, above all mortals beside I prize you. Surely the Muse, Zeus's daughter, or else Apollo has taught you, for all too right following the tale you sing the Achaians venture, all they did and had done to them, all the sufferings of these Achaians, as if you had been there yourself or heard it from one who has."[9] Odysseus was too tough-minded a critic to lay bare the emotional impact of Demodokos's recitation, but all his audience would have understood that "the muse taught you" really expressed affect. The second element of praise in this passage operates in exactly the same way, but a little more subtly. In praising Demodokos's recitation as true, Odysseus again meant that it had reduced him to tears. Living in a period when realism was inspiring great art but naive theory, Dostoevsky once claimed to Ivan Goncharov that a character was "caught from reality, like a photograph," although neither he nor Goncharov usually viewed the creative process so simply.[10] Working in a more sophisticated era, Aristotle understood that truth is no particular desideratum in literature; what matters is verisimilitude. Verisimilitude has had many meanings over the centuries, but the strongest among them may well be that quality in a text which moves readers and audiences to say "Gee whiz!" The simplest way to achieve verisimilitude is the blatant assertion of verity. Poets make the claim constantly in order to enlist in their favor the critical association between truth and literary power.

The third displacement of affect has its literal meaning in the history of literature and has ties with the romantic aesthetic. It can be summed up in the two words "How new!" Homer understood all three of these displacements. When Phemios, the other minstrel in the *Odyssey*, begs for his life, he claims divine inspiration, of course, but links it in a single sentence not with any claim to be masterful but with a claim of originality: "No one taught me: deep in my mind a god shaped all the various ways of life in song."[11] Phemios's position is straightforward: if a poet is an autodidact, the real source of his work is divine, much as a Homeric hero with no genealogy is often assumed to be the son of a god. The discovery of sources or teachers would deny the part some god had played and thus deny the strength and greatness of a hero or an artistic creation. In this context Freud's military metaphor is almost the equivalent of Diomedes's remark: "If you are some one of the immortals come down from the bright sky, know that I will not fight against any god of the heaven."[12]

This use of statements about literary history to displace statements about a reader's affect has as long a history as the other two displacements, but it has had no Aristotle to keep readers from taking it literally and believing the claims of authors who are trying

7

to put affect-loaded words in the mouths of readers and critics. At the beginning of the most magnificently derivative poem in English, Milton invokes his muse to help him sing things unattempted yet in prose or rhyme.[13] Horace sings *carmina non prius audita*,[14] and advertisers find that adding the word "new" to the label on a product increases sales by fourteen percent. In this tradition, a poet like Allen Tate rejects the discovery of antecedents as the detection of plagiarism or, at best, of inadequate imagination. Pascal recognized that many of his *Pensées* had been enunciated before and plainly felt uneasy if originality was to be identified with excellence:

> 65. Let men not say that I have said nothing new: the arrange-ment of the materials is new; when you play tennis, it is the same ball you're playing with, but one of you places it better.
> I would be as pleased to be told that I had used old words— as if the same thoughts did not form another body of discourse through a different arrangement just as well as the same words make other thoughts through their differing arrangements.
> 66. Diversely ordered words have diverse meanings, and di-versely ordered meanings have different effects.[15]

Pascal's first sentence reflects concern over accusations of unori-ginality but accepts the link between originality and excellence as a literary principle. To reconcile the reality of his highly derivative practice with this principle, he posits a special kind of originality that legitimizes his work. He is original in the disposition of his materials, not in the materials he has collected.

Horace, of course, could not have given Pascal's answer to charges of unoriginality, since stanzaic and metrical design were the most thoroughly derivative components of his unprecedented song; but even if he seriously linked originality with excellence, which I doubt, Horace never had to reconcile this inherited doctrine with insistent unmaskings by a band of positivist scholars. In recent times, one of the greatest such scholars also deferred to the belief in an inspired originality. To overcome the taboo against genetic scholarship which this idea implied, and to justify genetic studies of works he loved, Gustave Lanson argued as follows:

> The study of sources and influences, in which little-informed minds see only an occupation of pedants proud of sterile knowledge or working nastily to denigrate that genius which baffles them, this source study, carried out throughout the nineteenth century and more active, more methodical in the last thirty or forty years, is the best means that has been found to recognize, to define, to evaluate creative originality, its quality and its power. The materials of a work of genius are not genius. But by making an inventory

of these materials one succeeds in isolating by analysis an irreducible element in which will reside the novelty and the personality of the work. People felt that the *Meditations* contained something never heard before, but what? What had never been heard before? That is what the simple reader was unable to specify.[16]

This charming doctrine of residual originality as the locus of literary value is a heroic attempt to handle the continuing strength of a pattern of thought that has nothing to do with Lanson's rational approach. In today's journalism, as in Lanson's day, or in ancient Greece for that matter, critics love to use the words "first" or "never before" when they are demonstrably untrue in the literal sense. Sometimes they will reconcile the assertion of originality with the text by using a disclaimer that makes the literal claim meaningless: "This was the first time any author had seen this phenomenon in this way" means that no earlier author has written exactly this work. Lanson certainly understood that no scholar could be certain no sources remained undiscovered, and that literary value based on the absence of known sources would be tenuous indeed, but he could not shake himself free of millennia that linked originality with excellence.

Lanson, Pascal, and others could have justified their work by repudiating the cult of originality itself and turning to an equally honored tradition, one that valorizes texts in the name of their unoriginality. Lowes believed that *Kubla Khan* seemed richer and more remarkable when every line had one or more known sources than when it had been ascribed to the mysterious marvels of a befuddled brain.[17] Donald Stauffer made a similar remark in advocating study of the creative process: "Since the root meaning of poetry is 'to make,' perhaps such scrutiny of poetry-in-the-making insures most certainly that one is looking at the thing itself, and not at something off the track."[18] This sense that one can enhance a work of literature by disproving the originality of its materials suggests an expansion of the phrase "How true!" In this expansion fidelity to reality includes fidelity to any body of lore, whether it be holy, traditional, scholarly, or literary, so long as it represents some truth. This validating power of the source shapes Christ's use of the prophets and the prophets' use of the Torah, and probably at one time the Torah's use of its Mesopotamian sources. The less original a story was, the greater its claim upon men. "For verily I say unto you, till heaven and earth pass, one jot or one tittle shall in no wise pass from the law."[19] In this theory, whether a writer is thought of as embedded in a tradition, a psychology, or a society, his excellence lies in the accuracy with which he expresses what

9

already is. At this level the praise associated with "How true!" comes into potential conflict with that associated with "How new!"

This section modestly aspires to do for originality what Aristotle did for verity in literature. For two millennia now, sophisticated poesy has "claimed not to be true." For centuries, when readers picked up a book entitled "The true history of. . ." they knew from the very title that they were reading fiction, which if it was powerful would be characterized not by truth but by verisimilitude. In the same way, we must read our puffery about originality as claiming or honoring not real newness but the appearance of it. There is no more need for a text to be new than for it to be true. Just as verisimilitude names that which makes us say "How true!" so the long-needed word *novisimilitude* names that which makes us say "How new!" while both words really name that affect which makes us say "Gee whiz!"

IV

DOSTOEVSKY DEVELOPED THINKING ABOUT INSPIRATION TO RECONCILE ORIGINALITY WITH TRUTHFULNESS.

Dostoevsky understood but sometimes ignored the potential conflict between originality and truth as literary ideals. When writing to one of the great antiromantic writers of his time, he might claim to be acting like a camera, but one of his more romantic admirers quotes this conversation about inspiration:

> "Poetic labor, no matter how long it lasts, does not depend upon the will: it is moved by an unseen force. . . ."
>
> "People say that creation must reflect life, and so forth. That is all nonsense: the writer. . .creates a life himself, and such a one in its full sweep as never was before. . . ."[20]

This sense that creative inspiration leads to something grandly new might place him on the side of those romantics whose highest praise is "How original!" rather than of those realists who say "How true!"

For all his love of paradox, Dostoevsky did not invent this coupling of the demand for newness with the claim of trueness. Donald Fanger has called him one of a group of romantic realists,[21] and the tensions among his aesthetic doctrines reflect the shrewdness of this term. In his most lyrical treatment of the creative process, a letter to Apollon Maikov, Dostoevsky seems to be hovering between a superhuman and a subhuman center for the creative process:

I think a *poema* [In Dostoevsky's personal vocabulary this word meant any large and inspired piece of prose or verse.[22]] emerges like an autochthonous precious stone, a diamond, in the heart of the poet, altogether complete in all its essence, and right there is the first job of the poet *as a builder and creator*, the first part of his creation. If you like, then it is even not he that is the creator, but life, the mighty essence of life, a living and existing god which gathers its powers from the diversity of the creation into certain *places*, and most often of all in a great heart and a strong poet, so that even if the poet himself is not the creator...still, his heart at least is that very lode which gives birth to diamonds and without which they are never found. Afterward, of course, comes the *second* job of the poet, no longer so profound and mysterious, but simply as an artist: this is to work it up and arrange it.[23]

Dostoevsky wrote no isolated theoretical works, and the opinions in his letters, fiction, and journalism always contain dialogic adjustments to his reader, his literary persona, or his journalistic opponent. Scholars have to resist the temptation to treat letters, memoirs, or manifestos as less literary than works that bear the label of fiction. Dostoevsky's polemics especially demand great caution; his standard technique in debate was to concede far more than his opponent expected and then exact one damning admission from his opponent in return. Still, his position does emerge to some extent when he expresses virtually the same opinions in this letter to Maikov and in a polemic with N. K. Dobroliubov, who stood at the opposite pole from Maikov in his ideology and in Dostoevsky's affections:

Creation, the basis of all art, resides in a human being, as the revelation of a part of his organism, but it resides inseparable from the person. Consequently, art can have no different strivings than those to which the whole man strives. . . . It will always live with a man as his real life; it can do no more. Consequently it will always remain faithful to reality.

Of course, in his life, a person can depart from normal reality, from the laws of nature; his art will depart after him. But that is what proves its close, unbreakable tie with the man, its permanent fidelity to the man and his interests. . . . And since its interest and its goal are one with the goals of the person whom it serves, and with whom it is inseparably joined, the more freely it grows, the greater the service it will do for mankind.[24]

In this passage, as in the Maikov letter, Dostoevsky seems to be asserting an indissoluble link between the writer and his world and, at the same time, the impossibility of ever describing or prescribing that link. He is not claiming, with Tate, that genetic study

11

is distasteful, but he is expressing some sympathy with the old doctrine that it is impossible—expressed best, perhaps, by C. G. Jung, who believed that any reaction to stimulus may be causally explained, but the creative act, the absolute antithesis of mere reaction, will forever elude human understanding. Dostoevsky believed that this uncomprehended and unprescribed process would be faithful not only to the world that anybody might see better at firsthand, but to the world as it actually was, a truth that was not accessible without his special insights. This vatic doctrine enabled Dostoevsky to reconcile the claim of originality with the demand for realism. He could say that he invented nothing, but that he perceived things others did not. This claim implies a closer contact with reality than others had, and Dostoevsky was very proud that he could document the source of many items in his works. He would sometimes confirm his success by quoting people who had found his works "true," though I have suggested that this word may in fact express the integrity of the impact of the novel and not any correspondence with any world.

Dostoevsky made another partly verifiable boast about his realism. He claimed to present truths that were evident to others only later; that is, he claimed to prophesy. His opponents attacked both *Crime and Punishment* and *The Possessed* as vicious and libelous impossibilities, using the whole rhetorical force of the assertion of untruth to produce animus. Responding to many such attacks, Dostoevsky showed a certain morbid glee in pointing to crimes that closely matched those he described but that occurred between the writing and the publication of his novels, so that it was impossible for him to have either copied or caused the crime:

> I don't know whether I carried it out well, but I know that the character of my hero is real in the highest degree. (In *The Possessed*, there were many characters they attacked me for as fantastic, but later, believe me, they all were justified by reality, so they must have been imagined correctly. K. P. Pobedonostsev, for example, reported to me two or three events among the imprisoned anarchists which were strikingly similar to those I depicted in *The Possessed*.) All my hero says in the text I sent you is based on reality. All the stories about children occurred, were printed in the newspapers, and I can show where; nothing was invented by me.[25]

He carried this faith in his insight or prophetic power over into everyday life. His wife mentions a servant whose son had not been heard from for two years and who wished to have a funeral mass sung for him in the superstitious hope of supernaturally summoning him. Dostoevsky urged her to avoid this sacrilege because her son would appear in two weeks anyway. He did.[26] On another occasion, Dostoevsky warned his wife to watch their son carefully because he had dreamed that the boy suffered a bad fall. Some time later his son fell in an epileptic fit and died. There is something Darwinian in such accounts of fulfilled prophecies: unfulfilled ones tend to be forgotten. We do have, moreover, the statistical outcome of Dostoevsky's longest series of pure predictions, a series in which even flawless human intuition would have foreseen little: as a gambler, Dostoevsky confined himself to a game that depends entirely upon prediction, unlike bridge, where human communication matters, or twenty-one, at which even omniscience would not ensure success if one always received bad cards. At roulette, Dostoevsky's faith in his predictive capacity conflicted notoriously with his performance.

On many different occasions Dostoevsky's remarks show that he reconciled his claims to originality with those to truth by invoking claims to powers in which he genuinely believed. These powers came not from the muses, as Hesiod's did, but from a closeness of observation and contact with the world not given to ordinary mortals. The greater his fidelity to his sources, the greater his likelihood of seeing through them to that truth which was original because no one else could see it. At the same time, long after he had discovered the diamond, the essence of a novel, Dostoevsky would struggle with the plans for it, shifting characters and approaches, as his notebooks show.

Dostoevsky's own descriptions of his creative process were so close to the standard formulations of his time that it is hard to separate the introspective from the conventional. He probably could not distinguish between the two himself, for he naturally interpreted the existing understanding according to his own experience, and projected the categories he inherited upon his own experience. He may even have adjusted his practice to conform to the wisdom of his time. It is as important, therefore, to study what Dostoevsky did as to study what he said he did, though each subject throws light on the other and deserves study in itself.

Chapter Two

DOSTOEVSKY READ ENORMOUSLY IN BOOKS AND PERIODICALS OLD AND NEW, RUSSIAN AND EUROPEAN, GOOD AND BAD, LITERARY AND NONLITERARY.

I
FOR MANY YEARS SCHOLARS DID NOT REALIZE THAT DOSTOEVSKY READ BROADLY, ENTHUSIASTICALLY, AND PURPOSEFULLY.

In 1934 Compton Mackenzie described the impact of Dostoevsky upon his generation: "To the critic who pointed out that there was no evidence of such influence in our published work, I would reply that the evidence will be found in an anxiety to tell the truth."[1] I have already suggested that this ascription of truth to Dostoevsky might best be read as a praise of literary power by an author too sophisticated to say "Gee whiz!" and not sophisticated enough to say "What skill!" Mackenzie also implies that Dostoevsky is not a full member of the community of letters but direct and unprocessed, without recourse to the lore and the techniques worked out by centuries of writers. A legion of commentators have described Dostoevsky in this way. Perhaps the greatest and best known is Henry James, who wrote to Hugh Walpole,

When you ask me if I don't feel Dostoieffsky's "mad jumble, that flings things down in a heap," nearer truth and beauty than . . . picking and composing . . . I reply with emphasis that I feel nothing of the sort, and that the older I grow and the more I *go* the more sacred to me do the picking and composing become. . . . Form alone *takes*, and holds and preserves, substance—saves it from the welter of helpless verbiage that we swim in as in a sea of tasteless tepid pudding. . . . Tolstoi and D. are fluid puddings, though not tasteless, because the amount of their own minds and souls in solution in the broth gives it savour and flavour, thanks to the strong, rank quality of their genius and their experience.[2]

James's sense of Dostoevsky's art or lack of it comes in part from Eugène-Melchior de Vogüé, the diplomat, traveler, and observer whose *Roman russe* more than any other study introduced Russian literature to France. In 1886 de Vogüé had contrasted Dostoevsky with James's old dinner companion, the "Westerner" Turgenev, and called Dostoevsky a "Scythian, a true Scythian, who will revolutionize all our habitual intellectual attitudes."[3] Admitting that Dostoevsky had read Balzac, Eugène Sue, and George Sand, and that they seemed to have great dominion over his imagination, de Vogüé felt that Dostoevsky lacked control of his characters; they "rushed on, subject to the disordered impulses of their nerves, no brakes and no regulating reason; you could call them unfettered wills, elementary forces."[4] His central view emerges when he calls Dostoevsky

a phenomenon from another world, a monster incomplete and mighty, unique in his originality and intensity. The shiver you feel in approaching certain of his characters makes you ask whether you are in the presence of genius; but you remember quickly that genius does not exist in literature without two higher gifts, measure and universality; measure is the art of mastering one's thoughts, choosing among them, condensing all their brightness into several flashes. Universality is the art of seeing life in its entirety, representing it in all its harmonious manifestations.[5]

In later sections of this chapter, I will show that de Vogüé was simply wrong on the issues of condensation and alien cultural origins, but his view has flourished with a tenacity that has been ascribed to a desperate need in French literary circles to find—or failing that, to fabricate—an alien excellence to counterbalance the dominion of Zola's and Maupassant's naturalism, which was beyond the reach of most direct attacks in the 1880s.[6]

II
Substantial, but Incomplete, Information Survives about Dostoevsky's Reading.

In Russia, serious scholars before the First World War began to recognize Dostoevsky as a highly professional writer who had read broadly in the European tradition. In France, Germany, and Czechoslovakia, such scholarship flourished between the wars, and in England and America after the Second World War. Leonid Grossman wrote the first important articles to see Dostoevsky in his literary context and to stress the purposefulness with which he read, using both classics and current successes as reservoirs of literary technique. Grossman's work before and just after the Revolution constituted a program for the next generations to pursue.

Much of that work has been done by now, despite the long interruptions under Stalin and Hitler. We now know that Dostoevsky was an avid reader all his life, and that he was a lectatory genius, *genial'nyi chitatel'*, as A. L. Bem phrased it.[7] The full dimensions of Dostoevsky's reading deserve a full-scale study, and the work of Grossman, Bem, A. S. Dolinin, V. S. Nechaeva, V. L. Komarovich, Georgii Chulkov, V. V. Vinogradov, Iurii Tynianov, M. P. Alekseev, B. G. Reizov, L. M. Rozenblium, G. M. Fridlender, Vladimir Tunimanov, V. E. Vetlovskaia, S. V. Belov, Dmitrii Cyzewskij, Alfred Rammelmeyer, Jacques Catteau, Malcolm Jones, Charles Passage, Victor Terras, Olga Lyngstad, Donald Fanger, Nathalie Babel Brown, and a host of others has now made that enormous undertaking possible. I shall use the next few sections to set out a frame of reference for the detailed discussions that will come later, but will also try to give a sense of what manner of man Dostoevsky was when he had a text in his hand, and perhaps to provide some basic information for scholars whose access to the Russian texts does not match their curiosity about this richly cultivated field.

The data on Dostoevsky's reading are substantial but by no means exhaustive. At the military engineering academy where he was educated, he studied English, French, and German, and "the very first book" he claimed to need in his first letter to his brother after prison camp was a German lexicon.[8] His more expansive and youthful letters discuss reading E. T. A. Hoffmann or Shakespeare in the original, but most evidence suggests that he preferred to read German and English literature in French or Russian translations. His widow made a list of over seven hundred books he owned at the time of his death,[9] and the police cataloged the library of the Petrashevskii circle at the time of his arrest for membership in it.[10] His own writings mention two to three hundred authors, and memoirs and articles about him mention many more. But Dostoevsky's reading and constant rereading range far beyond the list of works that can be directly connected with him. Sometimes he made lists of books he intended to read or had read. In 1874 or 1875, for example, he made the following list:

NB. Books in the Ems library to read if there's time.

G. Sand. *Césarine Dietrich. Journal d'un voyageur pendant la guerre.* (Paris, 1870).

Erckmann-Chatrian. *Histoire d'un homme du peuple.* (Paris, 1865).

Belot. *L'article 47.* (Paris, 1870).

G. Sand. *La confession d'une jeune fille.* (Paris, 1865).

Erckmann-Chatrian. *Waterloo.* (Paris, 1865).

A. Dumas (fils). *Affaire Clémanceau.* (Paris, 1857).

Proudon (P.-J.). *La révolution sociale démontrée par le coup d'état du 2 Décembre.* (Paris, 1852).

Nb. *Musset Alfred. La confession d'un enfant du siècle.* (Paris, 1836).

Flaubert (G). *Madame Bovary.* (Paris, 1856).

Octave Feuillet. *Le roman d'un jeune homme pauvre.* (Paris, 1858).

Belot. *Le drame de la rue de la Paix.* (Paris, 1867).

Femme de feu. (Paris, 1872).

A. Dumas-fils. *L'Homme-Femme.* (Paris, 1864).[11]

This book list links the texts associatively, not systematically. Musset's *Confession d'un enfant du siècle,* for example, enters the list because of its resonance with George Sand's *Confession d'une jeune fille,* on the one hand, and with Erckmann-Chatrian's *Waterloo,* on the other, since the Musset begins with a description of post-Napoleonic neurasthenia. We know that Dostoevsky planned to reread this book, because it had already distinctly influenced the *Notes from Underground.* But the adultery theme in the Musset also leads to the great adultery novel of the century, *Madame Bovary,* as well as to such prurience as Adolphe Belot's *Femme de feu,* whose title alludes to both the fires of passion and the phosphorescent water in which the heroine swims. And all this sexism leads naturally to Dumas's *Homme-Femme,* which discusses adultery at great length, ending with a page-long sentence listing all the efforts a husband must make to regain an adulterous wife, and concluding with two words of instruction if all such efforts fail: "Kill her." In short, Dostoevsky's reading was like his writing. Tolstoi would read with a treatise in mind that he intended to write or at least work out with a clear sense of what had been said on the subject. Dostoevsky would read with a collection of themes in his mind that he did not know exactly how to use but that he knew were related in ways too intricate for the systematic part of his mind to handle.

Such information gives a clear indication of the dimensions of Dostoevsky's reading, but only an indication. He was constantly turning to the journals of the day, which were enormously rich in Russian and translated literature; in addition, he read trial proceedings, political disputes, psychological treatises, and other materials as avidly as he read literature. As Leonid Grossman put it three generations ago, in the best single article on Dostoevsky's reading, "The last twenty years of Dostoevsky's life were caught up as a whole in ceaseless feverish work as a journalist, novelist, and editor. It is hard to reckon all the printed material he saw and assimilated in this period."[12] With this richness of interests and this intensity of reading, one can almost argue that the burden of proof rests heavier on a scholar who hypothesizes that Dostoevsky had not read a given text than on one who claims he had.

III

THE FIRST, THE LAST, AND SOME OF THE MOST INFLUENTIAL TEXTS DOSTOEVSKY READ INVOLVED THE BIBLE AND RELIGION.

Dostoevsky's first recorded reading was a book of Bible stories, which he may have known already from his deeply religious mother or the churches where she took him. In book 6, chapter 2, part *b* of *The Brothers Karamazov*, Father Zosima recollects such a book, "a sacred history, with beautiful pictures entitled *A Hundred and Four Sacred Stories from the Old and New Testaments*," as the text he learned to read from (*Pss* 14:264).[13] Among the two dozen notes Dostoevsky's widow made on her copy of *The Brothers Karamazov* is one that says that Dostoevsky learned to read from a book of these stories.[14] He knew the Bible well, and during his years in prison camp there were periods when the authorities permitted him to read nothing but the Bible he had received from the widows of some of the Decembrists who had made the march to Siberia a generation earlier. His New Testament survives in the Lenin Library, heavily underlined and marked.[15] According to his wife's notes in this Bible, he asked her to read him Matthew 3:14–15 at three o'clock on the day he died. All his life Dostoevsky gave the Bible a central place. In one of his last letters, in response to a man who had written him for advice on what his son should read, he recommended a number of the classics but added, "Above all, of course, the Gospel, the New Testament in translation. If he can even read it in the original (that is, in Church Slavonic), that would be best of all. The Gospels and the Acts of the Apostles are the *sine qua non*."[16]

He also read broadly, though not systematically, among the theologians, hagiographers, and other Christian writers of his time and earlier. His first letter to his brother after the almost bookless years in prison camp requests writings of the church fathers and church history.[17] The catalog of his library lists more than two dozen religious titles, including several Bibles, psalters, commentaries, a missal, a lives of the saints in a dozen volumes, a life of the monk Leonid in the Optina Hermitage, a Koran, and writings by Christians as diverse as Simeon the New Theologian, Isaac Sirin, Parfenii the Monk of Athos, Jean Baptiste Massillon, Aleksei Khomiakov, and Vladimir Solovev.[18] Valentina Vetlovskaia, the strongest Soviet student of this side of Dostoevsky's reading, cannot find which life of Francis of Assisi he read but makes the connection between St. Francis and Father Zosima far richer than it had seemed before.[19] Dostoevsky mentions such great figures in the history of Orthodoxy as Gregory Palamas, Tikhon of Zadonsk, Sergius of Radonezh, Stefan Yavorskii, Archimandrite Photius, and Metropolitan Macarius, but also minor religious writers of his time like Nikolai Yakovlevich Ogloblin, Andrei Nikolaevich Muravev, Aleksandr Fedorovich Gusev, and Peter Mikhailovich Tseidler. He is equally interested in less conventional Orthodoxy, mentions Avvakum, and either mentions or corresponds with contemporary writers who treat the great schism, such as Vasilii Ivanovich Kelsiev, Pavel Prusskii, Vasilii Ivanovich Kalatyrov, or Pavel Ivanovich Melnikov. He also refers to I. G. Pryzhov, who was ruined through his contact with Nechaev, but who wrote a study of the *iurodivye*, or holy fools, who used provocative behavior with extraordinary effect. Dostoevsky's narrators and characters refer to other characters as resembling schismatics, *iurodivye*, or other religious eccentrics.

Further afield, he owned a book on spiritualism, attended a seance, and wrote three articles in *The Diary of a Writer* attacking both spiritualism and the positivist assault upon it. From Western Christianity, he owned a volume of Thomas à Kempis translated by his friend and great supporter Konstantin Pobedonostsev; mentioned Martin Luther several times; owned several Swedenborgian texts, which Czesław Miłosz has discussed; mocked Lord Radstock, the visiting evangelist; made literary use of Nikolai Savvich Tikhonravov's edition of medieval apocrypha; and referred on a number of important occasions to Ernst Renan's and David Friedrich Strauss's lives of Christ.

The scholarly world has brought much intellection to bear on these religious readings as sources for the novels. Sergei Hakel ascribes much of Zosima's teaching to Parfenii and Isaac Sirin, and Sven Linner finds equally much in Tikhon of Zadonsk and Ambrose in the Optina Hermitage, while both follow Konstantin Leontiev in tracing key elements of Zosima to Bishop Myriel in a secular source, Les misérables.[20] Vetlovskaia has explored much of Dostoevsky's religious reading and its impact on his work, but the subject has fascinated readers from all camps for over a century. M. A. Antonovich describes Dostoevsky's approach as "mystico-ascetic." From his position of rigorous eccentricity, Konstantin Leontiev attacked Dostoevsky for insufficient deference to the ascetic, sacramental, and disciplined component of Christianity in his depiction of Zosima, while church leaders who would rarely agree with Leontiev or Antonovich about anything agree in part with both about the centrality of Dostoevsky's religious position in all his mature writing.

Others have written on Dostoevsky's reading of—or more likely about—N. F. Fedorov, who believed that the common task of mankind is the literal resurrection of our ancestors through the resources of every available kind of knowlege and technique. More important, of course, were the writings of Dostoevsky's close friend, follower, and teacher, the religious philosopher Vladimir Solovev. The closeness of these two major figures has made it particularly difficult for scholars—and quite possibly for the authors themselves—to specify which direction the influences were flowing, but there can be no question that the religious discussions and the picture of the monastery itself in The Brothers Karamazov would have been very different if Dostoevsky had not been reading Solovev and seeing the religious world at least in part through his eyes. Religious teachings that Dostoevsky may never have encountered at firsthand, like those of Jakob Böhme, would have come to him through Solovev—and through Schelling, as Zdenek David showed in his 1960 Harvard dissertation.[21] In this area, as in so many others, mediated influences can be indistinguishable from direct ones.

IV
DOSTOEVSKY TREATED THE SECULAR CLASSICS WITH RESPECT AND OCCASIONALLY WITH DEEP LITERARY INVOLVEMENT.

After the Bible and other religious texts, Dostoevsky praised certain great established classics most of all. Sometimes this praise reads like a mixture of adolescent romanticism and preadolescent competitiveness, but at the very least it shows his clear sense of what he ought to like:

> Oh, how [Ivan Shidlovskii and I] spent that evening! We recalled those winter days when we talked about Homer, Shakespeare, Schiller, Hoffmann, whom we discussed as much as we read him. . . . You wrote to me, Brother, that I hadn't read Schiller. You're wrong, Brother. I crammed Schiller, talked him, ranted him; and I think fate has arranged nothing better in my life than letting me get to know the great poet at such a moment in my life; never could I have gotten to know him the way I did then. . . . Maybe in some discussion I juxtaposed Pushkin and Schiller, but I think that between those two words there's a comma. They don't resemble each other at all. The same for Pushkin and Byron. As for Homer and Victor Hugo I think you intentionally wanted to misunderstand me. Here's what I say. Homer (a fabulous human being, perhaps like Christ, incarnated by God and sent to us) can be paralleled only with Christ, and not with Goethe. Look into him, Brother, take the *Iliad*, and read it really well (so you haven't read it, own up). Because in the *Iliad*, Homer gave the whole ancient world its organization in its spiritual and secular life with just such power as Christ did the modern world. . . . As a lyricist Victor Hugo has a simply angelic character, a childlike Christian bent to his poetry, and no one equals him in this, neither Schiller (however Christian he be) nor Shakespeare as a lyricist, I read his sonnets in French, nor Byron, nor Pushkin. Only Homer has such unshaken sureness in his calling, such childlike faith in the god of poesy whom he serves, like Victor Hugo in his bent toward the wellsprings of poesy, but only in his bent, not in his concept, which was given him by nature and expressed by him. . . . I think Derzhavin can stand above them both in lyric. . . .
>
> Why did you take it into your head to say we couldn't like either Racine or *Corneille*(!?!?) because they had bad form. You're pathetic. . . . Racine, the ardent, passionate, enamored Racine has no poetry? . . . Now, as to Corneille. . . . Have you read *The Cid?* Read it, you poor wretch, read it and fall in the dust before Corneille. . . .[22]

This letter tells us more about how splendidly insufferable Dostoevsky must have been at eighteen than it does about his lifelong literary tastes or reading habits. It reveals no more knowledge of classical culture, for example, or even of Homer, than the Hegel twice (at least) warmed over that our most infuriating freshmen spout today, though later evidence in the novels confirms the admiration for Racine and Corneille. The editors of the 1972 *Complete Works* (*Polnoe sobranie sochinenii* [*Pss*]) suggest that Dostoevsky was rejecting the standard romantic scorn for "false classicism" almost a decade before Vissarion G. Belinskii did. He may also have been behind the times: Stendhal's essay on Shakespeare and Racine was only fifteen years old, and the neoclassical aesthetic never really died in France.

Dostoevsky acquired several Russian translations of the Greek and Roman classics in the last years of his life. These included the *Iliad*, the *Odyssey*, Pliny's letters, and the works of Aeschylus, Aristophanes, Plato, Xenophon, Virgil, Julius Caesar, and Tacitus. A quarter century earlier, in exile, he had asked his brother to send him, "As far as possible, all the ancients (Herodotus, Thucydides, Tacitus, Pliny, Flavius, Plutarch, and Diodorus)," revealing a fascinating bias toward historians.[23] He mentions Tacitus a dozen times, and Plutarch and Cornelius Nepos once or twice. Julius Caesar's name comes up fairly often, but more as a world conqueror and self-made leader than as a writer. He mentions Sappho, Diogenes, Socrates, Plato, Aristotle, Aesop, Virgil, Cicero, and Juvenal, but not in ways that demonstrate any serious interest. Sergei Belov has written on the possibility of a serious Platonic influence, and in chapter 7 this book will treat some striking parallels with Plato, but the absence of actual references or close verbal parallels leaves open the possibility that trains of thought converged, or that Plato reached Dostoevsky indirectly at one or more removes. Besides Homer, whom he continues to recommend in his more sober years, Dostoevsky writes little about the Greeks or Romans, except for passing references, like Fedor Karamazov's description of his thin, protruding nose, "Authentic Roman. . . together with the goiter, the authentic physiognomy of the ancient patrician of the time of the decline" (*Pss* 14:22), or Kolia Krasotkin's view of classical studies, which I will quote again later for its ideological implications: "I haven't much respect for world history. . . .the study of a series of human stupidities. . .again, these classical languages. . .are a police measure. . .cultivated because they're boring and therefore stultify our aptitudes" (*Pss* 14:498). Kolia is expressing a modish attitude that Dostoevsky deplored, but it may be safe to say that Dostoesky's upbringing, his education, and his omnivorous reading in his own generation and the one before it made him more likely to reinvent a classical insight or to take a modern version of it than to borrow it directly from its original text.

For the Middle Ages, the picture is more or less the same. He refers to medieval attitudes and folklore, mentions Augustine's *Confessions* once in a list of books, mentions the *Arabian Nights*, discusses Muhammad a dozen times, refers to Prince Kurbskii and half a dozen times to the *Lay of Igor's Troop*, but with no evidence of serious interest or hard reading except in the case of the religious works already discussed and one epic figure, Dante. Leonid Grossman outlined Dostoevsky's debt to Dante, which goes far beyond the tributes to an accepted masterpiece or the word *Dantesque*, which is sometimes applied to *The House of the Dead*.[24]

From the Renaissance, Dostoevsky mentions Petrarch, Machiavelli, Ronsard, Francis Bacon, and Thomas More, but he really found only two genuinely congenial figures, Shakespeare and Cervantes. He mentions Cervantes more than two dozen times. Grossman, Ludmilla Turkevich, and others have shown how the personalities and careers of Prince Myshkin and Alesha Karamazov reflect Don Quixote's selfless purity of heart and idealization of a far-from-flawless lady. Until now, however, insufficient attention has been paid to the influence on Dostoevsky of an equally important character in Don Quixote, Sidi Hamet Benegali, and the crowd of other narrators through whom we experience the novel.[25] Certainly, Cervantes showed as much sophistication in this area as Dostoevsky's models—Diderot, Hoffmann, or Poe—and even such grand masters at it as Sterne and Gogol owe Cervantes such a debt that it may prove impossible to clarify the later genealogy of narrative perversity.

Shakespeare meant even more to Dostoevsky. At the time of his death he owned two complete Russian editions of Shakespeare, and he mentions him over a hundred times in his letters, articles, and fiction.[26] Several of his characters cite Shakespeare, sometimes in ways that mock the misuse of Shakespeare's name. Opiskin, in *The Friend of the Family*, says, "Referring. . .to Shakespeare, I shall say that the future presented itself to me as a gloomy chasm of unknown depth, upon whose bottom lurked a crocodile"; a woman in *The Brothers Karamazov* casts herself from a precipitous riverbank solely to resemble Ophelia; Stavrogin's mother says that he resembles Hamlet more than he does Prince Hal. Such passages refer not so much to Shakespeare as to provincial Shakespeare productions, which doubtless resembled those in which Dickens's Mr. Wopsle played. Yet even Ivan Karamazov quotes Polonius as saying "How skillfully you can distort words," something Polonius never says.

Shakespeare, however, is far more than a name that Dostoevsky can use for its reverberations in the reader's literary consciousness. Both Shakespeare and Dostoevsky are generally considered to have written four enormous monuments, all murder stories. *Macbeth* and *Crime and Punishment* present crimes of ambition committed against helpless old people in high dark rooms by remarkable young men whose consciences prey on their sleep and waking behavior before and after the murder. *Othello* and *The Idiot* present the murders of extraordinary beauties by the powerful, dark, jealous outsiders who have run off with them. *Hamlet* and *The Possessed* show the inruption of a princely fatherless son and his friends from Western Europe into the provincial capital where his mother shares power with a weak leader, and the way these youths lay waste their cities, their women, and themselves. *King Lear* and *The Brothers Karamazov* trace the metamorphoses of parricide among siblings who range from almost implausible goodness to genuinely remarkable villainy. These parallels reflect neither conscious imitation nor pure coincidence, but rather the shaping of a deeply embedded body of concerns in the presence of a powerful model.

The indexes do not contain the names of Montaigne, Rabelais, the Carmina Burana, or a number of other early materials considered in later chapters of this book. But the mere mention of a book does not prove that Dostoevsky had read it, or had read a given page of it, and the failure to mention it in a surviving document does not prove that he had not read it. As this book explores the mechanisms of literary borrowing, I hope it will tighten some of the existing ways of detecting and verifying literary influence.

V

In His Youth, Dostoevsky Read Karamzin, Scott, and Schiller, and Later On, Voltaire, Diderot, and Rousseau.

For the period after the Renaissance, Dostoevsky's reading became more catholic, no longer restricted to a canon formed by others. He mentioned Milton and Pascal a couple of times, said the expected thing about Malherbe, made a dozen references to Lesage or *Gil Blas*, and respected Corneille and Racine all his life; but he mentioned Molière a dozen times and used his *Tartuffe* to great advantage, especially in constructing his own hypocrisy story, *The Friend of the Family*. Here the young lovers, the servants, and the aggressively credulous wife follow Molière's formula, as does the striking delay in the appearance of the hypocrite on stage. But Dostoevsky's Gogolian hypocrite transcends Molière's Plautine one by making his political tawdriness explicit and even eloquent; and Dostoevsky's foolish old patriarch actually embodies those virtues of dignity, decency, and simplicity of heart which Molière admired more than any others but represented only by lampooning their absence or by having a *raisonneur* proclaim their value abstractly.

From the eighteenth century, Dostoevsky possesses half a dozen authors so fully that he can elaborate such constructs out of elements that are only implicit in their texts, but he also has a dutiful control of all the established classics, as well as a substantial body of the kind of noncanonical works he seems not to know in the ancient and medieval periods. Among English authors, he mentions Defoe, Swift, and, most attentively, Richardson. Among the Russians he mentions Lomonosov, Khemnitser, Kheraskov, Dashkova, Radischchev, and Bogdanovich a few times, but as we have seen, Derzhavin seems to have produced the greatest impression upon him, at least as a young man. When the subject is fully studied, it may turn out that he did not use Derzhavin as he used most authors—for expertise in techniques he hoped to master—but simply bathed in him, as young men often do in very great poets, and that he carried from him little but a kindred irony about the utopian vision that was so fashionable in both their periods. Certainly his own two poems to Alexander II bear no mark of lessons learned from Russia's most sophisticated master of the panegyric.

From the French eighteenth century, he mentions such established classics as Saint-Simon, the Abbé Prévost, Boileau, Montesquieu, Beaumarchais, La Rochefoucault, and La Fontaine once or twice, but pays somewhat more attention to the more racy extracanonical figures of the end of the century: Chénier, the Marquis de Sade, and Louvet de Couvray or *Faublas*. William Brumfield and others have discussed his use of such libertine novels as *Thérèse Philosophe* and a questioner of received truths and moralities like Helvétius,[27] but for Dostoevsky the central figures of the mid-eighteenth century were certainly Voltaire, Diderot, and Rousseau.

Voltaire's novels were one of the first things he requested upon his return to Russia from Siberia,[28] and he refers to Voltaire over thirty times, including the passages in *The Brothers Karamazov* where he is referred to as the old sinner who averred that if God did not exist he would have to be invented. But Grossman shows that this novel rests in much more basic ways on questions that Voltaire raised.[29] Dostoevsky refers to Diderot less than a dozen times, but Diderot seems to have meant more to him in regard to the art of the novel than Voltaire did, experimenting in *Rameau's Nephew* with the relation between character and beliefs in ways that lead toward the *Notes from Underground*. Rousseau appears by name over two dozen times in Dostoevsky's writings and probably played an even larger role in Dostoevsky's thinking than this number indicates. Sven Linner argues that Rousseau's Savoy vicar is more important in establishing the tradition of the holy priest in the history of novels than Goldsmith's vicar of Wakefield, though Balzac's and Hugo's holy priests represented the true literary intertexts among which readers would place Zosima.[30] But Dostoevsky uses Rousseau for far more than character types. He engages in an ongoing polemic with him over the nature of confession, of goodness, of the church and nations, of education, and many other issues, at the same time that he draws from him a way of presenting landscapes, motives, and ideals that is most prominent in *The Idiot* but pervades all his works. Perhaps he mentions Rousseau comparatively seldom because Rousseau had penetrated the consciousness of so much of Europe in so many ways that Dostoevsky was aware of him more through George Sand, the utopian socialists, and a host of other writers than from repeated immersion in his works. The *Notes from Underground*, for example, responds to Rousseau's *Confessions* with particular savagery, but much of that investigation of willfulness and self-exposure derives not directly from Rousseau but from Karamzin's short story by the same title, "Moia ispoved'," and also from Musset's *Confession d'un enfant du siècle*.[31]

Karamzin and his whole generation formed the cultural center of the young Dostoevsky's life. His brother Andrei describes how his parents and later his older brothers would take turns reading aloud to the family:

> For the most part, we read historical works; Karamzin's *History of the Russian State* (we had our own copy), of which we read the last volumes most often, IX, X, XI, and XII, so that something of the histories of Godunov and the Pretender remains in my memory from these readings; Polevoi's *Biography of Mikhail Vasilevich Lomonosov* and many others. Among the purely literary works I remember we read Derzavin, especially his *Ode to God*, Zhukovsky, and his prose translations, Karamzin's *Letters of a Russian Traveler*, "Poor Liza," "Martha the Lady of the City," etc. Of Pushkin, mostly the prose. Later on they started reading novels too: *Yurii Miloslavskii*, *The Ice Palace*, *The Streltsy*, and a sentimental novel, *The Kholmskii Family*.... we also read the tales of the cossack Luganskii. All these works remained in my memory not merely as titles because these readings were often interrupted by

the reflections of my parents. . . . In Fedia's hands most often I saw Walter Scott—*Quentin Durward,* and *Waverley;* we had our own copies, and he read them more than once, in spite of the strange and heavy translation. All Pushkin's works underwent the same reading and rereading. My brother Fedor also loved the stories of Narezhnyi, of which he read *The Novice* more than once. I can't remember for sure whether he was reading something of Gogol's then...I remember only that he was delighted with Vel'tman's novel *Heart and Mind.* . . . In our house there also appeared the volumes of the *Library for Reading* which came out at that time. . . . These books were the exclusive property of my brothers. Our parents did not touch them.

In general, my brother Fedya read historical works, serious ones, and also the novels that turned up.[32]

Cyzewskij, Tunimanov, and others have worked on particular relationships between Karamzin and Dostoevsky, but both Karamzin and Scott deserve more attention from Dostoevsky scholars than they have received. Still, the general outline of his debt to them is plain. His sense of honor, of the virtues appropriate for men and women, his attention to the common people, his patriotism, and his belief that no one generation can afford to reject the accumulated wisdom of history all match central operating beliefs of these two great national authors whom he read as a child. In addition, he continued to read them; the stories of provincial life that he wrote in the 1860s depict a kind of silliness much like that which Scott explores in *St. Ronan's Well.*

In the same generation with Karamzin and Scott, and more important literarily for Dostoevsky, was Schiller, as the early letter quoted above and a hundred other specific allusions suggest. M. P. Alekseev explored this subject in 1921,[33] and both B. G. Reizov and Alexandra Lyngstad have discussed the intricate role of Schiller in *The Brothers Karamazov.*[34] Dostoevsky's characters talk more about Schiller's works than about any other writings except Pushkin's, Gogol's, possibly Shakespeare's, and the Bible.[35] These characters speak sometimes with the worldly irony of Svidrigailov, and sometimes with that youthful enthusiasm for the nobility and idealism of Schiller's characters that Dostoevsky himself displayed in his early letter. When Fedor Karamazov compares his family's situation to that in Schiller's *Robbers,* he is using a familiar allusion to influence Zosima and infuriate Mitia, while Dostoevsky is using the same allusion at the same time to complicate the reader's perception of old Fedor, and the reader is also trying to use it to clarify the role of Schiller's play in the genesis of the initial conflict in Dostoevsky's novel. A passage like this can illuminate the extraordinary intricacy of the relationship between Dostoevsky and his sources.

Like most observers, Dostoevsky tended to link the names of Schiller and Goethe, but the two authors meant very different things to him. Schiller may inspire devotion or irony in Dostoevsky or his characters, but either attitude will be excited and exciting; Goethe always inspires admiration for his genius and his greatness, but, as Arkadii Dolinin phrased it, he was "olympian, one of the few world geniuses who seemed the most alien to Dostoevsky's always troubled mind."[36] All educated readers in Dostoevsky's generation knew most of Goethe well, and Dostoevsky uses that knowledge to characterize the pawnbroker at the beginning of "The Gentle Creature," who has the bad taste to quote an overly familiar passage from *Faust,* calling himself a part of that part of the whole which intends evil and does good. In short, Goethe offered Dostoevsky an icon to allude to and a rich source of literary lore and technique but not a congenial literary mind, except, perhaps, in Goethe's stressed and stormy youth.

To summarize Dostoevsky's treatment of the generation that flourished during Goethe's long life, as it related to those before and after, I can quote a letter to one of the people he was afraid might visit him to consult on what her child should read:

> You say that up to now, you have not been giving your daughter anything literary to read, fearing to cultivate her fantasy. Now it seems to me that this is not altogether correct: fantasy is an inborn power in a human being, especially in a child, in whom it is primarily developed from the earliest age, before all other capacities, and demands satisfaction. Denying it satisfaction, you either crush it or on the contrary make it develop too much through its own powers (which really is bad). . . . The impression of the beautiful is just what's needed in childhood. In Moscow when I was ten years old, I saw a performance of Schiller's *Robbers* with Mochalov, and I assure you that that very strong impression which I experienced then has worked on the spiritual side of me with great fruits. At twelve, on vacation in the country, I read all of Walter Scott, and even if I cultivated my fantasy and impressionability, still, I set it on a good course and not a bad one, especially since I took into life with me from this reading so many beautiful and sublime impressions that they naturally established strength in my heart for the struggle with seductive, passionate, and corrupting impressions. I advise you too to give your daughter Walter Scott now especially because he is quite forgotten among us Russians, and later on, when she will be living on her own, she will find neither the means nor the need to make the acquaintance of this great writer herself. . . . Have her read all of Dickens without

exception. Acquaint her with the literature of earlier centuries (*Don Quixote* and even *Gil Blas*). Best of all, start off with verse. Of Pushkin, she must read everything, verse and prose. Gogol too. Turgenev, Goncharov, if you wish; my own works I don't think would all be right for her. It would be good to read Schlosser's whole history, and Solovev's history of Russia. It's good not to miss Karamzin. Don't give her Kostomarov yet. Prescott's conquests of Peru and Mexico are indispensable. In general, historical works have enormous educational significance. Leo Tolstoi must all be read. Shakespeare, Schiller, Goethe all exist in very good Russian translations. . . . Newspaper literature ought to be kept away, at least for now. . . . I don't think we need a face-to-face meeting at all now, especially since I am very busy.[37]

In short, as far as the writers who belonged primarily to the eighteenth century are concerned, although Dostoevsky certainly knew such figures as Richardson, Fielding, and Sterne in English; Kant, Hegel, and Herder in German; Radishchev, Denis Fon Vizin, and Alexander Sumarokov in Russian; or the Marquis de Sade in French, his references to them are cursory. He made real use of only half a dozen figures in this century, all of them established classical authors in his childhood.

VI

DOSTOEVSKY'S LITERARY IDENTITY RESTS HEAVILY ON THE GENERATION THAT FLOURISHED EARLY IN THE NINETEENTH CENTURY.

In Dostoevsky's childhood, Goethe and Karamzin were still alive, established as living monuments, but a whole array of newer authors caught the imagination of the younger generation. Dostoevsky mentions such romantics as Wordsworth, Chateaubriand, Mérimée, and Musset a few times, but the writers who really influenced his style were E. T. A. Hoffmann, Edgar Allen Poe, and the gothic novelists. These writers influenced him directly, as his letters and texts show on dozens of occasions, but also indirectly, through Gogol, Dickens, Hugo, and others who had absorbed their techniques and interests. Hoffmann's influence continued throughout Dostoevsky's life, as has been documented by many scholars, most amply by Charles Passage.[38] Dostoevsky mentions Frankenstein, and Robin Miller connects Charles Robert Maturin's *Melmoth* with *The Brothers Karamazov* as explorations of the problem of evil.[39] Dostoevsky himself discusses Ann Radcliffe in a letter to the poet Iakov P. Polonskii, who was abroad:

You're a lucky man. How often I have dreamed, from my very childhood, of visiting in Italy. Even from the novels of Ratclif [*sic*], which I read when I was still eight, various Alfonses, Katarinas, and Lucias gnawed their way into my head. And right down to the present, I'm still ecstatic over Don Pedros and Donna Claras. Then came Shakespeare—Verona, Romeo and Julietta, Lord knows whan an aura it had. To Italy, to Italy! and instead of Italy, I ended up in Semipalatinsk, and before that in the House of the Dead.[40]

Dostoevsky is rarely wistful and rarely mixes Spanish and Italian names, but even in his last piece of writing, the speech for the unveiling of the Pushkin monument, he discusses the Englishness of Shakespeare's Italians (*Pss* 26:145).

What Dostoevsky learned from Hoffmann and the Gothic novels, Edgar Allen Poe offered in a compressed, intensified, and highly psychological form, which also derived heavily from Hoffmann. Dostoevsky's journal *Time* (*Vremia*) introduced Poe to the Russian reading public, and scholars from Leonid Grossman to Joan Grossman have explored the Poe-Dostoevsky connection.[41] These studies show us the sources for many individual passages, but they also reveal the source of much of what is most "Dostoevskian": the exploration of the perverse, of abnormal mental states, the enunciation of emotions more intense than those of ordinary folk—as well as doubles; hallucinations; extraordinary holy figures; helpless women of great birth and beauty; flashing, often fearsome, hypnotic eyes; dark stairways and secret places in threatening buildings; and a host of other elements that de Vogüé and other Westerners have tended through ignorance or a need for alien excellence to call archetypically and exotically Russian.

Much of this influence cannot be isolated from that of Dickens, Hugo, Sue, and others who incorporated many of the same elements from the gothic novels, or from the influence of Byron, Lermontov, and others who drew not only from the gothic novels but also from the same well of romantic imagery and imagination on which the gothic novels drew. In many ways the most important lesson Dostoevsky learned from this immensely popular literature was the technique of keeping his readers in suspense, not only about what is going to happen in the next installment, but also about the very nature of the text they are reading. Tsvetan Todorov, and earlier Freud, discuss the impact upon readers of not knowing whether they are looking at a picture of a real world needing better interpretation, or a supernatural world running by different laws of nature, or some delirious intermediate or ambiguous experience, as in Dostoevsky's most Hoffmannesque stories, *The Double* and "The Landlady."[42]

The poets of this generation mattered to Dostoevsky in a rather different way. He mentions Heine a dozen times, and Pierre-Jean de Beranger four or five, but otherwise, except for Byron, he mentions only Russians. By Dostoevsky's time the struggle between poetic archaizers and innovators was a thing of the past, but Ivan Krylov, Ivan Dmitriev, and Vasilii Zhukovskii probably belong in the former camp; Dostoevsky mentions the last two several times each, and Krylov almost fifty times. This continuing interest comes partly from Krylov's longevity on the literary scene, but much of it doubtless comes from his sheer quotability. The hesitancies and incoherences of Dostoevsky's personae draw little from Krylov's directly, but they reflect the same sense that readers can be swayed more easily if they have worked to get at a point that is being made with apparent clumsiness. Dostoevsky's treatment of Krylov would bear ampler study than it has received. Among the innovators, he mentions Konstantin Batiushkov, Anton Del'vig, Peter Andreevich Viazemskii, and Alexander Polezhaev once or twice each, but Pushkin, Lermontov, and Byron are infinitely more important to him.

The two Russians matter to Dostoevsky as much for their drama and prose as for their verse, and all three entered his work as iconic figures in the national or international awareness. In the almost fifty times he mentions Byron, his interest lies in the Byronic hero or that hero's predicament. In general, he spoke of Byron in connection with Pushkin and Lermontov and not as an independent figure in his literary consciousness. When he mocks a pose as "something Manfredish," he is using Byron as a cultural referent, something so familiar to all his readers that it permits a whole world of emotion and moral and social attitude to be contained in a single word. Pushkin occupies a far more important place in Dostoevsky's literary mind. He mentions him over a hundred times—in letters, as we have seen, but in many articles and novels also, beginning with *Poor Folk*, whose poor hero cannot cope with his own resemblance to Pushkin's station agent, and ending with Dostoevsky's swan song, the speech that overwhelmed the flower of the Russian intelligentsia at the unveiling of the Pushkin monument in Moscow in 1880. He uses the "Egyptian Nights" or "The Gypsies" or the Belkin tales or *Boris Godunov* or most often *Eugene Onegin* not only as a world to which he can refer but for his plots and characters and their psychologies. Much has been written on Dostoevsky and Pushkin, and much remains to be said.[43]

Lermontov he admired and used and entered into dialogue with in many of his works. In *Poor Folk*, on the very first page, when Makar Devushkin, perhaps the least predatory of all literary heroes, says, "Why am I not a bird, not a bird of prey!" Lermontov's "Zachem ia ne ptitsa, ne ptitsa polei" is meant to resound ironically in the readers' ears, just as in Dostoevky's last novel, the encounter between Katerina Ivanovna and the young officer Mitia Karamazov is meant to reverberate that between Lermontov's Pechorin and Princess Mary. When Dostoevsky called Lermontov one of the two "demons" Russian literature had produced (the other being Gogol), he was thinking of his prose and his personality as well as his poetry, but Lermontov remains an underinvestigated source for Dostoevsky's writings.

VII
DOSTOEVSKY READ BROADLY BUT NOT SYSTEMATICALLY AMONG PHILOSOPHERS, SCIENTISTS, AND HISTORIANS.

Unlike Tolstoi, Dostoevsky did not set himself reading programs to master a given subject. The book list cited in section 2 above links the texts associatively, not systematically, reflecting the way Dostoevsky went about his reading in general.

He mentions systematic philosophers like Leibnitz, Spinoza, and Descartes, and his first letter to his brother after prison says, "Send me a Koran, Kant's *Critique de raison pure,* and if you're somehow in a position to send me something unofficially, be sure to send *Hegel,* especially Hegel's *History of Philosophy.* With that my whole future is linked!" (*Pss* 27, pt. 1: 173). Dostoevsky's needs are often passionate and should not be taken too literally. Ia. E. Golosovker's book on Dostoevsky and Kant, like Cyzewskij's and G. Belzer's work on Dostoevsky and Hegel, finds interesting parallels and similar structures but little direct literary connection.[44]

Among the social philosophers, he mentions Malthus and Mill several times and Karl Marx once, in an 1873 article on current events in which he says, "The Pope will have it in him to go out to the people, afoot, unshod, poor, and bare, with an army of twenty thousand Jesuit warriors, experienced in the angling for human souls. Will Karl Marx and Bakunin withstand this army? Hardly . . ." (*Pss* 21:203). A fine debate raged for many years over whether Dostoevsky met Bakunin in Switzerland, but plainly, for Dostoevsky, Bakunin and Nechaev constituted the Russian wing of a political philosophy that had its roots in France, in such figures as Louis Blanc, François Babeuf, whose names he uses, and Pierre Proudhon, whom he refers to more than a dozen times.[45] But the social thinkers who entered Dostoevsky's work most centrally were the utopians he had known in his youth in the Petrashevskii circle.

He mentions Victor Considerant and Etienne Cabet; and Charles Fourier's name appears two dozen times in his writings. V. L. Komarovich and Sergei Durylin have described the way utopian thinking and imagery entered Dostoevsky's novels, a matter that will concern us especially in chapters 5 and 7 of this study. These were the social thinkers Dostoevsky knew best; he used the Petrashevskii library, but the discussions at the meetings of the circle also made materials he had never read a part of his thinking.

In Dostoevsky's mind philosophers of voluntarism, materialism, positivism, or utilitarianism tended to fall together into a community that might best be characterized simply as the enemy. The *Notes from Underground* brings this community together in the clearest way, but on the few occasions that Dostoevsky mentions the names of Comte, Feuerbach, or the justifiers of the scientific approach, his language becomes at best ironic and more often vitriolic. He mentions such great figures in the history of science as Galileo, Copernicus, and Newton, but more as emblems of greatness than as discoverers of any particular scientific truth. In his own time, science was linked with the positivistic and rationalistic vision of the world, which he repudiated. Among the great figures, he pays surprisingly little attention to Darwin, considering Darwin's enormous importance in Russia.[46] Writing in the great days of chemistry, he attacks Liebig and Mendeleev with equal vehemence, but Mendeleev about a dozen times, primarily for the banality of his materialism. In the reverse pattern, the Russian neurologist Ivan Mikhailovich Sechenov receives a couple of attacks, but the grand attacks in *The Brothers Karamazov* are reserved for Claude Bernard. Lobachevskii's work in mathematics fares better, but it seems safe to say that in general Dostoevsky's experience of science came in engineering school, where he read widely at secondhand; from the hundreds of science articles in the journals he read; and from the books that explained or popularized the science of his time, by authors like Alexander von Humboldt, Karl Voght, Jakob Moleshott, or George Henry Lewes. Among Russian scientists, he mentions Pisarevskii's general physics course, and Aleksandr Dmitrievich Putyata, a writer on mathematics and astronomy with whom he exchanged letters at least once.

Like religion, science had a centrally moral meaning for Dostoevsky. The finest science of his time was reductionist, seeking simple material explanations for complicated biological, geological, mental, social, and even spiritual phenomena. Dostoevsky rejected this reductionism and the positivistic faith that went with it, but his training and reading in science left traces in his thinking and language which need further work. In an unpublished 1985 Columbia dissertation, Lisa Knapp has explored his use of the word *inertia* in his writings. She finds that it draws its meaning not only from the natural scientists, who describe the tendency of a body to remain at rest or in motion in a given direction unless some external force slows, speeds, turns, or stops it, but also from the church fathers, who describe the difficulty of changing our ways even when we have a new and clear idea of what is right. The enormous apostrophe to inertia at the end of "The Gentle Creature" brings the laws of science together with those of the spirit in a way that destroys any simple formulations about Dostoevsky's antiscientism:

> Inertia! Oh nature! People are alone on earth—that's the woe! "Is there any man alive in the field?" the Russian warrior cries out. I cry out too, though no warrior, and no one answers. They say the sun gives life to the universe. The sun is rising, and—look upon it, is it not dead? All dead, and everywhere the dead. There are only people, and around them silence—that's the world! "People, love one another"—who said that? Whose testament is that? The pendulum ticks feelinglessly, repulsively. It's two o'clock at night. Her little boots are at her little bed, as if awaiting her. . . . No, seriously, when they carry her away tomorrow, what will become of me? *(Pss* 24:35)

Here, in one of the most personal, most emotional, most religious, and intertextually most movingly allusive passages he ever wrote, Dostoevsky brings scientific lore about the sun into collision with a despairing man's perception of it and brings the sophisticated word *inertia* to bear on that man's perception of himself. Dostoevsky detested many scientists, but their offense was not science but scientism, the belief that science holds the solution to all practical, intellectual, and spiritual problems.

The historians had a different meaning for Dostoevsky. I have already quoted passages showing how much of Karamzin he read as a child; how much Greek and Roman history he owned and asked for; how strongly he recommended William Prescott, Fedor Solovev, and various historians of Europe; and how much Russian history he knew and understood. He also mentions Louis Thiers a score of times, Henry Buckle, Jean-Baptiste-Adolphe Charras, and Hippolyte Taine a few times, and he corresponded with the historian and journalist Evgenii Aleksandrovich Belov. In the nineteenth century the line between historians, journalists, and fiction writers was not as distinct as it is in American history departments. The major historians appeared in and sometimes published popular journals, and professional journalists like Faddei Bulgarin would enter actively into historical polemics. Gogol tried his hand at teaching history, and when Dostoevsky read novels like those of Dumas, he was doubtless reading them as history as well as fiction. In fact, the reverse is probably more true. When Dostoevsky read history, he was reading it for the plots, the stories, the characters, the insights into psychology in times of crisis or despair, or for examples to use in his polemics.

Dostoevsky's characters see history in a variety of ways. In the second chapter of *Crime and Punishment*, Marmeladov says, "As you can imagine, Sonia didn't receive any education. I tried four years ago to go through geography and world history with her. But since I wasn't strong myself in this realm of knowledge, and there were no decent guides for this, for what books were in our possession...hmm!...so that was the end of all her studies. We stopped at Cyrus of Persia" (*Pss* 6:16). This vision of history as a fixed part of a gentlewoman's upbringing, a body of knowledge to be taken out of a textbook, contrasts sharply with the Underground Man's search for terms to use about history in chapter 8 of part 1. He approves of grandeur, diversity, monotony, of everything except the assertion that history makes good sense (*Pss* 5:16). In *The Brothers Karamazov*, Smerdiakov's and Kolia Krasotkin's reading of history leads to a particular kind of pretentious ignorance, linked with a distrust of other literature and a tendency to bully one's interlocuter. In all these cases, Dostoevsky uses the character's attitude toward history as a sort of touchstone, testing the quality of mind of the speaker and in each case finding him wanting. In chapter 3 of book 5, Ivan Karamazov's attitude toward history also characterizes him, and in a far more endearing fashion:

> I want to get to Europe, Alesha, and I'll get away from here, although I know I'm only going to a graveyard; but to the most, most precious graveyard, that's it! The departed there are precious, and every stone above them witnesses to such an ardent ongoing life, to such a passionate faith in their exploit, their verity, their struggle, and their lore that I know beforehand I shall fall to the earth and kiss those stones and weep over them—at the same time convinced with all my heart that this long since has been a graveyard and nothing more. And I'll not weep from despair, but simply because I shall be happy at the tears I shed. I'll be intoxicated with my own adoration. The sticky spring leaves, the blue sky— That's what I love! Here is no mentality, no logic; here it's with your innards, with your gut you love, and love your own first youthful powers. (*Pss* 14:210)

Alesha agrees that one must love life first of all, more than the meaning of it, and at this point where the two brothers, each so admirable in his way, agree, history emerges in their minds as a storage place for life far richer than the official facts or scientific rules that other characters discover there. Like Ivan and Alesha, Dostoevsky recurs often to this theme of live life which is threatened by the inertia of our drives on one hand and the deadness of our theories on the other. Dostoevsky regarded history and most other honest texts as repositories for live life.

VIII

BALZAC, DICKENS, GOGOL, AND HUGO WERE DOSTOEVSKY'S CHIEF ACKNOWLEDGED MASTERS.

The authors I have discussed so far have belonged to many different parts of the world of letters, a world to which Dostoevsky turned for characters, events, dialogue, descriptions, imagery, ideas, or techniques. But he felt himself to belong to a very specific literary community, the group engaged in the development of the nineteenth-century novel. At the center of this group lay those whom Donald Fanger calls the romantic realists—Balzac, Gogol, and Dickens.[47] Hugo should join this list of great contemporary novelists to whom Dostoevsky often paid tribute and whom he mined for materials, ideas, attitudes, and literary tricks.

This territory has been well mapped in the critical literature. Dostoevsky began his career with a translation of Balzac's *Eugénie Grandet*, and in *The Brothers Karamazov* the temptations of Alesha by Ivan and of Christ by the Grand Inquisitor demand close comparison with the temptation scenes in *Père Goriot*. In the same way Dostoevsky enters into a polemic with Gogol in *Poor Folk* and continues it through the savage parody in *The Friend of the Family*, yet he never stops learning from him, down to *The Brothers Karamazov*, where the narrator says, "I really ought to tell something about [Smerdiakov] specifically, but I'm ashamed to divert the attention of my reader to such commonplace servants and therefore will revert to my account, trusting that somehow it will come out of itself in the further course of the story" (*Pss* 14:93). Like any literate Russian of his day, Dostoevsky would have read the parallel passage in the second chapter of *Dead Souls* in his youth, a period he claimed to remember with extraordinary clarity. In this passage, the narrator ends his discussion of the servant: "And so this is what can be said first thing about Petrushka. The coachman Selifan was an altogether different person. . . . But the author is quite ashamed to occupy the reader with people of the lower class, knowing by experience how unwillingly they become acquainted with lower estates."[48] This pair of passages belong to a rich tradition of texts that manipulate the real reader by deferring to an unenlightened imaginary reader. Karamzin, Pushkin, and many others had played with similar toys, but the deprecatory archness of these two passages suggests that Dostoevsky was striving for a Gogolian effect. I cannot strengthen this stylistic argument by claiming that Dostoevsky ever said "We all came out from Gogol's 'Overcoat.'" The chief evidence for this statement is in an article in *Le revue des deux mondes* in 1885 in which de Vogüé ascribes the remark to an author "closely linked to the literary history of the past forty years." S. A. Reiser points out that this characterization applies equally well to Turgenev and many others, and suggests that while de Vogüé might well have heard it from Dostoevsky, he was most probably quoting a remark that was in the air.[49]

Igor' Katarskii notes that before *Poor Folk*, Dostoevsky never mentions Dickens, but he describes things as Dickensian quite casually soon after that.[50] Dickens had been published in Russia for a decade before *Poor Folk* and had become a part of Russian culture even before his literary merit was recognized there. Certainly Dostoevsky used Dickens centrally in several of his works, such as *The Insulted and Injured*, whose ties with *The Old Curiosity Shop* have been well described. In general, it can be argued that the most Dickensian of Dostoevsky's novels are less successful than the four great murder novels, whose plots and sequences of thought and feeling come from other sources, though Steerforth may contribute to the creation of Stavrogin, or Mr. Pickwick to Prince Myshkin and the way people respond to him.

Several of my quotations have already illustrated Dostoevsky's early sense that Victor Hugo was a grand and noble master of the contemporary novel, but not to be compared with Shakespeare or Goethe. Those biographers of Dostoevsky who quote Myshkin's description of the moments before being executed need to come to terms with Hugo's *Dernier jour d'un condamné* as a source that interacted with Dostoevsky's personal experience. Nathalie Babel Brown has written a long and detailed plot summary that works equally well for *Crime and Punishment* and for *Les misérables*, and Dostoevsky himself commented on the relation between the two novels much later, when *The Brothers Karamazov* was taking shape:

> On the subject of Victor Hugo, I probably talked to you, but I see that you are still very young, since you place him on the level with Goethe and Shakespeare. I like *Les misérables* very much myself. It came out at the same time as my *Crime and Punishment*, that is, two years earlier. Our great poet, the late F. I. Tiutchev, and many others at the time ranked *Crime and Punishment* incomparably higher than *Les Misérables*; but I disputed them all

and proved to them all that *Les misérables* was higher than my poem, and I disputed them honestly, wholeheartedly, and even now am convinced of this, in the face of the general opinion of all our experts. But my love of *Les misérables* does not keep me from seeing its great flaws. The figure of Valjean is enchanting, as are a terrific number of most typical and splendid passages. . . . Still, how ridiculous his lovers are! what franco-bourgeois they are in the most ignoble way! How ridiculous are the endless babbling and sometimes the oratory in the novel, but especially ridiculous are his republicans, puffed up and implausible figures. His villains are far better. Where these fallen people are real, on Victor Hugo's part, there are always humaneness, love, and magnanimity, and you did very well to notice this and love it. Especially to love the figure of the Abbé Myriel.[51]

This curious mixture of genuine arrogance, genuine humility, and genuine literary evaluation gives a picture of where Dostoevsky's long and rather consistent concern with Victor Hugo had brought him by the time he was writing *The Brothers Karamazov*.

Of course, Dostoevsky did not have to like or admire an author to use him in his novels. He picked up Zola's *Ventre de Paris* and wrote to his wife, "I can scarcely read it, such filth [*gadost'*],"[52] but B. G. Reizov has shown the importance of Zola's ideas about social and genetic causation in the history of the Karamazov family,[53] and even on the verbal level he finds a passage in the very first pages of *The Brothers Karamazov* which shows that Dostoevsky had Zola in mind as he created a family that bears some resemblance to Zola's passionate, energetic, and disreputable Rougons: "Just how it happened that a girl with a dowry, and a beauty to boot, and one of those snappy wits on top of that, which are not so rare in our present generation, but were already making their appearance in the last one, could have married such an insignificant 'runt' [*mozgliak*], as they all called him, I shan't undertake to explain too much" (*Pss* 14:7–8). He would not have expected his readers to recognize the parallel passage in *The Rougon-Maquarts* but would have used it for its intrinsic literary appropriateness:

She had scarcely been alone in the world for six months, owner of a holding which made her an heiress who was sought after, when people learned of her marriage to a gardener's man named Rougon, a barely civilized peasant who came from the fore-Alps. . . . This marriage astonished local opinion. No one could imagine why Adelaide preferred this poor wretch, coarse, heavy, common, scarcely knowing how to speak French, to this or that person, children of comfortable farmers, who had been hovering about her for a long time.[54]

Dostoevsky uses this passage of Zola's not only for the name of a character and the themes of social inappropriateness, generational degeneracy, and incomprehensibly self-destructive marriages but also for the appeal to the puzzlement of the neighbors in introducing the account.

Dostoevsky did not have to consider authors great to depend on them heavily as sources. In his own generation, he admired and used George Sand and Eugène Sue, who both derived their immense popularity from a high moral and political idealism coupled with remarkable professional skill at storytelling. In the article just cited in reference to Zola, Reizov also dealt at some length with Sand's *Mauprat* as a source for the encounters between Dunia and Svidrigailov or Katerina Ivanovna and Mitia Karamazov when they stood helpless before an armed man in an isolated room.[55] Dostoevsky wrote a moving obituary for George Sand, which sets her in the context of the intellectual world of her time, where she was the bearer of major ideas and not just a masterful spinner of tales or a feminist icon, as she is for most readers today:

> I think I was sixteen the first time I read her story "L'Uscoque," one of the most charming of her first stories. I remember I was in a fever all night after it. I don't think I would be wrong to say that judging at least by my recollection, George Sand occupied just about the first rank in the whole *pléiade* of new writers who were suddenly glorified and reverberated over all of Europe. Even Dickens, who appeared here almost simultaneously with her, perhaps took second place to her in the attention of our readers. I am not talking about Balzac, who had appeared before her and produced such works as *Eugénie Grandet* and *Père Goriot.* . . . In the midforties, the glory of George Sand and the faith in her genius stood so high that we who were her contemporaries were all awaiting from her something incomparably greater in the future, an as-yet-unheard new word, even something decisive and definitive. These hopes were not fulfilled; it turned out that at that time, toward the end of the forties, that is, she had already said all she was fated and destined to enunciate. . . . George Sand was not a thinker, but one of the most clairvoyant foresensers (if I may express myself in such a contorted phrase) of the happier future awaiting humanity, to the attainment of whose ideals she boldly and nobly entrusted her life.[56]

Malcolm Jones has worked on the relationship between Sue and Dostoevsky with equal control and persuasiveness, but no work to date has exhausted the ways these two enormously prolific authors affected Dostoevsky.

The list of European novelists whom Dostoevsky read goes far beyond these important figures. No convincing evidence suggests that he knew George Eliot or Jane Austen, but Regis Messac makes a persuasive case that some part of Raskolnikov's identity comes from Bulwer-Lytton, whom Dostoevsky never mentions.[57] He certainly read Paul de Kock, Adolphe Belot, Frédéric Soulié, and a host of authors few read today except to earn a living.

In Russia, as an active editor and avid reader of many journals, Dostoevsky came in contact with virtually the entire literary community, great and small. Tolstoi he never met, but he wrote about him often, sometimes jealously, envying the time Tolstoi had available for reworking his novels; sometimes wondering about what really mattered in the shapely lives of the gentry Tolstoi usually depicted—or about the military and political implications of Tolstoianism—but at his best, especially in the years when *The Brothers Karamazov* was gestating, with a clear sense that the literary integrity of Tolstoy's works was matched only by the moral integrity of his positions:

> *Anna Karenina* is perfection as a work of art, appearing at just the right moment, unequaled by anything comparable in European literature at the present moment; and also its idea is really something of our own, our beloved own, the very thing that constitutes our particularity before the European world, that constitutes our nation's "new word," or at least the beginning of it—precisely such a word as you will never hear in Europe, but which Europe needs so much, notwithstanding all its pride.[58]

The large body of literature comparing, contrasting, and describing the relationship between Tolstoi and Dostoevsky suffers from the amplitude and ambiguity of the data available.[59]

The relation with Turgenev was more intense, more important, and full of contradictions. Each of these two very different authors influenced the other strongly as their literary consciousness was maturing, and each said savage things about the other and to the other; but the two became reconciled at the end of their careers.[60]

Nikolai Nekrasov was the other major literary figure who was personally close to Dostoevsky at certain points in his life, struggled with him ideologically, and eventually came to terms with him at some level. Joseph Frank has argued that Dostoevsky could not tolerate the anti-Russian attitude of radicals such as Nekrasov in the 1860s but was able to publish *The Raw Youth* in Nekrasov's journal in the seventies because Russian radicalism had again become nationalist. Ivan Karamazov's citation of him illustrates

Nekrasov's Russianness with particular irony: Dostoevsky had read Ivan's example of a peculiarly Russian brand of savagery both in Nekrasov and in *Les misérables,* which Nekrasov also used as a source, as Nathalie Babel Brown has shown.[61] Dostoevsky summed up his relation with Nekrasov in the moving beginning of his obituary of him in *The Diary of a Writer:*

> Nekrasov is dead. I saw him for the last time a month before his death. He seemed almost a corpse already then, so that it was even strange to see that such a corpse was talking, moving its lips. But he not only talked, but retained all his clarity of mind. He still seemed not to believe in the possibility of imminent death. . . . Returning home [after paying respects at his coffin] I couldn't start working and took all three volumes of Nekrasov and started reading from the first page. I sat all night till six in the morning, and seemed to live these thirty years all over again. Those first four poems with which the first volume of his verse begins appeared in the *Petersburg Miscellany,* where my first story appeared too. After that, as I read on (and I read in order) it was as if all my life passed before me. I also recognized and recollected those poems of his which I had read first in Siberia, when, emerging from my four-year incarceration in the camp, I achieved the right to take a book in hand. I recollected my impression at that time. In short, during that night, I reread almost two-thirds of all Nekrasov wrote and literally for the first time reckoned how great a place Nekrasov, as a poet, had occupied in my life throughout these thirty years! As a poet, of course. Personally, we were together rarely and not long, and only once with completely uncalculating, burning emotion, at just the very beginning of our acquaintance, in forty-five, when I was writing *Poor Folk.*[62]

Dostoevsky critized Nekrasov's character with severe compassion in this memoir, but here and elsewhere he ranks Nekrasov's vision of the Russian people in all its filth and greatness as a poetic achievement excelled only by Pushkin's and Lermontov's.

IX

AS A JOURNALIST, DOSTOEVSKY READ EVERYTHING HE COULD, GOOD OR BAD, PUBLISHED OR UNPUBLISHED, BY FRIEND OR FOE.

Dostoevsky's letters and journalism make it plain that he remained deeply involved in reading and rereading every kind of text at all points in his career. He mentions the names of far too many of his contemporaries to discuss in a book devoted to the fruits rather than the facts of his reading. The most important influence upon him may well have been that of his ideological and political enemies. Like many authors trained in journalism, Dostoevsky answered existing positions, particularly smug ones, better than he created new ones, and he interacted avidly with the writings of the radicals as he read them. For the purposes of this study, it makes better sense to discuss this community in connection with Ivan Karamazov, who was a member of it, so I shall simply mention some names here.

Dostoevsky's career spanned an extraordinary polarization of Russian intellectual life. In his youth, the struggle between the Slavophiles and the Westernizers had taken place within an intellectual world with more or less coherent manners and ideals. Dostoevsky cites Aleksei S. Khomiakov and the Aksakovs fairly often, and although he mentions Ivan Kireevsky only three times, their thinking often moves in parallel, perhaps, as V. A. Kotel'nikov suggests, because of common sources in European romanticism and Orthodox Christianity.[63] The great intellectual figures of Dostoevsky's youth—Peter Chaadaev, Timothy Granovsky, Yurii Samarin, and others—appear frequently in his writings, perhaps in some part out of nostalgia for a less viciously polemical period.

By the sixties and seventies, middle positions had become very hard to maintain. Dostoevsky read and used the antinihilist writers of his own time with much the same vigor as he did the nihilists. Charles Moser has treated the antinihilist novel as a clearly defined literary genre,[64] and in many ways Dostoevsky's *Possessed* is the best example of it. Two other major writers, Leskov and Pisemskii, wrote novels in this genre, and Dostoevsky drew a savage detail in Rakitin's life from Leskov's brilliant antinihilist memoir, *The Enigmatic Man*. The relation between Dostoevsky and Pisemskii deserves more attention than it has received. The other great conservative novelist of this period, Goncharov, exchanged cordial letters with Dostoevsky on several occasions and was a crucial figure in his literary consciousness, both as a writer and as a censor. Dostoevsky's scorn for the lesser antinihilists like V. I. Askochenskii and Vsevolod Krestovskii still left him in touch with their writings. The most influential conservative of Dostoevsky's time was not primarily a writer. Dostoevsky's letters to the great publisher Mikhail Katkov drip with civility when he needs a royalty advance from Katkov's enormously prosperous *Russian Messenger* (*Russkii vestnik*), where *The Brothers Karamazov* appeared. Dostoevsky might feel ironic about Katkov's personal concern with power, but he respected Katkov's views, appreciated his genuine support, and certainly read everything he wrote. Most of the writers for Dostoevsky's journals also stood far to the right on the issues of the day, and Nikolai Strakhov, Apollon Grigor'ev, and Dmitrii Averkiev provided considerable imagery and ideology for *The Brothers Karamazov*. Dostoevsky understood the limitations of these authors but liked and respected them through most of his career, corresponded with them about their work and his, and kept in close touch with their work.

Dostoevsky mentions or refers to over two hundred other Russian authors and editors or their publications, and no definable group seems to be absent from the list. In the case of Europe, on the other hand, as Grossman observed many years ago, Dostoevsky, who loved art and poetry, was in Paris in the full flower of impressionism and symbolism and ignored these artists and poets completely.[65] Baudelaire's name appears, but as a translator of Edgar Allen Poe. Dostoevsky simply did not have a modernist mind and did not need one in the Russian milieu in which he flourished. Alex de Jonge has compared Dostoevsky's treatment of emotional intensity with that of the symbolists, and although the parallels are strong, they are due not to literary influence but to a parallel grounding in European romanticism.

With this single revealing exclusion, it is safer in any given case to assume that Dostoevsky knew the writings of his contemporaries in Russia or France than to assume he did not.

CHAPTER
THREE

DOSTOEVSKY CONDENSED A LIFETIME OF PREPARATION INTO A YEAR OF PLANNING AND TWO YEARS OF WRITING.

I
DOSTOEVSKY BUILT *THE BROTHERS KARAMAZOV* OUT OF MANY EXPERIENCES THAT ARE PARTLY KNOWABLE, AS THEY ARE RESHAPED IN THE NOTEBOOKS FOR OTHER WRITINGS.

As chapters 1 and 2 of this study suggest, *The Brothers Karamazov*, like Dostoevsky's other novels, and much other literature, reworks an enormous body of literary and other experiences that were sometimes thousands of years old and often the common property of literate nineteenth-century Russians. Chapter 3 will summarize the thorough studies that have already been made on the chronology of this reworking.[1] Chapters 4 through 9 will discuss how this alchemy took place, examining *The Brothers Karamazov* not only as the product of the entire culture Dostoevsky knew but also as the artifact of his energetic literary mind.

The beginnings of *The Brothers Karamazov* are hard to date. Insofar as any life is a seamless whole, and this was Dostoevsky's last major work, much of what he wrote can be treated as a preparation for the novel. Iu. G. Oksman, Arkadii Dolinin, and others have described the ways Dostoevsky used his journalistic articles and letters along with his notebooks as early versions of the materials that would find their place in his novels.[2] Every novel or story he published contains elements that emerge again in *The*

Brothers Karamazov. It has even been suggested that the translation of Balzac's *Eugénie Grandet* with which he began his career may include work that would come to fruition in *The Brothers Karamazov*, with the traits of old Grandet already transformed in the direction of old Fedor Karamazov, who would emerge thirty years later.

Each of Dostoevsky's surviving notebooks has been published in association with the novel closest to it, but all of the notebooks also contain leftovers that went into later novels, including *The Brothers Karamazov.* Consider the 196th item of the 500 convict sayings that he wrote down in Siberia in the first of his notebooks that survives: "Hello!" "Well, hello, if you're not joking" (*Pss* 4:240). No information survives about the circumstances of this interchange, or about whether it was recorded in the notes a helpful orderly in the prison hospital kept for Dostoevsky or whether he wrote it down himself from memory after his release from the camp. We do know that a quarter-century later Dostoevsky expanded the note into a scene that characterizes Kolia Krasotkin, the magnificently objectionable leader of the schoolboys:

> "I love to shake up fools in all classes of society. . . . Take note of it; they say there's nothing stupider than a stupid Frenchman, but the Russian physiognomy gives itself away, too. Now, isn't it written all over that guy's face that he's a fool, look, that peasant there, well? . . . Hey, hello, my good man!"
>
> A slowly passing peasant, who must have had a drink or two already, with a round, simpleminded face and a graying beard, lifted his head and looked at the young fellow. "Well, hello, if you're not joking," he answered unhurriedly.
>
> "And if I am?" Kolia laughed.
>
> "If you're joking, then joke, God bless you. Doesn't matter; that's allowed. Joking's always allowed."
>
> "I'm afraid, my friend, that I was joking."
>
> "Well, God forgive you."
>
> "And will you too?"
>
> "Very much so. Now, get going."
>
> "Well then, you're a real smart peasant."
>
> "Smarter than you," the peasant answered unexpectedly, and gravely, as before.
>
> "Hardly," Kolia was rather disconcerted.
>
> "I'm saying the truth."
>
> "And maybe you're right."
>
> "Good-bye, boy."
>
> "Good-bye, my good man."

"Peasants are diverse," Kolia observed after some silence. . . .
"How was I to know that I would hit upon one with real wits? I
am always prepared to recognize wits in the populace." (Pss 14:477)

There is no way of knowing how much of this particular in-
terlude has its source in the prison camp; how much in figures like
Bazarov and the radicals of the forties or the sixties, who also
patronized the peasants; and how much in the sequence of the
dialogue itself, where, even if Dostoevsky had no outside source,
"If you're not joking" could provoke "And if I am?" by the sheer
perversity of a preadolescent's logic. In any case, the notebooks for
all of Dostoevsky's other works reecho in *The Brothers Karamazov*,
and the more recent they are, the more influential, with *The Diary
of a Writer* notebooks and those for *The Raw Youth* most important
and those for *The Possessed* and *The Idiot* somewhat less so.

But long before Dostoevsky began writing novels, notebooks, or
even letters, he was accumulating and processing data about key
themes and elements in *The Brothers Karamazov*. (In a later chapter
I will discuss his claim that he drew one scene in the novel from
a recollection dating to the age of two.) Among other things, the
novel recounts a parricide, a murderous confrontation between a
son and his father over a beautiful woman, many deaths, murders,
abandonments, and mistreatments of children, and many richly
moving encounters between children and wisely or hysterically
loving parents, as well as several variants on the relationships that
develop among the united and separated siblings in the families of
Zosima, the Snegirevs, and the Karamazovs. Jolan Neufeld, Sigmund
Freud, Dominique Arban, and many others have argued persuasively
that Dostoevsky began working on these aspects of *The Brothers
Karamazov* at the traumatic moments in his own life: the murder
of his difficult father; the early loss of his mother; the long sickness
and the death of a wife he had loved and also found almost insufferable; the death of his brother Mikhail, with whom he had shared
his childhood; his education and his first forays into literature,
socialism, and journalism; and very probably his infantile experience
of helplessness in the face of perceived or fancied parental and
sibling threats or rivalries. These beginnings for the novel are log-
ically and biographically prior to the literary ones; they sensitized
him to certain readings, led him to others, and shaped his response
to all that he read, but in general, for the purposes of this study, I
will treat most such early moments as establishing patterns that
were part of Dostoevsky's processing mechanism rather than of his
process of creation as he set to work on *The Brothers Karamazov*.

II

IT EMERGES FROM A CLUSTER OF WORKS HE PLANNED BUT NEVER WROTE.

Dostoevsky planned many works of literature that he never wrote, and a number of them have been recognized as early efforts to make artistic use of materials that eventually emerged in one or more of the novels, often including *The Brothers Karamazov*. For many artists, creativity comes in bursts. Dostoevsky experienced such a burst in the late 1860s. His new wife, his children, his prolonged encounter with Europe, and his solving of the difficult narrative and other problems of *The Idiot* gave him the strength to put behind him the miseries of Siberia and of his first marriage, his gambling, his affair with Suslova, the loss of his brother and first wife, and the many financial, political, and other anxieties of the 1860s that had helped to give his writings of that period their capacity to hover on the edge of hysteria. The release of energy and the readiness for new tasks led him to conceive a collection of projects far beyond his capacity to carry out.

In 1867, for example, he planned a work on Ivan VI, the emperor who was deposed at the age of one in 1741 and incarcerated alone until an attempt to enthrone him in 1764 brought him "grandly and sadly" to his death. From an attic window the adjutant who tempts him to sponsor this insurrection shows him the outer world, "All thine, if only thou desirest. Let us be off!" (*Pss* 9:113). The emperor, an innocent, refuses because the enterprise risks the lives of his friend, himself, and the prison commandant's daughter, whom he has seen once or twice through the window. This piece of minimalist psychology comes primarily from contemporary historical accounts of Ivan VI, perhaps with literary reinforcement from *The Charterhouse of Parma, The Man in the Iron Mask,* or a life of the Buddha, but alongside these sources is the biblical temptation of Christ in the Wilderness, which was to be represented in the great temptation scene in the legend of the Grand Inquisitor. The editors of the *Pss* point out that this temptation to exchange innocent blood for the power to do great good runs through many of Dostoevsky's works (*Pss* 9:489). An unwritten novel like this forms one of the links between Raskolnikov's acceptance of this temptation in *Crime and Punishment* and Ivan's rhetorical rejection of it in the "Mutiny" chapter of *The Brothers Karamazov*.

Other planned works contain individual elements that enter the later novel—the killing of a father, the education of children (*Pss* 9:115), or a vignette from the late 1860s that would help to generate Snegirev's behavior when Alesha gives him a hundred rubles: "They found 3,000, and delivered it. The recipient gave them a scolding and 25 rubles. Out of poverty, he took it. He couldn't *refuse*. In the midst of his fearsome need, he and his wife decide to take it back. He crumpled the paper and threw it in his snout" (*Pss* 9:120). In the case of another unwritten novel, *The Prince and the Moneylender*, the editors call attention to the parallels between the state of mind of an innocent convict and that of Mitia Karamazov after his conviction (*Pss* 9:124). Dostoevsky's notes, of course, are reminders, not instruments of communication; they are sometimes condensed to a line or two, and sometimes to a page or two, but in many cases his letters show that a few words in the notebook stand for a clearly visualized scene or sequence.

The most famous and probably the most complete of Dostoevsky's unexecuted plans was *The Life of a Great Sinner* (*Pss* 9:125–38), which seems to have emerged from another unwritten novel, *Atheism*, at the very end of the 1860s, as he was finishing *The Idiot*. These unwritten novels remained in flux, but the best account of *Atheism* probably comes from a well-known letter to Apollon Maikov from Florence on 11 December 1868:

> I now have in mind here 1) an enormous novel named *Atheism* (between you and me, for goodness sake), but before undertaking it, I have to read almost a whole library of atheists, catholics, and orthodox. It will come to fruition, even if my work is fully supported, no sooner than three years from now. A character exists: a Russian man, out of our society, *middle-aged*, not very educated, but also not uneducated, not without rank—*suddenly*, already middle-aged, he loses faith in God. All his life, he has considered only his government job, has not stood out, and till 45 has been notable for nothing. . . . He bustles among the new generation, the atheists, the Slavs and the Europeans, among the Russian bigots, anchorites, and priests; he is firmly hooked, incidentally, by a Polish Jesuit who propagates the faith; he sinks from him into the depths of the flagellants—and finally regains Christ, the Russian land, the Russian Christ, and the Russian God. (*Pss* 28, pt. 2:329)

Dostoevsky refers to this novel many times, and its central theme of a conventional life, a loss of faith, a traumatic search for faith, and a return to faith shapes the lives of the three brothers Karamazov, Zosima, his brother, the mysterious stranger, and, in more problematic ways, several other characters in *The Brothers Karamazov. The Life of a Great Sinner* has the same central theme but elaborates it into the whole life of a character, in a work to be called a *zhitie*, or hagiography, but planned on an enormous scale—five related novels, the whole as long as *War and Peace*. The plan constitutes a major effort to bring together many of the elements that would later appear in *The Brothers Karamazov*, but it is most important as the fullest documentation of a moment when Dostoevsky, almost fifty, formulated the techniques, themes, and literary goals that would be central in the thousands of pages he wrote during the last decade of his life.

On 13 September 1874 Dostoevsky laid out the plan for a drama, set in Tobolsk, that reworked the experience of the convict Il'inskii, whom he had described in *The House of the Dead* a decade earlier. As it stands it is a melodrama, not fleshed out with the social, political, religious, and other implications that fill the other planned works I have mentioned. It played a central place in the plot of *The Brothers Karamazov*, and I will deal with it at length in the next chapter in connection with the career of Mitia Karamazov.

Early in 1876, Dostoevsky wrote, "I always have watched children before, too, but now I keep an eye on them especially. For a long time I've made it my ideal goal to write a novel about the Russian children of our day—about their parents too, of course—in their present-day interrelation" (*Pss* 29, pt. 2:72). In his introduction to *The Brothers Karamazov* notebooks, Dolinin cites this and other passages, and the notebooks for *The Idiot*, *The Possessed*, and *The Raw Youth* confirm Dostoevsky's statement that he has had such a plan for a long time.[3] This rich and often-reorganized body of material emerged in extended form in *The Raw Youth* and in a planned novel with the original title of *Fathers and Children*, probably conceived in March 1876. But as the quotation implies, he was always adding new materials to the complex of characters, events, remarks, and ideas that would take new form in *The Brothers Karamazov*, not only in the youth of Alesha and his encounters with the schoolboys, in which context I will discuss it later, but also in the accounts of the other brothers and many other characters.

In December of 1877 Dostoevsky wrote himself a memorandum "for my whole life" that contained four items and a note:

1) Write the Russian Candide.
2) Write the book about Jesus Christ.
3) Write my memoirs.
4) Write the poema *The Memorial Service*.
N.B. (All this in addition to the last novel and the proposed edition of the *Diary*, i.e., a minimum of ten years work, and I'm now 56.)
(*Pss* 17:14)

Most scholars think the "last novel" referred to is *The Brothers Karamazov*, but that belief may merely project backward the fact that he died three years later, which he plainly did not intend to do, although certain letters show that he knew his health was bad.[4] I am more inclined to treat it as a vast shadowy project that Dostoevsky promised himself to write if he could ever escape the pressure of monthly deadlines. In one of the seminal articles on Dostoevsky, Leonid Grossman argued that "the Russian Candide" emerged as that part of *The Brothers Karamazov* which examines the question of how a benevolent and almighty God permitted innocent suffering.[5] Some part of the book about Jesus may also have entered *The Brothers Karamazov,* as may the other works. It is impossible, however, to know whether these works were well formed in Dostoevsky's mind or not, that is, whether I should have translated "the book about Jesus Christ" as "a book about Jesus Christ," since Russian does not use articles. Like *The Life of a Great Sinner,* this document is not a master plan for Dostoevsky's late novels but rather a piece of evidence about the way the materials in his mind would crystallize into the outline of works of literature. These outlines might then redissolve, returning their materials somewhat transformed for future use, or might form the beginning of a novel that he carried to completion. They constitute scraps surviving from an enormous body of literary intellection, much of which was never committed to paper, and some of which was written and lost. Scholars always long to leave no surviving item unconnected with other items, but in studies of this sort, the absence of a key connection may prompt us to ascribe incorrect meanings to the pieces we have.

III
THE NOVEL INCLUDES LEFTOVER MATERIALS FROM EARLIER WRITING AND OFTEN RUNS EARLIER LITERARY EXPERIMENTS WITH ONE VARIABLE CHANGED.

Like Shakespeare, as Keats understood him, Dostoevsky had the "negative capability" of publishing works that did not exhaust the possibilities of a given character, event, situation, idea, or technique; and like Shakespeare, he would return to such elements in subsequent works until they had no more to offer him. In this sense, Murin in "The Landlady" has been treated as a first draft for the physical figure of the Grand Inquisitor, Myshkin as an early transformation of many of those sources that fed into Alesha Karamazov, Raskolnikov as a trial run for important elements in the career of Mitia Karamazov and the ideas of Ivan Karamazov, and so on. Certain character types recur in many Dostoevsky works. Rakitin grows out of a lineage of cheap, stupid, repulsive, socially insecure but sexually insolent radicals who constitute the petty villains in Dostoevsky's three other great murder novels: Luzhin in *Crime and Punishment*, Verkhovensky in *The Possessed*, and the collection of nihilistic villains in *The Idiot*. The grand, fascinating, murderous, mysterious sensualists in these novels—Svidrigailov, Rogozhin, and Stavrogin—all rework earlier materials in preparation for their appearance in the sensualist Mitia Karamazov, the mysterious murderer Smerdiakov, and the grand, fascinating Ivan. Events also have their antecedents; when Katerina Ivanovna comes to Mitia Karamazov's quarters, risking her honor for the sake of her father's, Dostoevsky is reworking materials he has already reworked in *Crime and Punishment*, when Dunia visits Svidrigailov in the hope of protecting her brother.

Dostoevsky had been processing and reprocessing the ideas in *The Brothers Karamazov* for many years, as we have already seen, but the most important and best studied earlier work on them appeared in *The Diary of a Writer*. His stature as a novelist often makes us forget that he was one of the important journalists of his time, publishing and editing *Time* and the *Epoch* (*Epokha*) with his brother in the 1860s; editing the *Citizen* for the deeply conservative Prince Meshcherskii in 1873–74; and then expanding his *Diary of a Writer* from a column in that journal into a separate monthly, which he and his wife published and he not only edited but also wrote in its entirety in 1876, 1877, and for two issues between the end of *The Brothers Karamazov* and his death. With a press run of six thousand copies, this was one of the most successful Russian journals of the period. It contained two of Dostoevsky's greatest short stories, "The Gentle Creature" and "The Dream of a Ridiculous Man," and a number of other memoiristic or fictional pieces, but most of the thirty-five-page (in *Pss*) issues consisted of essays on the legal, social, or international questions of the day.[6] In these pages Dostoevsky wrote the first draft of many of the ideas that would later be enunciated by Ivan Karamazov, the monastery folk, and the narrator of *The Brothers Karamazov*. *The Diary of a Writer* will play a large part in the pages that follow.

During the year 1877 Dostoevsky reached the decision to interrupt a journal that was strongly serving his ideological and financial needs. The only plausible reason for doing so would be the birth or discovery of that "diamond," the living center of a novel, which he described in his lyrical letter to Maikov already discussed in chapter 1, section 4, and discussed again at the end of this book. In the August issue he announced to his readers that he would cease publication "for reasons of health," and in the December issue he said he was interrupting publication to begin work on "a certain artistic work which has been forming for these two years unnoticed and unwilled." Dolinin quotes these last three words and explains them as follows:

> In these words is contained a particularly precious indication of the creative process of the artist, the *prehistory* of the creation of the Karamazovs. There wandered in the sphere of awareness the embryos of figures, separate, dispersed traits, situations not organized into any united whole, emerging to meet the facts of the surrounding reality. These are still not elements of plot, but they can become so. They have appeared so far always subordinated to enunciated ideas. Summoned to the surface by ideas and thoughts of another, nonartistic order, they immediately sank back again into the sphere of ideas. But the artistic work continued all the same.[7]

Dolinin is describing the subject of my book, and I would agree with him that the crucial assemblages and transformations of material took place in 1875 and 1876, although, as I have suggested, some parts of the creative process date far back, and others took place during the period 1878–80, when Dostoevsky was actively planning and writing the novel. I will summarize the amply established information about this period in the next section, using the notes in volume 15 of *Pss* as the most recent and authoritative study.

IV
DOSTOEVSKY DEVOTED MOST OF 1878 TO PLANNING *THE BROTHERS KARAMAZOV,* AND MOST OF 1879 AND 1880 TO WRITING IT.

The earliest notes for *The Brothers Karamazov* are lost, but the memoirs of Dostoevsky's wife and his appeal for lore about children in his farewell to the readers of *The Diary of a Writer* both show that he was hard at work on the new novel before the end of 1877. On 16 March he wrote to the teacher Mikhailov:

> Here is my request, dear Vladimir Vasilevich: I have conceived and soon will begin a big novel in which, among others, children will play a large part, and particularly young ones, from 7 to 15, for example. Many children will be introduced. I am studying them, have studied them all my life, love them greatly, and have my own. But the observations of a person like you . . . will be precious for me. So write me about *children* what you know yourself. Both about Petersburg children who have known you as uncle, and about Elizabethgrad children, and *what you know about.* (Events, practices,

answers, words and sayings, peculiarities, family life, faith, evil-doing and innocence, nature and teacher, the Latin language, etc., etc.—in a word, what you know yourself.) You will help me greatly, and I will wait hungrily for it.[8]

Dolinin argues that this letter marks the end of a second stage in the creative process, the final arrival at what Dostoevsky sometimes called a "plan" and sometimes an "idea." For *The Idiot* and *The Raw Youth*, a large body of notes survive in which Dostoevsky tried out different patterns of organization for the characters and episodes that hovered in his reservoir of materials for the novel. Scholars have not decided exactly what Dostoevsky meant by the words "plan" and "idea," but it does not seem to be the plot, as some have thought, because virtually all the elements in the plot appear earlier, and major rearrangements of them take place after the "plan" has crystallized. In the final chapter of this study, I shall be in a position to speculate on the nature of this moment, after which Dostoevsky was able to begin writing continuous text for the novel.

By April 1878, when the first surviving sheet of notes was written, the novel involved not only children but also the Il'inskii melodrama he had conceived several years earlier, and doubtless other elements that did not appear on the isolated sheet. On 18 May, however, Dostoevsky suffered a wrenching shock, which interrupted all productive work for weeks. His son Aleksei died of an epileptic fit, his first. In Dostoevsky's mind, epilepsy was his legacy to his son, since it had played such a destructive role in his own life. He had always been deeply devoted to his family, worried about their health, and wrote many passages in his letters like this one from 10 June 1875: "I saw Fedya and Lili in my dream today, and worry whether something has happened to them! Ah, Ania, I think about them day and night" (*Pss* 29, pt. 2: 47). It has been suggested that *Hamlet* is the longest of Shakespeare's plays because Shakespeare became involved in creating a rich identity for the namesake of his own son Hamnet, who died soon before he wrote the play. *The Brothers Karamazov* is Dostoevsky's longest work in part, perhaps, because Dostoevsky found it hard to stop making a life for Aleksei Karamazov.

On 22 June, on a trip to Moscow, he sold the periodical rights to *The Brothers Karamazov* to Mikhail Katkov's *Russian Messenger*. The price was generous, three hundred rubles per printer's sheet (approximately five hundred 1989 dollars for approximately twenty modern pages). Such terms from a hardheaded, remarkably effective publisher like Katkov, who had lived with Dostoevsky's crises and delays for fifteen years, demonstrates that the novel was well under way. On 25 June in Moscow, Dostoevsky joined his friend the philosopher Vladimir Solovev for a week's trip to the Optina Hermitage, where the famous Elder Ambrose comforted him over the loss of his son. Anna Grigorievna, who understood the interplay between religion and emotion in her husband's mind, had urged Solovev to take him there. She records that many details of the monastery in *The Brothers Karamazov* were drawn from what Dostoevsky saw on this visit, and that Zosima's words of comfort to the peasant woman who has lost her son (also named Aleksei) are those of Father Ambrose to her husband.

From the Optina, Dostoevsky returned to St. Petersburg and to his country home at Staraia Russa and devoted himself to writing. At this stage, his basic schedule was to work most of the night on detailed notes for a chapter, to sleep all morning, and then to dictate what he had composed to his wife, who was a trained stenographer. She would make a copy, which he would correct, and from his corrected copy she would make the fair copy for the publisher. He was still sketching outlines for parts of book 1 on an envelope dated 1 September and seems to have spent most of October on book 2. On 7 November he delivered the fair copy of books 1 and 2 to his publisher, and they appeared in the January issue. He spent the end of November and most of December and January on book 3, which he sent to Moscow at the beginning of February, in time for publication in the February issue. Late in February, he was at work on book 4 but unable to meet the March deadline, so it did not come out until April. Book 5 came out in the May and June issues, with the break between the chapters "Mutiny" and "The Grand Inquisitor." Dostoevsky justified the delay to his editor on the grounds of the immense importance of these chapters. In July he traveled to Bad Ems to take the waters for his emphysema, missing that issue but continuing work on book 6, which came out in August.

On 8 July 1879 he wrote to his editor that it would be impossible to finish the novel in 1879 and offered to take the blame upon himself so that the *Russian Messenger* would not be criticized for prolonging a work that attracted readers, as they had been with *Anna Karenina*. In the months that followed, the plans for book 7, which had originally centered on Grushenka, expanded into books 7, 8, and 9. He completed book 7, "Alesha," in mid-September, and it appeared in the September issue. The first four chapters of book 8 appeared in the October issue, and in a naively revealing passage of a letter written 16 November, Dostoevsky apologized for delaying chapters 5 through 8:

> Yesterday I sent you the ending of the 8th book of the Karamazovs, which has probably been received in the office already. Again I beg you to excuse my delay. All through the 8th Book there suddenly appeared many altogether new characters, and at least in passing, each had to be sketched as fully as possible, and therefore this book turned out bigger than I had originally indicated and took more time too, so that this time I was late, altogether unexpectedly for myself too. . . . The 9th book also emerged for me suddenly and unexpectedly.[9]

He began working on book 9 late in November 1879 and sent it to Moscow on 14 January 1880, in time for the January issue. Book 10, "The Schoolboys," which included passages from all stages of the evolution of the novel, took until April to complete and appeared that month. From 23 May to 10 June Dostoevsky was in Moscow for the unveiling of the monument to Pushkin; as a result, he missed the issues for those two months and published only the first five chapters of book 11, "Ivan," in the July issue. The great scenes between Ivan and Smerdiakov and then the Devil were written in July and the first ten days of August, appearing in the August issue. The long account of the trial in book 12 also took two months to complete, with chapters 1–5 appearing in September and 6–14 in October. He had outlined the epilogue as early as April, but it was 8 November 1880 when he sent it to his editor, saying, "Well, the novel's done. I worked on it three years, wrote it two— a remarkable moment for me."[10]

In short, the emergence of *The Brothers Karamazov* can be divided into four stages, whose boundaries are not sharp.

1. 1821–80: The unstructured accumulation of materials.

2. 1876–77: The crystallization of these materials about certain changing foci of interest.

3. Late 1877–78: Planning.

4. Mid-1878–late 1880: Writing.

I will return to all the subjects introduced here but felt the need for a chronology at this point.

CHAPTER
FOUR

DOSTOEVSKY KEPT MERGING AND REWORKING THE SOURCES OF MITIA KARAMAZOV TO FORM A NEW CHARACTER AND A NEW PLOT.

I
THE CONVICT IL'INSKII'S GUILT AND INNOCENCE SERVED DIFFERENT PURPOSES IN *THE HOUSE OF THE DEAD*.

In the first chapter of *The House of the Dead*, Dostoevsky makes one of his strongest criticisms of the prisons he has known. "In the course of several years, I did not see among these [people] the slightest sign of repentance. . . . In the convict, the prison and the most intense hard labor develop only hatred, craving for forbidden pleasures, and an awful frivolity" (*Pss* 4:15). To make this critique indisputable, he concedes that there are indeed viewpoints that might lead one to justify many crimes but recoups this concession with the following assertion:

> Regardless of all possible viewpoints, everyone will agree that there
> are crimes which always and everywhere, under all possible laws,
> from the beginning of the world, have been considered undoubtedly
> crimes, and will be so considered as long as men are men. Only
> in the prison did I hear accounts of the most fearsome, the most
> unnatural deeds, the most monstrous murders, told with the most
> unconstrained, with the most childishly happy laugh.

57

Then, with no transition, not even a break in the paragraph, he continues with his first example, the Il'inskii story:

> One parricide especially haunts my memory [*ne vykhodit u menia iz pamiati*]. He was of the gentry, and had been in the service and more or less played the prodigal son to his sixty-year-old father. His behavior had been altogether wild, and he was deep in debt. His father restrained him, reproved him; but his father had a house, a farm and was considered to have money; and his son killed him, longing for the inheritance. The crime was only discovered a month later. The murderer himself had made a declaration to the police that his father had disappeared without a trace. Finally, while he was away, the police discovered the body. Across the whole length of his courtyard ran a board-covered ditch for flushing dirt. The body was lying in this ditch. It was dressed and tidy. The grey head was cut right off, reset on the trunk, and under the head the murderer had placed a pillow. He admitted nothing, was deprived of his rank and his gentry status, and exiled to twenty years hard labor. The whole time I lived with him, he was in the most excellent, cheerful spirits. This was a self-willed, flighty, extremely irresponsible person, although far from a fool. I never observed any particular cruelty about him. The convicts despised him not for his crime, to which no one referred, but for his willfulness, for not knowing how to behave himself. In conversation, he sometimes recalled his father. Once when talking with me about the healthy constitution which ran in his family, he added, "You know, my father never complained of any sickness at all to the end of his days." Such bestial insensibility, of course, is impossible. This is a phenomenon; there's some flaw in his composition here, some physical and moral monstrosity not yet known to science, and not a simple crime. Of course, I did not believe in his crime, but people from his town who must have known all the details of his story told me the whole affair. The facts were so clear that it was impossible not to believe them.
>
> The convicts once heard him cry out at night in his sleep: "Hold him, hold! His head there, cut it off, the head, the head!" (*Pss* 4:15–16)

We know that Mitia shares with Il'inskii his involvement in parricide, his membership in the gentry, his position as a prodigal son to a sixty-year-old father, his wildness, his debts, and the restraint and reproofs of a father who possesses a house and considerable wealth. Like Il'inskii, Mitia also passes the period between the murder and its discovery in debauchery and then is tried and exiled to twenty years hard labor in Siberia. Both are in excellent spirits after the sentence; both have healthy constitutions, and neither one is either a fool or visibly depraved.

These parallels are plain and are well known, but one can hardly say that Mitia Karamazov "was" Dostoevsky's fellow convict Il'inskii, for that Il'inskii was already hidden under the beginnings of a series of transformations that would eventually include his name itself. *The House of the Dead* is not a simple memoir. Among other things, it is a cautious but telling polemic against the Russian penal theories and practices of Dostoevsky's time. As a pure example of an unrepentant murderer in the passage quoted, Il'inskii demonstrates the ineffectiveness of this penal system. Yet much of what we learn about him after the statement "This is a phenomenon" runs skew or even counter to this argument. The impossibility of Il'inskii's bestial insensibility, the sense of his unique monstrosity, the possibility of disbelief in his crime, all weaken the reader's tendency to generalize Il'inskii into a thoroughly convincing proof that the Russian penal system could not reform criminals. Indeed, the first part of the Il'inskii passage is a far more effective argument than the whole. This pattern often occurs in Dostoevskian polemic, and it deserves explanation.

Several reasons why Dostoevsky elaborates the Il'inskii account enough to damage his own point can be suggested, and they do not exclude one another. The first might be Dostoevsky's simple fidelity to his experience. His aesthetic and his creative practice dictated that he show the truth more fully and accurately than the first half of the passage had done. It can also be argued that any paragraph in this initial chapter has special introductory functions. To catch and keep the attention of his readers, Dostoevsky may have needed to spice the sensationalism of a hideous crime with a little gruesome incongruity. He does not, moreover, offer *The House of the Dead* as a personal memoir, but rather as the report of a fictional character, the murderer Gorianchikov, whose condition is in itself an indictment of the Russian prison camps. Gorianchikov's human qualities have been destroyed by his prison experience, and he lives on the borders of sanity. The first chapter of most works must begin to characterize certain figures, and most especially the narrator. We could therefore ascribe the extra information on Il'inskii to Dostoevsky's effort to show the obsessive quality of his narrator's mind by dramatizing the first sentence of the Il'inskii passage: "One parricide especially haunts my memory."

The doubt about Il'inskii's guilt might also be considered compulsive, a way of asserting Dostoevsky's own innocence for his father's murder, which he could not have committed but could have felt guilt for psychologically. From the point of view of this study, as he writes this essentially journalistic passage (and others like it) Dostoevsky gets carried away in the direction of something that will be important in *The Brothers Karamazov*. The impossibility of imagining Il'inskii's guilt is a step in the direction of the judicial error that convicts Mitia Karamazov. The idea of an innocent convict floats into this account of Il'inskii's life and then is promptly made incredible, much as separate voices in *The Brothers Karamazov*, such as that of the Prosecutor and Madame Khokhlakova recount alternative plots in which Mitia is guilty, although the full authority of the novel makes them incredible. In *The House of the Dead* the dialogue between guilt and innocence takes place in the mind of a single narrator, while in the elaborated fiction of *The Brothers Karamazov* it is acted out between different characters, in court and elsewhere. In both these cases, however, an unconscious mind, which lacks the apparatus for *either/or*, would link the whole context of events and ideas with guilt that had both a plus and a minus sign attached to it, much as the absolute value of a number exists independent of its sign. Indeed, one might speculate that the "physical and moral monstrosity not yet known to science" became embodied in the figure of Smerdiakov, who actually commits the murder in *The Brothers Karamazov*, and who expresses not the slightest remorse in discussing it.

The actual development of Mitia Karamazov turns out to be far more intricate than this tempting picture of a dialogue between belief and disbelief in one man's guilt developing into a pair of characters, one guilty and one not. A year and a half later, at the beginning of the seventh chapter of part 2 of *The House of the Dead*, Dostoevsky inserts a note as follows:

> In beginning this chapter, the publisher of the notes of the late Aleksandr Petrovich Gorianchikov considers himself obliged to make the following announcement to his readers.
>
> In the first chapter of *The House of the Dead*, something was said about one parricide, a member of the gentry. He was offered, incidentally, as an example of the lack of feeling with which the convicts sometimes talk about the crimes they have committed. It was also mentioned that the murderer did not admit his crime before the court, but that the facts were so clear from the accounts of the people who knew all the details of his story that it was impossible not to believe in the crime. These same people told the author...that the convict was completely dissipated, deeply in debt, and killed his father, craving his inheritance. The whole town where this man had worked told the identical story. As to this last fact, this publisher has rather accurate information. Finally, it was stated that in the prison camp the murderer was constantly in the happiest, pleasantest state of mind, that he was a man who was unpredictable, frivolous, and unthinking in the highest degree, although not a fool at all, and that the author never noticed any

especial cruelty in him. And here the words were added, "Of course I did not believe in this crime."

The publisher of *The House of the Dead* has recently received word from Siberia that the criminal was actually in the right and had suffered ten years penal servitude for nothing; that his innocence had been established in court officially; that the real criminals had been found and had confessed, and that the unfortunate man had already been freed from the prison. The publisher cannot have the slightest doubt of the reliability of the information.

There is nothing to add; there is nothing to say to expand on the full depth of the tragedy in this case, on the life ruined still in its youth by means of such an accusation. The fact is too clear, too striking by itself.

We also think that if such a fact should be possible, that very possibility adds a new and extraordinarily vivid feature to the character and the fullness of the picture of the house of the dead. (*Pss* 4:194–95)

This passage enables us to trace the erroneous conviction of Mitia Karamazov not only to hints but to actual statements in *The House of the Dead*.

The passage does not, however, enable us to trace Mitia's erroneous conviction to the real Il'inskii, for the real Il'inskii was never convicted of murder at all. B. G. Reizov, after dealing with all the materials discussed in this section, calls the attention of modern scholars to a passage in the memoirs of P. K. Mart'ianov, who was in the prison camp with Dostoevsky.[1] Mart'ianov reports that this man, whom he calls Il'in, had been tried for parricide, but the court found insufficient evidence to convict. Emperor Nicholas I himself, coming upon the record of this case, had him sentenced to twenty years in prison camp because parricide was too horrible a crime to go unpunished, even if unproved. Such intervention would be the mirror image of Nicholas's treatment of the Petrashevskii group, in whose case he had impeccable proof from interrogations and at least one spy, but the group had committed nothing resembling a horrible crime. Since Reizov's day, B. V. Fedorenko has found the record of Il'inskii's trial. The *Pss* summarizes his findings. The initial inquiry commission had decided that even though there was only circumstantial evidence, Il'inskii should be sent indefinitely to the mines as a criminal laborer. The commander of the Siberian army corps, however, recommended that "Il'inskii remain under strong suspicion" and be sent "to reside in the town of Berezov in the Tobolsk district under strict police supervision." Nicholas then stated that having a person in the army under such awful suspicion was impossible, and that Il'inskii should be "remanded among the convicts in the life category, and lose his membership in the gentry."[2] No account questions that Il'inskii's father was actually murdered by local peasants, much as Dostoevsky's had probably been when Dostoevsky was eighteen years old.[3] It is thoroughly in character for Nicholas I to have seen his status as a father figure sufficiently threatened by a case like this to warrant intervention. And the obsessive power that Il'inskii had over Gorianchikov, "haunting his memory," could be traced to a kinship of misfortune that Gorianchikov's creator might have felt with Il'inskii.

Reizov takes Mart'ianov's account as probably accurate and feels that Dostoevsky, fresh from Siberia himself, suppressed the tale of imperial meddling out of political prudence. There would be no dishonesty in this reticence, for *The House of the Dead* "claims not to be true," has a fictional narrator, and never mentions Il'inskii's name. Another hypothesis might be simpler. It was Gorianchikov, not Dostoevsky, who claimed to have talked with Il'inskii, and the "publisher" of the second passage (who is also a persona of Dostoevsky's) takes great pains to indicate the second- or thirdhand quality of all his information. Much of Mart'ianov's information about Dostoevsky, moreover, is carefully labeled as secondhand.[4] From this we could infer that although Mart'ianov was in camp with Dostoevsky and with Il'inskii, these last may not themselves have been together in camp very much, and Dostoevsky might simply have made good use of a story he knew only in part.

Reizov makes one strong argument against this hypothesis. Dostoevsky, an ex-convict and a habitué of trials in St. Petersburg, must have known that the penalty for premeditated parricide was life imprisonment, but Mitia was sentenced to only twenty years, the same term Mart'ianov gives Il'inskii, that other innocent convict. The court records confuse the issue even more. On the one hand, the emperor's call for a life term seems to deprive us of any common source for Mart'ianov's and Dostoevsky's mention of twenty years. On the other, Mitia's aggrieved behavior at the trial and the preliminary investigation resembles Il'inskii's in ways that Dostoevsky could hardly have learned from any source but Il'inskii, unless he imagined them on the basis of his understanding of such an undisciplined character (*Pss* 4:284). In the same way, the complicated financial dealings between Mitia, his father, and Grushenka seem to find a curious parallel in parts of the record: "Whether there were house visits to my father by the settler Paulina Nekrasov I could not tell. Whether or not she had money, and how much, about which she never talked to me, just as she never entrusted any to my care, and whether she entrusted any to my father's care,

I do not know; likewise on the matter of whether my father gave the above money to my brother, I do not know."[5]

In any case either the initial incongruity between Il'inskii's character and his crime, or the shared experience of having a father murdered before whom one has groveled for money, or the wildly romantic revelation of his total innocence, or perhaps the comradeship as victims of a busybody emperor who appeared like a *diabolus ex machina*, or probably some combination of these features made Il'inskii haunt Dostoevsky's memory much as he had Gorianchikov's. All this is the stuff of melodrama, and as melodrama Dostoevsky set out to exploit it fifteen years later.

II
Dostoevsky Reworked the Il'inskii Story in the Plan for a Melodrama.

On 13 September 1874 Dostoevsky wrote the plan for a drama along the lines of the Il'inskii story to be set in Tobolsk twenty years earlier (*Pss* 17:5). There were to be two brothers, the older one with a fiancée whom the younger loved secretly and jealously, though she loved the older. The older is a young lieutenant, who runs wild and senseless and quarrels with his father. His father disappears for several days without a trace. The brothers are discussing the inheritance when suddenly the authorities dig up the body from under the house. The evidence is against the older. (The younger does not live there.) The older brother is tried and condemned to prison camp. (He had quarreled with his father, boasted about the inheritance from his deceased mother, etc.) When he goes to prison, and even his fiancée avoids him, he says tipsily, "Can it be that they believe this? Do you?" As a matter of fact, the evidence has been excellently fabricated by the younger. People do not know for sure who committed the murder.

There follows a scene in the prison camp. There is a plan to kill him. It's the administration. He does not give in, and the convicts swear their brotherhood with him. The administration reproaches him for having killed his father.

Twelve years later, his brother travels out to see him. There is a scene where they understand each other *without a word*. After seven more years, the younger brother is an official, a man of rank, but he tortures himself with guilt, and, suffering from depression, reveals to his wife, his brother's ex-fiancée, that he was the killer. She answers, "Why did you tell me?" He goes to his brother, and his wife chases after him. On her knees, she begs the convict to hold his peace and save her husband. The convict says, "I'm used to this." The brothers make their peace together, and the convict says, "You've had your punishment anyway." But on his birthday, the younger, before all the guests, steps out and says, "I killed him." People think he has had a stroke. At the end, the younger brother, on his way into exile, asks the older brother, who is returning, to be a father to his children: "Setting out upon the proper course."

Dostoevsky was interested in drama all his life. It has been suggested that he was moved to translate *Eugénie Grandet* because he had seen a dramatization of the novel as a young man, when he was working on his three lost plays, *Boris Godunov, Maria Stuart,* and *Iankel' the Jew*. He also first conceived of *Crime and Punishment* as a drama. Had Dostoevsky written more of this play, it might well have embodied all the weaknesses and none of the greatness of Tolstoi's *Resurrection* and *Power of Darkness* combined, an alarming thought. Like Tolstoi as he shifted from a novel about the Decembrists to *War and Peace*, however, Dostoevsky gradually shifted his efforts to the antecedents of this account of an exile.

We now have at least seven versions of the Il'inskii story: the real Il'inskii, who knew he was innocent; Dostoevsky's direct impressions of him when they met, which probably included some doubt about his guilt; the information he received about Il'inskii in Siberia, which seems to have confirmed guilt unambiguously; the first account in *The House of the Dead*, which touches on innocence but confirms guilt; the letter from Siberia, which is not extant but probably ascribes guilt to the servants; the second passage in *The House of the Dead*, which shifts all guilt to unnamed persons; and the melodrama in Tobolsk, which shifts guilt to an innocent-seeming but evil brother. In these several versions the Il'inskii story accounts for Mitia's frank and charming but wild and passionate nature, for his drinking and debauchery, for the binge immediately after the death of his father, for the trial for parricide and the conviction, for the true murderer being a servant, and perhaps for the physical and moral monstrosity of that servant. Mart'ianov's version of the Il'inskii story, if Dostoevsky knew it, may also account for the twenty-year sentence and the hostile meddling of the administration, closely linked in the drama with the charge of parricide. By the time Dostoevsky conceived his drama in 1874, however, he had added two other central figures, a woman and another brother. Whether the real Il'inskii suspected his brother of complicity in the murder, or whether his brother played an unhelpful part at the time of Il'inskii's trial, or whether there was enunciated or unenunciated rivalry between Il'inskii and his brother or his father over a woman, or whether Dostoevsky was in a position to know such things seems to be unknowable at present. In the play, the brother is also the murderer. In the finished novel, Mitia is involved with two women and two brothers, and the murderer is no more than a half brother, a relationship that enables him to be a servant too. The plot of this melodrama is almost archetypal, in part: the wild brother is innocent, loving, and considered guilty; the tame one loves only the inheritance, is murderous, ingeniously deceitful, or both, and looks dutiful. Schiller, Shakespeare, and Sheridan dramatize this same plot, which is at least as old as Israel.

King Lear, The School for Scandal, and the Esau story share this plot, but in The Brothers Karamazov Mitia makes specific references to Schiller. Cyzewskij has discussed his long quotations from "An die Freude" and "Das eleusische Fest" as well as the passage where old Fedor Karamazov compares his two sons to those in Schiller's Robbers. Here is a very different use of a source from Dostoevsky's use of the Il'inskii story. The figure of the elegant and devious brother in Dostoevsky's 1874 drama very likely does originate in Schiller. We know that as a very young man Dostoevsky loved Schiller, and that as he grew older this fondness remained, although tinged with the irony that came to characterize the Russian attitude toward Schiller in general as the century progressed. The most crucial references to Schiller are put in the mouths of Mitia and old Fedor when they are quite drunk. In fact Schiller's name and Schiller's verse represent not so much a literary source as a literary instrument, a way of summoning into the reader's mind a collection of associations, a whole romantic world of high ideals and high villainy, of beauty as the educator of mankind, of tragic passions and great moments of decision, of abstract nouns that suddenly take on an immense loading of emotion—in short, Schiller enables Dostoevsky to exploit preestablished reverberations and recedes as a source for the Karamazov brothers, although the remark of old Karamazov survives to remind us of the Schilleresque drama out of which the novel grew, hinting at a conservation of literary matter that I will be in a position to describe more accurately in later chapters.

Let us then take Schiller first as a source for the drama that preceded The Brothers Karamazov, but also as a resource for the novel, a situation and a set of values which had surfaced and were being exploited in full view of the reader, using what the reader already knew and felt to characterize Mitia, old Fedor, and the plot they both help generate.[6]

III

THE RESTRAINT THAT CHARACTERIZES MITIA'S ACTIONS COMES IN PART FROM GEORGE SAND.

The fiancée in the drama Dostoevsky projected has far fewer of the romantic vices and virtues than either brother. She abandons the man who loves her when authority declares him guilty. When she learns that she has committed a terrible injustice, she says, "Why did you tell me?" and does nothing to help either of the two men who need her help desperately. Some of Grushenka's fiscal practicality, and some part of Katerina Ivanovna's abandonment of Mitia, may be traced to this figure in the drama, but the haunting inhumanity of her answer to a confessional cry for help seems to have no close correspondence in the novel. Ivan and Katerina Ivanovna both try to isolate themselves from the murder, but they lack the coldness to succeed.

Katia develops in many ways, but the earliest episode in her encounter with Mitia illustrates the basic pattern. This scene might be summarized as follows: The dissipated, ill-bred, conceited, but attractive young battler encounters a beauty who is infinitely his superior in birth, education, and social grace. He intentionally affronts her and takes her answering arrogance as a challenge to his gallantry. Suddenly thrust into a position alone with her where she is totally in his power, he contemplates rape, with an acute awareness of his brutishness and her noble beauty. She is desperately concerned over the well-being of her father and is willing to sacrifice herself to prevent his being shot. The man describes his impulses as those of a bloodily vicious beast, but the scene ends with her peaceful departure, and the blade that was drawn for suicide goes unused.

This summary omits certain points and covers others in ambiguous fashion, but it is a recognizable account of the first meeting between Mitia and Katerina Ivanovna in *The Brother Karamazov.* It is also, as V. L. Komarovich has shown, a recognizable account of the first meeting between the hero and the heroine of another novel about a strong and passionate and accursed family, George Sand's *Mauprat.*[7] *Mauprat* is not only the story of an accursed family but also a novel about the education of a virtual savage in an atmosphere of nobility, sacrifice, adventure, and villainy—secret and overt—culminating in a trial where the question of a judicial error takes a central place. The educational component has its eventual antecedents in Rousseau, but the villainy, the band of brigands that demands the hero's loyalty, can convincingly be traced to the same source for the pair of brothers in the drama Dostoevsky planned, to Schiller's *Robbers*.

In this first meeting between Mitia and Katia, then, Dostoevsky drew on a novel that was already relevant to his purpose and related to his other sources. But Komarovich shows that this scene of the near rape of the heroine had caught Dostoevsky's attention earlier, that the first meeting between Mitia and Katia is drawn not only from *Mauprat* but from the last meeting between Svidrigailov and Dunia in *Crime and Punishment*, which in turn was derived from *Mauprat*. This complex of sources is obviously not exhaustive. Lermontov contributes to the scene at the watering place, and to the magnificent scorn that the aristocratic girl displays for the young officer. These and other scenes are certainly sources for the Svidrigailov scene and probably directly underlie both *Mauprat* and *The Brothers Karamazov*.

But at this point it becomes plain that Dostoevsky was working here with a stylized melodramatic situation, much as he had worked with the name of Schiller earlier. His readers need not recognize Svidrigailov or Bernard Mauprat or any other single source for this passage; they would still feel that the anecdotes in which Mitia's passionate heart confesses itself partake of the same literary nature as the verse he uses in the chapter before. Dostoevsky maneuvers within a formula whose virtues for his purposes include familiarity, as well as suspense, moral certainty, and the arousal that attends the rescue fantasy. But the formula admits of many variants. Mitia and Svidrigailov, for example, are spoiled, dissipated, attractive, self-impoverished members of the rural gentry, but Svidrigailov has all the outward qualities of a gentleman—looks, manners, clothes, handsome gestures with his money when he has it, and so on—while at this period Mitia's behavior, manners, and general way of life are all disreputable, though he can dress and act very well on some occasions. Inwardly, on the other hand, Svidrigailov glories in his perversions, has destroyed human lives in the pursuit of them, and is totally depraved, while Mitia has a restraining impulse that sets the "ideal of the Madonna" in his heart. In this sense Mitia is the last of Dostoevsky's spoiled, lecherous, spendthrift, dissipated, yet attractive heroes. He follows Svidrigailov, Rogozhin, Stavrogin, and Versilov. Each of these figures exists in opposition to a younger, sexually purer man who offers him some special kind of moral understanding.

In adapting this literary formula to the needs of his successive novels, Dostoevsky varies his pattern. Svidrigailov is the only member of this group who lacks "the ideal of the Madonna";

Stavrogin lacks the capacity for informal intimacy that marks the others; and Versilov lacks the youth that Svidrigailov has in appearance and the others have in fact, with all that youth implies. Rogozhin lacks the curious restraining impulse that on occasion makes Svidrigailov, Stavrogin, and Versilov accept shocking insults, that characterizes much of Mitia's career, and that helps explain why Mitia lacks that touch of the demonic that makes the others fascinating.

IV

BUT DOSTOEVSKY HAD ALREADY REWORKED IT IN *CRIME AND PUNISHMENT*

In respect to this restraining impulse, however, Mitia's dialectical relation with his sources in *Crime and Punishment* extends beyond Svidrigailov. Mitia, as we have said, has an impulse that keeps him from raping Katerina Ivanovna, keeps him from killing himself afterward, keeps him from immediately spending all the money he steals from her, and most important of all keeps him from murdering his father when he creeps up to the old reprobate's window, weapon in hand. In the 1870s Dostoevsky was fascinated by the court trials of two apparently violent, unrestrained women who failed when they attempted murderous assaults—Kairova, who slashed her rival superficially with a knife, and Kornilova, who threw her stepdaughter out of a fourth-story window without harming her. He wrote extensively on both cases in his *Diary of a Writer* and considered the whole question of murderous intent. He concluded that in both these cases it was virtually impossible to assert that the nonfatal assault was made with intent to kill. He arrived at this position partly by considering Raskolnikov:

> Of course, he knows that he is going to commit murder, but whether he will do it, he does not know for sure until the very time. . . . Could not even say whether he might simply go to the apartment and return.
>
> Now when the old woman has already turned to the window, and there cannot be another second's delay, when he has already taken out and raised the ax—will he bring it down or not? Of course, he will. Note that, make no mistake. But what if suddenly he should cry out and fall at the old lady's feet and tell her all, and not in order that she might forgive, but on the contrary, begging her to send for the police as quickly as possible. These people are awfully strange. (*Pss* 23:213–14)

This alternative experience for Raskolnikov is part of the genesis for Dostoevsky's attitudes toward Kairova and Kornilova. He excluded this passage from the final version of *The Diary of a Writer*, but in the third section of the May 1876 issue he elaborated on the same scene with respect to Kairova:

> Kairova herself could quite well have not known whether she would slash her to death or not, and they demanded that the jury assert "whether she would have slashed her to death if she hadn't been stopped." And she, when she bought the razor a day before, although she knew what she bought it for, still might not have known "not only whether she would slash her to death, but even whether she would start slashing at all." . . . And what if after one razor slash at Velikanova's throat, she had cried out, quivered, and dashed away. What makes you think that wouldn't have happened? And if it had, it might well be that nothing would have come to trial at all. . . . And what if it had turned out that after slashing once and panicking, she had started to slash herself, and maybe slaughtered herself right there. And finally, what if she not only had not panicked, but rather, feeling the first spurt of hot blood, had jumped up in a rage and not only completed the slashing of Velikanova, but also had begun to taunt the corpse, had cut her head right off. (*Pss* 23:9–10)

The end of this passage does little to advance Dostoevsky's argument for the acquittal of Kairova. Rather it suggests the complexity of the images that were conjured up in his mind by the Kairova trial. The severed head could have many sources, but the trial of Il'inskii would not have been absent from his mind. A year and a half earlier, he had written the sketch for the melodrama in Tobolsk, recollecting the strange, irresponsible figure of Il'inskii as he had known him but also as he had imagined him in the first chapter of *The House of the Dead*. The explanation of that most gruesome detail in the Il'inskii story preoccupied Dostoevsky, as is shown by his recounting of Il'inskii's cries in his sleep; and this picture of the murderous passion aroused by the feel of the blood one has already spilled belongs to that period in the evolution of Dostoevsky's imagination when he was writing about the murderers in *The House of the Dead*.

If this article relates to a court trial that summoned into Dostoevsky's mind the trials of Raskolnikov and Il'inskii, it also reminded him of the trial of Bernard Mauprat, certainly, and of the moment when his own fate was in the hands of the legal authorities, as well as of passages in Victor Hugo's *Dernier jour d'un condamné* and his own *Idiot*, in which Ippolit, Myshkin, and Lebedev all discuss such moments. In discussing Kairova's victim in section 5 of this issue, he continues:

> She endured several minutes (too many minutes) of *mortal terror.* Do you know what *mortal terror* is? For one who has not been close to death, it is hard to understand it. She waked up in the night, wakened by the razor of her own murderess, who had slashed her about the throat, she saw the fierce face above her; she struggled and the other kept on slashing her. . . this was almost the same as the death sentence to a man tied to the stake for execution when they are pulling on the sack. (*Pss* 23:18)

At the journalistic level, this passage helps to establish Dostoevsky's authority over his readers who have not been so close to an unjust execution for a liberal cause. From the point of view of this study, it shows at least one source of the involvement that drew Dostoevsky's attention to this particular trial: he saw himself in the position of both the accused and the victim. This emotional loading may explain how it is that a single journalistic passage contains so much of Mitia Karamazov's experience when he obtains a weapon, raises it to commit a murder, turns and runs, raises it again, commits a near murder, but casts it away and leaps down to see if there is any hope for his victim, and then runs off with suicide at the center of his plans, although in fact he has committed no murder. In his unpublished draft, Dostoevsky the journalist describes Raskolnikov's murderous attack as an alternative to falling at the old lady's feet at the last moment. In the published version he describes as alternatives Kairova's interrupted attack, her hypothetical attack that is not carried to completion, and her attack that she turns on herself. In *The Brothers Karamazov,* Dostoevsky the novelist combines these alternatives into a sequence, much as Freud claims that the dreaming mind presents alternatives as a sequence.

Dostoevsky had recounted the trials of Raskolnikov and Il'inskii very briefly, but he made the trial of Mitia the longest episode in *The Brothers Karamazov,* elaborating the reasoning and the eloquence of the lawyers with an irony reminiscent of *The Diary of a Writer.* The trial of Kairova played a real role in *The Brothers Karamazov,* but it entered the novel both directly from Dostoevsky's memory, and as processed through an article that already linked it with other trials and other crimes in the complex of unassembled elements that later on became the novel. As a conscious craftsman, Dostoevsky sometimes used his own life for rhetorical effect and sometimes entered into a dialogue with an earlier text, as he had in speculating what would happen if Raskolnikov had not committed the murder. Mitia Karamazov has many other sources, and other parts of this chapter in *The Diary of a Writer* enter *The Brothers Karamazov*, but these passages give an initial picture of the ways Dostoevsky formed characters and introduced plots into "journalistic" works like *The House of the Dead* and *The Diary of a Writer*, and carried ideological arguments on into a "literary" work like *The Brothers Karamazov*.

Chapter Five

THE THEME OF MEMORY ENTERS THE NOVEL FROM A RICH BODY OF READING AND OTHER EXPERIENCE.

I
DOSTOEVSKY WAS INTERESTED IN NINETEENTH-CENTURY RESEARCH INTO THE SUBJECTS OF COGNITION AND MEMORY.

Scholars have traced characters, events, and arguments to their sources for many generations, but the best thematic studies have less often been intertextual. To see how *The Brothers Karamazov* coalesces thematically out of a collection of readings and other experiences, it makes sense to deal with a central but neglected theme—memory—rather than treat the well-studied themes of parricide, child abuse, faith and miracles, grace and redemption, and so on. During Dostoevsky's lifetime, memory became a respectable subject for experimental inquiry, after centuries as the object of religious or physiological speculation or of practical brochures on how not to forget names, books, or speeches. The new mnemonics came to Russia at the hands of two competing schools of psychology, the neurologists and the alienists. Each group had its eighteenth-century antecedents, its nineteenth-century clinical and theoretical achievements, and its special techniques for investigating the mind.

Most literary scholars find the beginnings of the neurological approach in a famous passage in the dialogue between d'Alembert and Diderot:

Diderot: Could you tell me what is the existence of a sentient being, with respect to itself?

D'Alembert: It is the consciousness of having been itself, from the first instant of its thinking to the present moment.

Diderot: And on what is this consciousness based?

D'Alembert: On the memory of its actions.

Diderot: And without this memory?

D'Alembert: Without this memory, it would have no self at all, for feeling its existence only in the moment of the impression, it would have no account of its life. Its life would be an interrupted series of sensations linked by nothing.

Diderot: Well, what is memory? Where does it come from?

D'Alembert: From a certain accretive system which grows strong or weak and sometimes is altogether lost.

Diderot: So if a sentient being with this system appropriate for memory links the impressions it receives and by this linkage forms an account which is that of its life, and acquires the consciousness of itself, then it denies, affirms, concludes, and thinks?

D'Alembert: It seems so to me; I have just one more problem.

Diderot: You're wrong; you've lots more.

D'Alembert: But one principal one; it seems to me that we can only think of a single thing at a time and that in order to form a simple proposition, not to speak of these enormous chains of reasoning which embrace in their orbit thousands of ideas, it is necessary to have at least two things present, the object which seems to fall under the eye of predication, and the quality which is affirmed or denied with reference to it.

Diderot: I agree; and that has sometimes made me compare the fibres in our organs to sentient vibrating strings. The sentient vibrating string oscillates, resounds for a long time after being plucked. This oscillation, this sort of inevitable resonance is what keeps the object present while the predicating understanding is occupied with the qualities appropriate to it. But vibrating strings have still another quality; they make others tremble and this is how a first idea recalls a second, the two a third, all three a fourth, and so on without our being able to set limits to the awakened, enchained ideas of a philosopher meditating or listening to himself in silence and darkness. This instrument makes astounding leaps, and an idea once awakened can make a harmonic tremble at an incomprehensible interval from it. If the phenomenon is observed among sounding strings, inanimate and separated, how would it fail

to occur among points that are animate and linked, among
continuous and sentient fibres.[1]

Diderot's generating analogy in this passage resonates through
the history of thought from Pythagoras's strings to Pavlov's bells,
but in the nineteenth century it took on a special connection with
positivism and materialism all over Europe. While *The Brothers
Karamazov* was gestating, Hippolyte Taine published his article
"Cerebral Vibrations and Thought," which can exemplify the approach taken by the many proponents of neurology whom Dostoevsky knew, ranging from I. M. Sechenov, to N. G. Chernyshevskii,
to Claude Bernard.

> Since mental phenomena are only more or less deformed or trans-
> formed sensations, let us compare a sensation with a molecular
> movement of the nervous centres. Let us take the sensation of the
> yellow of gold, of a sound like "ut," of that which the emanations
> of the lily produce, of the taste of sugar, the pain of a cut, the
> sensation of tickling, of heat, of cold. The necessary and sufficient
> condition of such a sensation is an intestine movement in the grey
> substance of the annular protuberance, of the tubercula quadrigem-
> ina, perhaps of the thalamus opticus—in short, in the cells of the
> sensory centre; that this movement is unknown is of little con-
> sequence; whatever it be, it is always a displacement of molecules,
> more or less complicated and propagated; nothing more. Now what
> relation can we imagine between this displacement and a sensa-
> tion? Cells, formed of a membrane and of one or several nuclei,
> are scattered through a granular substance, a sort of pulp or greyish
> jelly composed of nuclei and innumerable fibrils.[2]

When juxtaposed with the Diderot passage, the Taine passage
shows a smug mind affirming its authority as opposed to a playful
mind confronting a real problem, but it also shows what had happened to vibrational neurology in a century. For Diderot, the vibrations constitute an elaborated and illuminating simile for the re-
tentive and associative powers of the mind. Taine realizes the trope:
the microscope and the scalpel have anatomized the fibers, and
Taine is certain that the movements are there merely awaiting
discovery. Diderot is exploring the nature of thought through memory, which distinguishes beings that have a self from others. Taine
is exploring it through sensation, which blurs any such distinction.
Most important of all, from Dostoevsky's point of view, Diderot is
engaged in dialogue on a genuine puzzle with his intellectual equal.
Taine's monologic scientism is as patronizing and as unsophisticated
as Bazarov's. The creator of Fedor Karamazov could respect the
creator of Rameau's nephew for his psychological insights, although

Fedor himself might use Diderot as the emblematic unbeliever in mocking the gathering at the monastery; but the detestation with which the underground man approached piano keys and organ stops, or with which Mitia Karamazov approached Claude Bernard, was borrowed from Dostoevsky's own attitude toward the psychological reductionism of the neurologists. The purest example of this attitude is probably his obsessively angry series of references in the 1877 notebooks to the sentence "He is not a man but a lyre," which had been intended as praise for a public speaker (*Pss* 24:131, 139ff.). When Dostoevsky needed expert advice on a psychological question, he therefore wrote, not to a neurologist, but to an alienist.[3]

Eighteenth-century forerunners had also provided the alienists with an underlying metaphor, which in this case was hydraulic rather than vibrational and which persists in Freudian thinking to this day. By mid-century Russian journals were comparing hallucinations to bursting artesian waters, discussing the pressure of unfulfilled needs, and so on. This way of thinking came more from Friedrich Anton Mesmer's thin magnetic fluid than from the older doctrines of the humors or the still older Epicurean idea of flux among the atoms of spirit.

In the 1820s James Braid had divorced Mesmer's practice of hypnotism from his suspect doctrines of magnetism, and John Elliotson and others in England had begun using hypnotism for anesthesia and therapy; in the medical journals, accounts of amputations under hypnosis began to appear, until ether superseded hypnosis. By the 1870s Ambrose Auguste Liébault and Henri Bernheim at Nancy were working to separate the phenomena of suggestion from those of hypnotic sleep, or "somnambulism" as they called it. This distinction opened the way for Jean-Martin Charcot, already a leading neurologist, to adopt hypnotism as one of his tools, and Charcot's work helped produce the Freudian synthesis, which eventually drove both reflex conditioning and hypnotism out of most therapy for half a century.

The central technique of the hypnotists focused on the direct power of the repeated word. As one of its best practitioners described it in the 1880s,

> I place myself facing the subject, seated or standing, and I invite him to look fixedly at me, without any extraordinary effort; after a few moments, I say to him, "You are going to feel a drowsiness; an imperious need of sleep is taking possession of you; your eyelids are becoming heavy. They are coming down. Your eyes are closing. You are going to sleep, sleep." Then a light pressure is brought to bear on the eyeballs, covered by the lowered eyelids, and the above

suggestion is repeated several times as needed, or else a similar one.[4]

These techniques of suggestion through repetition gave the hypnotists the tool they needed to explore memory through amnesia and to attack the opinion Diderot had ascribed to d'Alembert, that a memory may be "altogether lost." In the 1850s most of this community agreed that "every sleeper remembers things far more exactly than when he is awake. What he has once known he recovers in somnambulism."[5]

Although the hypnotists and alienists and their intellectual descendants have continued to examine and generalize this problem of latency, they have tended to explain it by analogies until the last decade or two. In 1919, for example, Bernheim's book *Automatism and Suggestion* contained the following passage:

> In all these states, the amnesia is neither constant nor absolute. . . .
> Even in the case of memories apparently erased, one can always, as I have determined, revive them by verbal suggestion. I tell the subject to shut his eyes and to recollect. I concentrate his attention in this way, I say to him "You are going to recollect everything," and the memories reappear sometimes instantly or quickly; other times more slowly, through gradual evocation. One would say that the impressions from a state of sleep or of somnambulism, produced in a special state of consciousness where the attention is concentrated like a nervous light, are no longer illuminated in the normal state of consciousness, when the light is no longer concentrated upon them; they have become latent; they again become luminous, conscious, if suggestion again concentrates on these dim impressions the light of cerebral attention. . . . [He rejects a neurological explanation, and continues:] The evocation of a memory would therefore not be the revival of a localized imprint, but the reproduction of the special cellular modality that created the impression or the idea in the first place. The latent memory does not exist as long as it is latent. It can be awakened by the cellular modality the same way a remembered motion does not exist but can be awakened by a muscular contraction.[6]

This formulation that in amnesia, natural or hypnotic, memories are latent, not lost, was available to Dostoevsky long before he undertook *The Brothers Karamazov*. As a part of his regular reading, he would have read the following statement in the *Fatherland Notes* for 1861, volume 136, in an article on current psychological developments: "In somnambulism, memories not only appear with great liveliness; they even pass from one session of sleep to another, so that somnambulists sometimes continue in one session activities that were begun in another; in the waking interval of consciousness, the memory of these actions is lost." He need not, however, have read articles on science to learn about the need to revive a situation in order to revive a memory. In *The Mystery of Edwin Drood* his favorite English author, Charles Dickens, has a character say, "If I hide my watch when I am drunk, I must be drunk again before I find it." Dickens was enormously interested in hypnotism, and his friend Wilkie Collins made the regeneration of a latent memory the climactic episode in *The Moonstone*. In short, long before *The Brothers Karamazov*, Dostoevsky had as a part of his intellectual background the doctrine of persistent latency and the evidence that a situation, real or hypnotically induced, would help recall a memory if it resembled it.

Quite apart from its appeal to his scientific, literary, and journalistic contemporaries, the problem of memory concerned Dostoevsky personally for two reasons. The first was his worry about his own memory, his dread of the effect upon it of each epileptic fit. He told his wife about the lost feeling during the period of recuperation, before the memories were restored, and summarized his symptoms to a virtual stranger as follows:

> I must tell you that I suffer from epilepsy and it takes away my memory completely, especially for certain events. Can you believe I constantly can't recognize people I've met the month before? Moreover—I forget my own works entirely. This winter, I read one of my novels, *Crime and Punishment*, which I wrote ten years ago, and read two-thirds of the novel as new, unfamiliar, as if it were not I who had written it, I'd managed to forget it so thoroughly.[7]

If this statement can be taken literally in an author who was apologizing for a piece of discourteous forgetfulness, and whose characters change eye color or patronymics astonishingly seldom in his long novels, then Dostoevsky himself agonizingly went through his own investigation of amnesia many times a year. His friends— and enemies—confirm the basic experience he describes, adding that the amnesia was selective, according to a pattern that is familiar to neurologists:

> Everything that happened to me before this first epileptic seizure, every minutest event of my life, every face I met, all that I read or heard, I remember down to the most trivial detail. Everything that began after the first seizure, I often forget; I sometimes quite forget people whom I have known well; I forget faces. I have forgotten all that I have written after the prison camp; when I was finishing *The Possessed*, I had to reread it all from the beginning, because I had forgotten even the names of the characters.[8]

This ongoing experience would have led Dostoevsky to read the current scientific work on memory, not with the detached curiosity of any alert observer, but with the kind of emotional loading that would fix it in his own memory and link it with other elements that had acquired similar loading.

Dostoevsky's second reason for being concerned with memory involves his deep personal concern with immortality. In the life of a man or a nation, he attached great importance to the "opportunity to utter one's own word," not so much to acquire fame as to enter into the community of mankind. In the most famous passage in his 1863–64 notebook, he meditates as follows on this problem:

> Is there a future life for every "I"? People say a man collapses and dies altogether. We already know it isn't altogether, because just as a person giving physical birth to a son transmits to him a part of his identity, so in the moral world, he leaves a memory of himself to people, that is, he enters into the future development of mankind with a part of his former identity that had been alive on earth. (N.B. The desire for eternal memory in the funeral service is indicative of this.) (Pss. 20:172)

Dostoevsky wrote this passage at his wife's bier. The *non omnis moriar* formulation had been trite for millennia, but here he links it by analogy with familial immortality and notes that his religion sanctions this kind of immortality along with its own. This gathering of the concepts of parenthood, religious ceremony, and earthly immortality about that of memory in the presence of the emotional complexity of mourning marks an important stage in the thematic development of *The Brothers Karamazov*. This interest in one's survival in the memory of others made Dostoevsky especially responsive to N. F. Fedorov's projects for the resurrection of one's ancestors. In his letter about Fedorov, however, which is often quoted as a source for *The Brothers Karamazov*, Dostoevsky also discusses the risk of substituting the earthly process for the divine one.[9]

II

DOSTOEVSKY'S CONCERN WITH MEMORY HELPS TO SHAPE THE THEMATIC STRUCTURE OF *THE BROTHERS KARAMAZOV*.

With this background and these concerns of Dostoevsky's in mind, I should like to examine *The Brothers Karamazov* as an essay on remembering and forgetting. The theme of memory emerges in the first sentence of the first chapter with the statement that Fedor

Karamazov's death was still recollected after thirteen years. It keeps recurring until the last chapter of the novel, which begins with a service of eternal memory for the dead Iliusha and ends with a speech about childhood memories, which I will discuss presently.

Book 1 of the novel sets up a careful opposition between the way old Fedor forgets and the way Alesha remembers. Early in chapter 2 Fedor had cast off his son Mitia, "not out of cruelty toward him, nor from any insulted conjugal feelings, but simply because he forgot about him altogether" (*Pss* 14:10). A few lines later, the narrator states, "If Papa should remember him (and he couldn't actually fail to know about his existence) then he would himself send him off to [Grigory's] hut." In chapter 3, when Fedor's second wife dies, Alesha is only four, "but strange though it is, I know he remembered his mother all his life, as if through a dream, of course. After her death, it happened with [Ivan and Alesha] just the same as with the first child, Mitia. They were altogether forgotten and cast out by their father" (*Pss* 14:13). Later, Alesha admits that he has returned to his father's house in order to find his mother's grave, but his father has already forgotten where they buried her (*Pss* 14:21). In book 3, chapter 8, when Fedor describes in disgusting detail how he had reduced Alesha's mother to hysterics by spitting on her icon, Dostoevsky carefully marks a mysterious lapse in Fedor's memory: "Something very strange occurred—only for a second, it's true. The realization had actually, apparently, escaped the old fellow's mind that Alesha's mother was Ivan's mother too. 'How do you mean, your mother?' he muttered" (*Pss* 14:127).

Presented in contrast to Fedor's forgetting, Alesha's remembering appears most elaborately at the start of chapter 4 of book 1 in a passage whose sources and structure I will discuss in the following chapters.

> I have already recalled that although [Alesha] had lost his mother when only four, he remembered her from then on, for his whole life, her face, her caresses, "just as if she stood before me alive." Such recollections (as we all know) can be remembered from an even earlier age, even from two years, but only emerging all one's life as bright spots from the murk, as if they were corners torn from a great picture which is extinguished and lost except for just that corner. Just so it was with him: he remembered one quiet summer evening, an open window, the slanting beams of the setting sun (these slanting beams were what he most remembered), in a room, in the corner, an image, a lamp lighted before it, and before the image his mother, on her knees, sobbing as if in hysterics, shrieking and wailing, clasping him in both arms, embracing him tightly, till it hurt, and praying to the Virgin for him, stretching

him from her embrace with both hands toward the image as if for the Virgin's protection. Suddenly the nurse runs in and snatches him from her in terror. There's the picture! In that instant Alesha also remembered his mother's face: he said it was ecstatic but beautiful, judging by as much as he could remember. But he seldom liked to confide this memory to anyone. (*Pss* 14:18)

For the purposes of this chapter, the passage not only distinguishes Alesha, the rememberer, from his father, the forgetter, but also links remembering with two other central businesses of book 1, the abandonment and the blessing of children.

Out of these early encounters with the theme of memory comes a secondary, moral association with memory. Dostoevsky is conditioning his reader to connect memory with love, attention, and family, while forgetting is connected with neglect and debauchery. This particular associative loading of memory is by no means automatic for Dostoevsky. In *The Possessed*, for example, the vindictive whim of a spoiled eccentric leads Madame Stavrogina to tell Verkhovensky, "I will never forget this." But in *The Brothers Karamazov* this key passage gives memory a rich meaning at the start; Dostoevsky can later use the established associations to load other elements with beauty or horror. At the beginning of the Grand Inquisitor chapter, for example, Ivan discusses sinners immersed inextricably in the burning lake and cites "an expression of extraordinary profundity and power": "These, God just forgets" (*Pss* 14:225). In contrast to this forgetting, Ivan has made a comment two chapters earlier that links exploits with memory: "I treasure that certain human exploit in which you may long since have even stopped believing, but still honor in your heart for old memory's sake" (*Pss* 14:210).

This association between preciousness and an exploit whose life resides not in any validity but merely in being remembered shapes our whole understanding of the legend of the Grand Inquisitor. At the end of the legend, when Alesha says that the Grand Inquisitor does not believe in God, Ivan portrays the Inquisitor's whole life as an exploit: "Suppose that should be true. You've finally solved the problem. And actually the whole secret is just that, but isn't that suffering, for such a man as he, who has destroyed his whole life on an exploit in the desert and not cured his love for humanity" (*Pss* 14:238). This double exploit, sacrificing one's life first for salvation and then for humanity, embodies that romantic beauty that Dostoevsky often ascribed to the great Russian radicals, as I will show in chapter 7, section 3. Such an exploit makes the tremendous power and appeal of the Grand Inquisitor in some sense a commentary on Alexander Herzen, Vissarion Belinskii, and the others whose beauty and language are incorporated into his makeup. By associating such exploits with memory, and by involving memory with families and blessings earlier in the novel, Dostoevsky has used this association to manipulate his reader's instincts into that sympathy with the Grand Inquisitor which he sets about destroying in ways I will describe later.

The association of memory with good things and forgetting with evil ones prevails at the end of book 5, chapter 5, after the legend, when Alesha mysteriously forgets his brother Dmitrii, although Ivan has mentioned his name three times on the preceding page and has left Alesha in a manner reminiscent of Mitia's departure from Alesha the day before: "Later on, he recollected several times in his life with great puzzlement how he had managed suddenly after parting with Ivan to forget completely about his brother Dmitrii, whom he had decided that morning, only a few hours earlier, to track down before leaving, even if that meant not getting back to the monastery that night" (*Pss* 14:241).

The next rich and vivid collection of memories occurs in book 6, chapter 2, section *b*, when Zosima discusses his dying brother Markel:

> I remember, once I went into him alone when no one was with him. It was in the evening, clear; the sun was setting and illuminated the whole room with a slanting ray. He beckoned to me; I saw and went to him; he took me by the shoulders with both hands, looked me in the face ecstatically, lovingly; he said nothing, just looked thus for a moment or so. "So," he said, "go now, play, live for me." I went out and went to play. And since then in my life I have recollected many times with tears the way he ordered me to play for him. (*Pss* 14:263)

This childhood memory of a laying on of hands is followed by twelve sentences that bracket a chapter break and deal with plot, not memory. The first two of these sentences treat Markel's death, and the next five describe the impact of this death on the neighbors and on Zosima, immediately and later. The five sentences in the next chapter begin with Zosima's mother, who responds to the urging of neighbors and sends him to the cadet school in St. Petersburg. The last of these twelve sentences records her death and is followed by a rather abrupt return to the subject of memory:

> From my father's house I carried only precious memories, for men have no more precious memories than those from their first childhood in the parental home, and this is almost always so, if the family contained even a little bit of love and unity. And even from the worst of families, precious memories can be preserved if only

your spirit is willing and able to seek the precious. Among my memories of home, I reckon also memories about sacred stories which I was curious to get to know in my parental home, while still a child. I had a book then, sacred stories with beautiful pictures, called *A Hundred Sacred Stories from the Old and New Testament*, and I even learned to read from it. It is still lying now on my shelf; I keep it as a precious memento. But even before I began to read, I remember how I first was visited by the influence of the spirit, when I was still eight years old. My mother took me alone (I don't remember where my brother was) into the temple of the Lord, in holy week on Monday for the Mass. The day was clear, and recollecting it now, I seem to see again the way the incense rose from the censer and from above in the dome, through a little window, there poured upon us in the Church the rays of God, and rising up to them in waves, the incense seemed to melt into them. I gazed in holy wonder, and for the first time in my life, received the seed of God's Word consciously into my heart. (*Pss* 14:264)

This passage reintroduces the theme of memory in its full vividness with the same collection of associations as in Alesha's early recollections—a mother with a child, a consecration, slanting sunlight. But here, instead of an icon there are holy scriptures, and instead of an essay on the dreamlike vividness and isolation of early memories there is an essay on their moral importance.

Memory is not confined to passages of high seriousness in the novel, but its presence as a theme can shape our awareness of sentimental or misleadingly comfortable passages. For example, at Mitia's trial, at the end of book 12, chapter 3, when Dr. Herzenstube reminisces about Mitia's childhood, he clearly remembers the lad's behavior but takes several lines of text in his effort to remember the Russian word for *nuts*. He tells of giving Mitia a pound of nuts and instructing him in the formula of consecration at baptism, "Gott der Vater, Gott der Sohn, und Gott der Heilige Geist." Next time Mitia sees him, he remembers the beginning of the formula but has forgotten the Holy Ghost and has to be retaught.

Twenty-three years later, I was sitting one morning in my office, my hair already white, and suddenly a blooming youth came in whom I couldn't recognize at all, but he raised his finger and said, "Gott der Vater, Gott der Sohn, und Gott der Heilige Geist! I've just arrived and came to thank you for the pound of nuts, for no one had ever bought me a pound of nuts at that time, and you alone bought me a pound of nuts." And then I recollected my happy youth and the poor boy outdoors with no shoes, and my heart was moved, and I said, "You are a noble young person, for you have remembered all your life that pound of nuts which I brought you in your childhood." And I embraced him and blessed him. And I wept. He was laughing, but he was weeping too. (*Pss* 15:106–7)

This passage can be taken as a splendid piece of tear-jerking at a moment in the novel that has been rather dry of emotion, and a moment when relief is necessary before the catastrophe. But for the purposes of this book, it is more interesting to treat the passage as a minuet about the themes of remembering and forgetting. Both Herzenstube and Mitia begin by forgetting words. Herzenstube begins by reminiscing about Mitia's childhood and ends with a sentence whose crucial word is the conjunction "for" (*ibo*). "You are a noble young person, for you have remembered all your life that pound of nuts which I brought you in your childhood." This "for" can mean either that the remembering is evidence of nobility or that the remembering led to the nobility, but in either case, it enacts the principle Zosima had enunciated concerning the importance of even a single precious childhood recollection, if one's spirit is willing and able to seek the precious. The themes of childhood, abandonment, and consecration gather about the theme of memory in the same emotionally loaded configuration as in the notes Dostoevsky wrote at his wife's bier. This time the mood of sentimental nostalgia takes the place of the big emotions connected with mourning, but the complex of themes has a continuing identity.

This collection of passages raises an interesting question: what is the connection between memory, consecration, and suffering children? Ivan Karamazov linked the suffering of children to the question of the theodicy—how does one justify a God who permits innocent suffering? In book 6, chapter 3, section *zh*, Zosima's answer to this question is essentially rhetorical, as I shall show when I discuss rhetorical matters in this book, but for the purposes of this chapter it rests on a vision of a causal universe which runs counter to many observations:

> My brother used to ask the birds for forgiveness; that, however mindless it may be, is also true, for everything is like an ocean; everything is interflowing and in contact: you touch it in one place and it gives at the opposite end of the world. Suppose it is insane to ask birds for forgiveness; still it would be better for the birds and for the child, and for every living thing around you if you yourself were better than you are now, even just one drop better. Everything is like an ocean, I say unto you. (*Pss* 14:290)

Zosima takes the first creature one can think of that is more innocent than a child and blames its suffering not on God but on himself and his interlocutors, using a doctrine of universal causal linkage which the materialists and determinists of Dostoevsky's day could hardly deny. The argument is ingenious, but it is abstract and mystical as expressed here and conflicts with the evidence of our own experience: we have all done good deeds that conferred no visible benefit upon bird, beast, or fish. Zosima must therefore adduce a second doctrine to handle good deeds that seem to be lost:

> Even if you have given of light but see that people are not saved even in the presence of your light, still, remain firm in the power of the light of heaven; believe that even if they have not been saved now, they will be saved; and if they are not saved, their sons will be saved, for the light will not die, although you may be dead. The righteous departs, but his light remains. The salvation always comes after the death of the savior. (*Pss* 14:292)

This denial that good deeds are ever lost has nothing of the mystical about it. It relates to the practical efficacy of good on earth. It therefore is subject to the questions of mechanism which Zosima's more mystical insights bypass because they come from direct experience. Dostoevsky had to deal with practical, skeptical readers who would say, "Religious devotees may care more about spiritual states than about deeds and their effects, but I need to be shown just how a good deed of mine can ever help if it affects a child who dies, or who later commits murder—and if my good deeds can be lost, just how can I be guilty of a sparrow's fall." In this way a rational opponent of Dostoevsky's could challenge only half of the determinist position and say that every good or evil deed is socially determined, as is argued by certain characters in *Crime and Punishment*, but that while its causes are determined, its moral effects may be lost. Dostoevsky had to confront this problem of lost good in order to make his essentially rhetorical attack on the problem of evil cogent among a rationalist readership. But in saying that good deeds were latent, not lost, he had to name a repository for the good while it is not visible in a child, or after the child has died. The repository he names is intuitively acceptable, and anything but original. He could have drawn it from chapter 54 of one of his favorite books, *The Old Curiosity Shop:*

> There is nothing...no, nothing innocent or good, that dies, and is forgotten. Let us hold to that faith, or none. An infant, a prattling child, dying in its cradle, will live again in the better thoughts of those who loved it; and play its part, through them, in the redeeming actions of the world, though its body be burnt to ashes or drowned in the deepest sea. . . . Forgotten! Oh if the good deeds

of human creatures could be traced to their source, how beautifully would even death appear; for how much charity, mercy, and purified affection would be seen to have their growth in dusty graves.

In this passage Dickens names the repository of good that appears to be lost. He makes the same connection between memory and immortality on earth, and the same connection between memory and a dying child. Taking this familiar linkage, Dostoevsky introduced a series of children into *The Brothers Karamazov*, including Alesha, Markel, Zosima, and Mitia. Each of these children goes through a consecration in a passage cited in this chapter: Markel dies, and in each of the others the good to which he was consecrated becomes latent. But latency, as Dostoevsky knew from the psychology of his times, was not loss, and the memory of Markel, the figure of Zosima appearing in a dream after death, and Alesha's ability to help Iliusha, Kolia, and the boys are all examples of the persistence and indeed the enhanced contagiousness of good beyond its apparent death. Dostoevsky indicated his biblical source for this pattern in his epigraph to *The Brothers Karamazov*, which equates this good with a seed. "Except a corn of wheat fall upon the ground and die, it abideth alone, but if it die, it bringeth forth much fruit." *The Brothers Karamazov* enacts the second part of this epigraph; the first part does not deny the salvation of those who do not die or fall; it simply sees their salvation as individual, bearing no fruit in the lives of others, and therefore less novelistic, at least in the Dostoevskian mode. Alesha's insemination with grace begins a process that becomes latent when he tells Ivan a general should be shot and when he accepts Rakitin's offer of forbidden food and drink and sex; and it ends on the last pages of the novel, as he implants a memory in the boys by means of his funeral oration after the service of eternal memory:

> We are about to part, gentlemen. Let us agree right here at Iliusha's stone that we shall never forget—first of all, Iliushechka, and second, one another. And whatever may happen to us after this in life, though we might not meet for twenty years after this, we will still remember how we buried this poor boy at whom we had thrown stones earlier, do you remember the bridge, there, and after that all came to love him so. He was a wonderful boy, a good, brave boy, he had a sense of honor and felt for the bitter insult to his father, against which he rebelled. So first, we will remember him, gentlemen, all our life. And though you may be busy with the most important matters, may have attained repute or fallen into the greatest misfortune, never forget the way it once was well with us here, all in communion. What I say to you may be unclear, but you still will remember it, and sometime after this will agree

with my words. Know, then, that there is nothing higher or stronger—or healthier, or more useful for the life ahead than good memories of any sort, and especially those carried out of childhood, from your parental home. People will tell you a lot about your education, but maybe this sort of beautiful, holy memory is the best education of all. If a person can take such memories along through life, then he is saved for life. And even if but one good memory remains with us in our heart, that may someday serve as our education. We may grow vicious after this, but still, however vicious we may be, which God forbid, yet as we remember how we buried Iliusha...the most savage and mocking person among us will not be able to laugh inwardly at his kindness and goodness at this current moment. Moreover, maybe just this memory alone will hold him back from some great evil. (Pss 15:195)

In this final speech in *The Brothers Karamazov*, Dostoevsky presents memory as an actual moral force, latent for years, perhaps, as science, literature, and personal experience had taught him it could be, but offering the immortality on earth that had concerned him early in his career, and at the same time offering a rationally acceptable repository for the good whose preservation was indispensable to his theodicy.

But rational answers never sufficed for Dostoevsky. He was always seeking ways to put his reader in the position of his characters, to carry the reader beyond the position of a listener or a bystander. As a moral and manipulative novelist, he was not content to describe precious memories. He was setting out to create them in his readers, and one technique he used calls to mind the works on hypnotism I have sampled earlier in this chapter. The hypnotists had learned that repetition produces suggestion, and in the sixty sentences from *The Brothers Karamazov* I have quoted in this chapter on memory, Dostoevsky used words directly relating to memory, permanence, or clarity sixty times. The theme of memory, rich as it was in meanings for him, became not only a central element of doctrine but also a powerful technique for fixing thoughts and feelings in his readers.

Chapter Six

THE ORIGINS OF A SINGLE PARAGRAPH REVEAL THE UNCONSCIOUS TRANSFORMATIONS THAT SHAPE ALESHA KARAMAZOV.

I

THE FIRST INTERTEXTUALLY RICH AND THEMATICALLY CENTRAL PASSAGE IN THE NOVEL RESTS ON A STORY DOSTOEVSKY HAD FORGOTTEN.

I have discussed the way Dostoevsky, like many of his contemporaries, claimed not to invent but to record what he presented in his fiction. This fidelity to reality often takes the form of fidelity to written experiences that can be compared with the final text. In making such comparisons, it makes sense to study, not a character like Mitia, or a chain of events like the murder and the judicial error, or a theme like memory, but something much smaller, a passage of text that has some internal coherence and some inherent interest.

As Dostoevsky wrote a particularly moving passage or one of critical importance in the novel, he seems to have drawn on more sources than in the more prosaic, "working" passages. This observation raises some methodological questions. First, the words "moving" and "critical" are hard to verify, although the responses of readers in several generations and countries can offer a consensus. Second, the richness of sources for a famous passage might be an artifact of our scholarly practices. Most scholars discover sources by accident: when reading Dostoevsky, they remember a parallel passage, or when reading a parallel passage, they remember the one in Dostoevsky. The second kind of accident would lead scholars to find more sources for those passages memorable enough to be recalled when the scholar came upon the source. While it is hard to demonstrate unambiguously, this literary density of the strong passages is pronounced enough to warrant special attention to them in a study like this one. I have already quoted the middle of the first rich, resonant passage in *The Brothers Karamazov*. This paragraph shows how Alesha's mother and Father Zosima instilled the grace of God in Alesha, and how Alesha's loving faith in his fellow men, coupled with a capacity not to judge or fear or wonder, though not naively ignorant of faults, awakened in old Fedor a more "sincere and profound" love than people like him ever feel. The paragraph is organized chiastically, with Alesha's childhood recollection of his mother sandwiched between two discussions of his eccentricity, and these in turn between two discussions of his loving-kindness and religious involvement. Each half of this paragraph begins analytically, discussing the relation between Alesha's loving-kindness and his eccentricity, and ends narratively, presenting his actual experience with his parent:

ТРЕТИЙ СЫН АЛЕША

Было ему тогда всего двадцать лет (брату его Ивану шел тогда двадцать четвертый год, а старшему их брату, Дмитрию — двадцать восьмой). Прежде всего объявляю что этот юноша, Алеша, был вовсе не фанатик, и, по-моему по крайней мере, даже и не мистик вовсе. Заранее скажу мое полное мнение: был он просто ранний человеколюбец, и если ударился на монастырскую дорогу, то потому только, что в то время она одна поразила его и представила ему, так сказать, идеал исхода рвавшейся нз мрака мирской злобы к свету любви души его. И поразила-то его эта дорога лишь потому, что на ней он встретил тогда необыкновенное, по его мнению, существо — нашего знаменитого монастырского старца Зосиму, к которому привязался всею горячею первою любовыю своего неутолимого сердца. Впрочем, я не спорю, что был он и тогда уже очень странен, начав даже с колыбели. Кстати, я уже упоминал про него, что, оставшись после матери всего лишь по четвертому году, он запомнил ее потом на всю жизнь, ее лицо, ее ласки, "точно как будто она стоит предо мной живая". Такие воспоминания могут запомипаться (и зто всем известпо) даже и из более раннего возраста, даже с двухлетнего, но лишь выступая всю жизнь как бы светлыми точками из мрака, как бы вырванным уголком из огромной картины, которая вся погасла и исчезла, кроме этого только уголочка. Так точно было и с ним: он запомнил один вечер, летний, тихий, отворенное окно, косые лучи заходящего солнца (косые-то лучи и запомнились всего более), в комнате в углу образ, пред ним зажженную лампадку, а пред образом на коленях рыдающую в истерике, со взвизгиваниями и вскрикиваниями, мать свою, схватившую его в обе руки, обнявшую его крепко до боли и молящую за него богородицу, протягивающую его из объятий своих обеими руками к образу как бы под покров богородице . . . и вдруг вбегает нянька и вырывает его у нее в испуге. Вот картина! Алеша запомнил в тот миг и лицо своей матери: он говорил, что оно было исступленное, но прекрасное, судя по тому, сколько мог он припомнить. Но он редко кому любил поверять это воспоминание. В детстве и юности он был мало экспансивен и даже мало разговорчив, но не от недоверия, не от робости или угрюмой нелюдимости, вовсе даже напротив, а от чего-то другого, от какой-то как бы внутренней заботы, собственно личной, до других не касавшейся, но столь для него важной, что он из-за нее как бы забывал других. Но людей он любил: он, казалось, всю жнзнь жил, совершенно веря в людей, а между тем никто и никогда не считал его ни простячком, ни наивным человеком. Что-то было в нем, что говорило и внушало (да и всю жизнь потом), что он не хочет быть судьей людей, что он не захочет взять на себя осуждения и ни за что не осудит. Казалось даже, что он все допускал, нимало не осуждая, хотя часто очень горько грустя. Мало того, в этом смысле он до того дошел, что его никто не мог ни удивить, ни испугать, и это даже в самой ранней своей молодости. Явясь по двадцатому году к отцу, положительно в вертеп грязного разврата, он, целомудренный н чистый, лишь молча удалялся, когда глядеть было нестерпимо, но без малейшего вида презрения или осуждения кому бы то ни было. Отец же, бывший когда-то приживальщик, а потому человек чуткий и тонкий на обиду, сначала недоверчиво и угрюмо его встретивший ("много, дескать, молчит и много про себя рассуждает"), скоро кончил, однакоже, тем, что стал его ужасно часто обнимать и целовать, не далее как через две какиенибудь недели, правда с пьяными слезами, в хмельной чувствительности, но видно, что полюбив его искренно и глубоко и так, как никогла, конечно, не удавалось такому, как он, никого любить . . . (*Pss* 14:17–19)

This paragraph can be traced to so many sources that the first few sentences will bear separate translation and examination. In English they read as follows:

He was just twenty years old at the time (his brother Ivan was in his twenty-fourth year, and their older brother, Dmitrii, twenty-eight). First of all, I shall state that this youth, Alesha, was not a fanatic at all, and in my opinion, at least, not even a mystic at all. I'll say my full opinion in advance; he was simply precocious in his love of people, and if he had set out on the monastic way, that was just because right then it was the only one that struck him, offering his heart what one might call the ideal of escape as it struggled out of the murk of worldly nastiness toward the light of love. And this way had caught his imagination just because at that moment he encountered upon it what he considered a rare being, our monastery's well-known elder, Zosima, to whom he bound himself with all the burning first love of his unjaded heart. Still, I do not dispute that he already was very strange at that time, and had been from his cradle on.

One of the best-known sources for Alesha is Michael, the hero of the story "Mixail" by Dostoevsky's close friend Anna Korvin-Krukovskaia. Dostoevsky read this story in 1864 and liked it well enough to print it on the first fifty-eight pages of his journal the *Epoch* for September of that year. The author's sister called his attention to the parallel between Michael and Alesha and quotes him as responding: "'You know, it's really true!' said Fedor Mikhailovich, striking his hand against his forehead, 'but, believe me, I had forgotten about Michael when I thought up my Alesha. Still, couldn't I have had him in my mind unconsciously,' he added after thinking a little."[1]

The story of Michael is simple. At the age of seven or eight, Michael is taken by his nurse from the country to Moscow to see his dying father, whose kind and frivolous brother and nephews comfort the boy. The nurse takes him to a moving church service in the Cathedral of the Assumption. Eleven years elapse, during which Michael abandons society, where he has been ill at ease, for the Trinity Monastery, to which another uncle of his has retired into sumptuous austerity after years of social success followed by political exile. Two years later Michael guides a princess and her daughter about the monastery, discovers that they are family acquaintances, and becomes enchanted with the daughter. Two weeks later he leaves the monastery and is kindly received by his uncle and cousins in Moscow; but a morbid shyness and revulsion at the bewildering pointlessness and corruptness of Moscow drive him back to the monastery. Three months later he dies apathetically of tuberculosis.

Little in the story is unique. The neglected child, the dying aristocrat, the visit to the church, the monastic exemplar, the gentlewoman traveling with her daughter, the country cousin's revulsion at city life, and the death from tuberculosis are standard subject matter for the nineteenth-century novel anywhere in Europe. The parallels, however, are important and numerous. Alesha, like Michael, is specifically called a *chudak*,[2] an odd character, and has a curiously self-contained quality and a reluctance to handle everyday practicalities. He is the motherless son of a rich and pleasure-loving father who abandons him in childhood to the care of a faithful servant. Early exposures to religious symbols and emotions, coupled with a rather maidenly delicacy, lead him toward a monastery, where he enters the tutelage of a remarkable and holy man (in the early notes for *The Brothers Karamazov*, an uncle, as in "Mixail"; *Pss.* 15:199) with a deep awareness of the ways of the world. In a later chapter, when he reaches twenty this novice is allowed by his mentor to leave the monastery and be drawn to a capricious girl who has visited the monastery with her mother, but the temptations of the world do not corrupt him.

These parallels startled Dostoevsky, and it startles us also to see the subconscious operate in such a workmanlike way.

II

DOSTOEVSKY TRANSFORMED PASSAGES SUBCONSCIOUSLY IN THE DIRECTION OF *THE BROTHERS KARAMAZOV.*

To avoid positing such a methodical operation for the unconscious memory, it seems natural to look for a common source or for an intermediate source, a work influenced by "Mixail" which in turn influenced *The Brothers Karamazov*. Postponing consideration of common sources, I shall cite a book by Dostoevsky's favorite author which also contains the arrival of a sickly, otherworldly cousin in a great city house; his warm but puzzled reception; the kind, vague, frivolous mother and the aggressive, attractive daughter; the gauche irresolution or sexual terror that isolates him from the girl he loves; his bewilderment in the streets of the great city; and his flight back to seclusion and sickness. This intermediate source is Dostoevsky's own *Idiot*, which he wrote less than four years after publishing "Mixail." If Michael is a source for Myshkin and Myshkin is a source for Alesha, the unconscious influence of Michael on Alesha is comprehensible. His own more recent and more powerful vision of the man too excellent for this world had simply eclipsed its sources in Dostoevsky's mind.

There can be no doubt that Myshkin is a source for Alesha. The early notes for *The Brothers Karamazov* use the name "Idiot" for Alesha. Except perhaps for the monastic details, all the traits and experiences shared by Michael and Alesha also belong to Myshkin. In addition, Alesha inherits Myshkin's tendency to love and trust those around him and to inspire answering love, and his related tendency not to notice insults. He also inherits Myshkin's shamefacedness and chastity, which produce experiences with Lize Xoxlakova and Grushenka analogous to those with Aglaia Epanchina and Nastasia Filipovna, whose respective roles as inaccessible aristocrat and vengeful kept woman are also comparable in the two novels. Finally, Myshkin's and Alesha's impracticality in financial matters and their disinterest in the problems of their own support inspire hospitality, helpfulness, and good humor in those around them. Even certain events in the novels are closely parallel. Both Myshkin and Alesha befriend an outcast who is attacked and teased and pelted by the children of the town, and finally bring the children to love and help this pitiable creature, whose death from tuberculosis draws all the children to the burial, where they shout, "Hurrah!" (*Pss* 6:69, 15:197).

The differences between these two sources and Alesha are rather more interesting than the similarities. Michael is not a mystic but could fairly be called a fanatic; he is characterized as "one of those rare natures which proceed unwaveringly under the influence of an abstract idea, never giving way, to the end of their powers, and are broken irreparably," and sometimes "there flashed through his mind a confused idea of distant wanderings in foreign lands and exploits in the name of Christ and all-forgiving love."[3] Myshkin lacks the purposefulness of a fanatic but does have basically mystical experiences before his epileptic fits or when it seems to him "that if I should walk straight on, walk a long time, and get up to that line, the very one where the sky meets the earth, then there would be the solution to it all, and you would see a new life straightaway a thousand times more powerful and tumultuous than ours" (*Pss* 6:54). We have seen that Alesha is "not a fanatic at all, and in my opinion, at least, not even a mystic at all," and we know that this is no casual remark, because as part of the second sentence, it occupies one of the most strategic positions in chapter 4, and because Dostoevsky's early notes for the novel contain the phrase "by no means a fanatic: by no means a mystic" (*Pss* 15:200). Rhetorically, moreover, the statement is redundant, a litotes denying the opposite of the qualities ascribed to Alesha in the next sentence.

Dostoevsky's ideological polemic offers the easiest explanation for such an emphatic denial of Myshkin's and Michael's predicates. In a period when mysticism was suspect and fanaticism fashionable only in politics, Dostoevsky's opponents found it useful to label as mystics or fanatics all believers who could not be dismissed as hypocrites. Dostoevsky naturally used all available resources to protect his hero from such a standardized attack. To do so, he had to deny these two attributes of Alesha's sources.

This dialectical relation to his sources can be expressed in another way. Dostoevsky published "Mixail" for many reasons, including his fondness for the author, but it seems likely that she fascinated him in large part because of her writing, and because he shared her interest in certain problems. Among those that appear in "Mixail" were such technical problems as the creation of an unremarkable hero, about which Dostoevsky wrote a digression in *The Idiot* and again at the start of *The Brothers Karamazov;* social questions, such as the uselessness of monasticism; moral questions, such as the ineffectiveness of a really good man or the danger implicit in isolation from frivolity; and ethical questions, involving the tension between Christian love and sexual love. This collection of problems lies somewhere near the center of *The Idiot,* relating it to "Mixail" not as to a mere source of detail, nor yet dialectically, as *The Brothers Karamazov* seems to be, but rather in the manner of Zola's experimental novels. Drawing from "Mixail," from Dickens, Cervantes, Pushkin, the Bible, a series of trials reported in the newspapers, and his own observations, Dostoevsky assembled the materials for a positively good man, set them to interact, and described the result of the experiment in *The Idiot.* Having carried out this experiment, he turned to other problems but continued to seek conditions in which such a figure could be more positively effective. With children and the childlike, Myshkin is effective, and Dostoevsky decided to write the novel about children that I mentioned in an earlier chapter. This idea dates back at least as far as the plan for the life of a great sinner, and the "teacher" plays a prominent part in the early notes for *The Possessed* and *The Raw Youth.*[4] A decisive moment in the genesis of Alesha may be the note Dostoevsky wrote to himself, "find out whether the Idiot has the right to maintain such a hoard of adopted children, have a school etc." (*Pss* 15:199). In this note, the novel about children and *The Idiot* merge into an entity that combines attributes of both.

This polemical relation between Alesha and Myshkin makes Alesha an assertion that Myshkin's failures and passive successes are accidental and not generic, and that his active successes could hold a central position. Myshkin's brief account of converting schoolchildren to love the dying Maria is thus expanded into the major episode of Iliusha and the boys. Alesha and Myshkin both sense the danger but cannot prevent the murder of a person close to them; the failure drives Myshkin out of the world and Alesha into it. In the same way, Myshkin's loss of the fierce and beautiful kept woman to a strong and violently passionate rival splits into three separate episodes. The first is an active success for Alesha, when his love transforms Grushenka's plan to seduce him; the fact that he is never her suitor makes the other two episodes, Grushenka's flight to her Polish lover and her rapprochement with Mitia, irrelevant to Alesha's career.

Dostoevsky's desire to show the practical power of love in action explains more obviously how the plot and the rhetoric of *The Brothers Karamazov* developed than it explains how the imagery of the novel is related to its sources. The passage that follows the sentences discussed so far is particularly rich in imagery, and it seems to be only incidentally related to Michael or Myshkin. I have already discussed it as an insemination with grace which remained in Alesha's memory all his life, but we should now look at its sources in a narrower way:

> I have already recalled that although [Alesha] had lost his mother when only four, he remembered her from then on, for his whole life, her face, her caresses, "just as if she stood before me alive." Such recollections (as we all know) can be remembered from an even earlier age, even from two years, but only emerging all one's life as bright spots from the murk, as if they were corners torn from a great picture which is extinguished and lost except for just that corner. Just so it was with him: he remembered one quiet summer evening, an open window, the slanting beams of the setting sun (these slanting beams were what he most remembered), in a room, in the corner, an image, a lamp lighted before it, and before the image his mother, on her knees, sobbing as if in hysterics, shrieking and wailing, clasping him in both arms, embracing him tightly, till it hurt, and praying to the Virgin for him, stretching him from her embrace with both hands toward the image as if for the Virgin's protection. Suddenly the nurse runs in and snatches him from her in terror. There's the picture! In that instant Alesha also remembered his mother's face: he said it was ecstatic but beautiful, judging by as much as he could remember. But he seldom liked to confide this memory to anyone.

Different parts of this passage have different sources. Various sources can be found even for the figure of the beautiful mother weeping in the slanting sunlight before an icon and separated from her son. Having used *The Idiot* as one of the major sources for Alesha, I should like to look at Dostoevsky's recent journalistic work, which we have already discussed as one of the chief workshops in which Dostoevsky's novels were initially wrought.

In *The Diary of a Writer* for April 1876 (part 3 of chapter 1) Dostoevsky introduced a weeping mother in a curiously revealing passage. Seeking an example of peasant benevolence and acuity in understanding human needs, he asks his readers,

Don't you remember how in Aksakov's *Family Chronicle* the mother tearfully begged the peasants to take her across the wide Volga to Kazan', to her sick child, across the thin ice, in the spring, when it had been several days since anyone had dared to step on the ice, which crashed and washed out just a few hours after her crossing? Do you remember the charming description of this crossing, the way afterward, when they had crossed, the peasants did not want to take any money, understanding that they had done it all because of the mother's tears and for the sake of our Jesus Christ. (*Pss* 11:257)

Writing *The Brothers Karamazov* only three years after this passage, Dostoevsky would have been hard put to think about a desperate weeping mother separated from her son without involving the picture he had made so vividly in *The Diary of a Writer*. The passage presents several problems, however. The nicest problem is that there is no such passage in Sergei Aksakov's *Family Chronicle*. Dostoevsky probably owned a copy of this memoir in the 1856 edition, which contains Aksakov's *Reminiscences* in the same volume,[5] and the *Reminiscences* contains the following passage:

The river Kama had not yet broken up, but had swelled and turned blue; the day before, they had carried the mail across on foot, but that night it had rained, and no one agreed to take my mother and her company across to the other side. My mother had to spend the night in Murzikha, dreading every moment's delay; she herself went from house to house through the village and begged the good people to help her, telling her woe and offering as recompense all that she had. Good and daring people were found, who understood a mother's heart, and promised her that if the rain stopped in the night and it froze just a bit in the morning, they would undertake to get her to the other side and accept what she offered for their labors. Till dawn my mother prayed, kneeling in the corner in front of the icon in the house where she was staying. . . .

[When she had crossed the river] my mother gave a hundred rubles to those who had taken her, that is, half the money she had, but these honorable people did not want to take them; they took only [five rubles each]. In astonishment, they heard her glowing expressions of gratitude and benediction. . . and promptly set out for home, because there was no time to delay: the river broke up the next day.[6]

The trivial error about the title is clearly not the only evidence that Dostoevsky was quoting from memory. He naturally shortened and simplified this passage, but he also changed it in a curiously systematic way. The wide Volga replaces its tributary the Kama. The last earlier crossing shifts from the previous day to several days ago. Dostoevsky's river burst and washed out (*vzlomavsiisia i pro-shedshii*) just a few hours later, while Aksakov's went out (*proshla*) the next day. Dostoevsky's peasants did not want to take any money; Aksakov's took five rubles each. Each of these changes amplifies the risk or the nobility of the peasants, supporting Dostoevsky's argument. The other changes lack such a polemical explanation, while those maternal tears which are so decisive in the peasants' decision actually tend to weaken his argument, since the instinctive comprehension of a brave mother's heart impresses us rather more than a surrender to a woman's weapons, water drops.

Emerging into Dostoevsky's memory for no polemical reason, and not from the passage he was citing, these maternal tears seem more closely related to *The Brothers Karamazov* than to Aksakov. For the tears of Alesha's mother are closely related to the tears of the believing woman who has also lost a son, the tears of a woman Ivan described whose son has been hunted to death by dogs, the tears of the woman in Seville before Christ resurrects her child, the tears of Markel's and Iliusha's mothers at the deaths of their sons.

In *The Diary of a Writer*, then, are these proleptic tears? Did they come, not from Aksakov, as Dostoevsky imagined, but from *The Brothers Karamazov*, or, to be more precise, from the collection of energies, ideas, images, and memories that would generate *The Brothers Karamazov* three years later? If so, the obvious question remains, Where did *that* weeping mother come from? One answer is the book that Dostoevsky believed he was citing, Aksakov's *Family Chronicle*, where we have not a weeping mother but an unfortunate wife, Praskovia Ivanovna Kurolesova, married, like Alesha's mother, below her station, although technically within the gentry, to a depraved, vicious, shrewd, suddenly successful master; on one occasion "it was already light, and the sun was even up... Praskovia Ivanovna knelt and tearfully prayed to a new church cross, which burned with the rising sun by the very windows of the house."[7]

Even closer to *The Brothers Karamazov* than this nonmother weeping for very different reasons before the icon in the slanting sunlight, but perhaps not uninfluenced by the Aksakov passage, is Arkadii's description of his earliest memories in book 1, chapter 6, section 3 of *The Raw Youth:*

> ...something of your face remained in my heart my whole life, and besides that, there remained the knowledge that you were my mother. I see that whole village as if in a dream, now, and I have even forgotten my nurse....I still remember the huge trees near the house, willows, I guess, then sometimes the strong light of

the sun through the open windows, the fenced flower garden, the path, and you, Mother, I remember only at one moment, when they held communion in the local church, and you took me up to receive the sacrament and kiss the cup; it was summer, and a dove flew through across the dome, from window to window.... Your face, or something about it, the expression, stayed so in my memory that five years later, in Moscow, I knew you right away. (Pss 13:92)

Here, not only the mother and child, the season, the window, the sunlight, the expression on her face, the son's lifelong remembrance, but also the mother's separation from her son thereafter—all find echoes in *The Brothers Karamazov*. Certain components of this scene, however, could not possibly have come from Aksakov, since Dostoevsky was already using them before Aksakov wrote. In "The Landlady" (1847), part 1, 1,

The service had just ended; . . . The rays of the setting sun streamed broadly down through the narrow window of the dome and lit one of the chapels with a sea of brilliance, but they kept weakening, and the blacker the gloom became, thickening under the vaults of the church, the more brightly shone the occasional gilded icons, bathed in the trembling glow of lamps and candles. In a fit of profoundly troubled pain, and somehow overwhelming feeling, Ordynov leaned against the wall in the darkest corner of the church and forgot himself for a moment. [Murin and Katerina entered. She] prostrated herself before the icon. The old man took the end of the cover hanging from the icon support, and covered her head. A stifled sobbing sounded through the church. . . .

Two minutes later she raised her head and again the bright light of the lamps bathed her charming face. . . . Tears boiled in her dark blue eyes. (Pss 1:298–99)

Already in the 1840s, Dostoevsky had begun reworking much of this material at a number of points in *Netochka Nezvanova*, whose second chapter begins:

My memories began very late, from my ninth year only. I do not know how everything that happened to me before that age left no clear impression I can now recall. But from the middle of my ninth year I recall everything exactly, day by day, uninterruptedly, as if everything that happened after that had occurred only yesterday. True, I can remember something earlier as if through a dream: the lamp always lighted in the dark corner by the old-fashioned icon; then, a horse once hit me on the street, and I was sick in bed for three months, as people told me later; also that during this sickness I once woke up at night beside Mother, sleeping together, and the way I suddenly was terrified of my sickbed nightmares, the silence of the night, the mice scraping in the corner, and how I trembled in terror all night. *(Pss* 2:158)

Taken together, these two works of Dostoevsky's early period contain the essay on infantile memory, the summer evening, the quiet of the slanting rays of the setting sun, the lamplit icon in the corner, and the beautiful woman kneeling before an icon, wailing hysterically. Sergei Durylin has traced the sequence of passages running through Dostoevsky's works where the slanting rays of sunlight appear, and V. L. Komarovich has linked these with the writings of the utopian socialists and others.[8]

The particular elements that are relevant to the scene in *The Brothers Karamazov* can perhaps also be traced to an author whom Dostoevsky claimed to have read completely, in Russian or in German, as a very young man, and whom he certainly admired deeply. E. T. A. Hoffmann's *Devil's Elixirs*, the story of a great sinner, parallels *The Brothers Karamazov* in its involvement with miracles, monasticism, and the operation of grace in the world, and it also begins with the childhood recollections of its hero.[9] The first few pages of these recollections contain the following passages:

> The first conscious impressions that dawn in my mind are of the monastery and the wonderful chapel of the Holy Linden. . . . The stillness is broken only by the devout chanting of the priests who, together with the pilgrims, file past in long lines, swinging golden censers from which ascends the odour of sacrificial incense. . . . The shining figures of saints and angels still smile down upon me. . . . Yet my memory cannot possibly reach back so far, for my mother left that holy city after a year and a half. . . .
>
> My clear recollection of personal experience begins with the occasion when, on the journey home, my mother came to a Cistercian convent where the Abbess—by birth a princess—who had known my father, received her kindly. . . .
>
> Holding my mother's hand, I mounted the wide stone steps and entered the high, arched chamber adorned with paintings of the saints, where we found the Abbess. . . . The bell sounded for vespers. The Abbess rose, and said to my mother: "Good lady, I regard your son as my protege, and from now on I will provide for him."
>
> My mother was unable to speak for emotion. Sobbing violently, she kissed the Abbess's hands.
>
> Just as we were about to go out of the door, the Abbess came after us, lifted me up again and, carefully moving the Crucifix to one side, embraced me. As her burning tears fell on my brow, she cried:
>
> "Franciscus—Be kind and good." . . .
>
> . . . St. Bernard's day falls in August, and I cannot recall the

weather ever proving unfavorable in that most favored of seasons;...I remember beautifully the feelings summoned up in me by the singing of the "Gloria."...It seemed as if the sky itself had opened at that moment above the altar, and the representations of the seraphim and cherubim on the walls were spreading their wings as if called to life by a divine miracle, and flapping them, flew through the shrine praising the Lord with song and wondrous lute-playing. Plunging into meditative contemplation of the service, my soul was carried off on the clouds of incense to a distant home.[10]

Hoffmann's scene contains many elements that Dostoevsky used over and over—the little discussion of early recollections from the second year of one's life, the peace of a monastery, silence, chanting, incense rising, holy images that glow, mother and child entering a holy place, church bells, hospitality and protection offered at the first encounter, maternal tears, a cross and a blessing, and the angels flying about the temple, if indeed these last are a source for that image in *The Raw Youth* which is at once closer to earth and closer to the absolute, the dove.

III

HE THEREFORE CONDENSED IN WAYS POSSIBLE ONLY IF HE PERCEIVED A COMMON SOURCE.

If the first description of Alesha incorporates works by Anna Korvin-Krukovskaia, as transformed in *The Idiot*; by Aksakov, as transformed in *The Diary of a Writer*; and by Hoffmann, transformed many times, the overdetermination demands a search for some redundancy or other organizing principle among the sources, as well as a search for some pattern of exclusion, abstraction, or condensation that makes the process work without overburdening Dostoevsky's text. To begin with, let us examine certain of Dostoevsky's omissions, since we have already considered the omission of Myshkin's mysticism and Michael's fanaticism.

The most obvious omission from all the sources named so far is their sickness. Even the chief nonliterary source for Alesha, Dostoevsky's own son Alesha, died of a seizure, apparently epileptic, while still a child. Medardus and Myshkin were similarly afflicted, although Medardus recovered, and Myshkin did not disintegrate mentally and physically until his constitutional weakness was aggravated by his failure to prevent a crucial murder. Aksakov was a nervous and sickly child and dangerously ill the time his mother crossed the Kama, while Michael, long before his youthful death from tuberculosis, has "a pale, feeble face, large, dark blue eyes. . . . He seemed a fragile, feeble boy, in whom a natural meditativeness and a habit-reinforced tendency toward daydreaming and fixation had undermined a constitution feeble to start with, and had stamped his early childhood with sickliness and weakness."[11] Faithfulness to his sources would demand that Dostoevsky somehow connect all this disease and death with Alesha; but, polemically, Alesha is Dostoevsky's final attempt to divorce an essentially religious excellence from the weakness, asceticism, submissiveness, and general unfitness for this world with which it was associated in the minds not only of his ideological enemies but also of his romantic predecessors, who loved to attribute inspiration to a wound or a disease such as tuberculosis.

And indeed, the first physical description of Alesha Karamazov begins with a redundant litotes startlingly like the one at the start of his spiritual description: "It may be that some reader will think my young man was of a sickly, ecstatic, poorly developed nature, a pale daydreamer, a wasted, worn-out person. On the contrary . . ." Here are the terms that could not be ascribed to Alesha, retaining what we have called their absolute value but entering the description with their sign changed. To the polemical explanation of that other redundant litotes, which denied Alesha's mysticism and fanaticism, we can now add this genetic one, that such a figure that would otherwise be excluded by Dostoevsky's ideological goals could be included with a minus sign and still retain a presence of a kind. Freud holds that our dreaming mind does not have the capacity to negate things or to forget them; it represents them indiscriminately, and the interpreter has the difficult task of affixing positive or negative signs to these floating meanings. When Dostoevsky reworked "Mixail" without realizing it, and the Aksakov passage in ways that ran counter to his argument, the unconscious processing retained many elements from his overlapping sources but sometimes with the negative marker that his conscious ideology demanded. The polemical and the genetic explanation, taken together, explain why Dostoevsky's reluctance to ignore his sources or his goals sometimes led him into a polemic with his own sources.

This single litotes hardly seems commensurate with the long list of sicknesses and deaths just cited. But Alesha Karamazov does not exist alone. He is primarily a member of two groups, of the Karamazov family and of those touched with the grace of God, and these two groups seem to act as Alesha's attic, the repositories for those attributes he inherits but cannot use. Thus, within the Karamazov family, Smerdiakov receives the epilepsy, and the failure to prevent a crucial murder precipitates Ivan's mental and physical disintegration. Among those touched with grace, Alesha's mother is weak and ecstatic and dies young. Iliusha is sickly and over-emotional and dies of tuberculosis as a child, while Zosima's brother Markel and the believing peasant's son Alesha die in childhood of unspecified causes, and Zosima himself is weak and dying at the time of the novel.

This transformation of attributes into their opposite, taken together with their redistribution among related characters, allows Dostoevsky to borrow extensively without being constrained by his sources. It also offers a genetic explanation for certain of the "doubles" who have received so much attention in Dostoevsky criticism. The double contains the leftovers or, in Zola's terms, the alternative ingredients that might have gone into the makeup of a given character if Dostoevsky's artistic and ideological goals had been different.

Alesha thus receives Myshkin's and Medardus's capacity to inspire instant hospitality, but Markel receives Myshkin's love of birds. The scenes in Aksakov and *Netochka Nezvanova* may be sources for the household icons in the passage at hand, but the church scenes in Hoffmann, "Mixail," and *The Raw Youth* are not wasted: we read how Zosima's mother led him alone "into the Lord's temple, in Holy Week, to the Monday mass. The day was clear, and recollecting, now, I see anew exactly how the incense mounted from the censer, and silently rose, and from above in the dome through a narrow slit, there poured upon us in the church the divine rays, and, rising to them in waves, the incense seemed to melt among them" (*Pss* 14:264).

On the basis of this rather neat relationship between the description of Alesha and its sources, a pattern of conservation seems to emerge which might be phrased as follows: "In Dostoevsky's creative laboratory, literary matter is neither created nor destroyed." This "law," of course, is little but a literary restatement of the attitude toward originality enunciated earlier in this book, or even of Dostoevsky's claim to invent nothing and represent the world more closely than others can, but this pseudoscientific formulation breaks down into two laws that make explicit the assumptions underlying most studies of realism.

The first law has been a materialist's commonplace for millennia: Lucretius, Lear, and Livingston Lowes,[12] for example, accepted it as a long-established truth that "nothing comes out of nothing." This law makes explicit the assumption underlying my recurrent question, Where did this come from? as well as the limitations that the length and the aesthetic identity of a nineteenth-century novel impose on such an inquiry. Any effort to write *The Road to*

Skotoprigonevsk would prove as hopeless as the title, because even if my conservation law were literally true, no one could prove scientifically that nothing in *The Brothers Karamazov* emerged from nothing.

The second law is the converse of the first: "Nothing returns to nothing," which again was old for Democritus and fresh for Freud. In literary terms, this means that once Dostoevsky had adopted a passage for use, he felt some aesthetic, doctrinal, or psychological need to retain it in its entirety, although, as we have seen, he might present parts of it in a negative form, like Michael's fanaticism, or redistributed to parallel characters or "doubles," like the sickness of many of Alesha's sources. For the verification of this law a nineteenth-century novel gives a more natural scope than a lyric. If Kubla Khan contains all of Bartram, the mechanisms of condensation are largely inaccessible. In one way or another, however, the description of Alesha does contain enough of the items in his sources to warrant further testing of this law: In a known source for *The Brothers Karamazov*, one should look for the disposition of every element somewhere in the novel. In a probable or possible source, the presence or absence of incidental elements may help determine whether the passage is a source. In human affairs, of course, "laws" of this sort sound more precise and elegant than they are. At best they may suggest methodologies and lines of inquiry in a world that is hopelessly confused without them. At worst, they can lead to the kind of pedantic casuistry that artificially reconciles reality with theory.

The first of these two conservation laws suggests a look at certain items in the passage being studied that have not yet been accounted for. The most striking of these is perhaps the simile the narrator applies to Alesha's memory: "as if [recollections] were corners torn from a great picture which is extinguished and lost except for just that corner." There are magnificent pictures in the Hoffmann passages, but not the image of a surviving fragment.

Dostoevsky once wrote, "In getting ready to write, I reread my previous observations in my notebooks, and besides that, reread all the correspondence I had with me" (*Pss* 29, pt. 2: 99–100). If he reread his correspondence in this way while the plan for *The Brothers Karamazov* was crystallizing in his mind, in the spring and early summer of 1878, he came upon a letter he had solicited himself, as we have seen earlier. The schoolteacher Vladimir Mikhailov, whom Dostoevsky had recently claimed to treasure and reread as a correspondent, had written this letter in response to Dostoevsky's request for materials about children for the new novel.[13] Mikhailov ends his long and dreary catalog of personal, political, and pedagogical disasters with an apology for being too distraught to supply the accounts of children Dostoevsky wanted. One child, however, does appear in the letter, and in a way that echoed one of Dostoevsky's own haunting fears, the death or misfortune of one of his own children:

> It is a good thing that there are just two of us. We had a little son, but 13 years ago he died. And before me hangs a portrait of that lad, his whole four-year-old figure. Kramskoi did it. Like a living being, he stands before me and gazes caressingly. Yes, had you lived to the present, would you still have looked at me that way, my precious? God bless you. I see you not crippled by the latest quasi-pedagogical formula; from you, at 17, I hear no speeches striking for their bitterness; I see no conceit at your own ignorance, no sarcastic smile at a mushy-hearted old man. God bless you, my dear, glowing boy. You do not see how badly your old folks are doing. Oh, we're tired, sinners that we are, how tired we are. But one must live. None of that. And live we will, we will!
>
> Thank you, my dear Fedor Mikhailovich, for writing your warm note at just such a moment. The response of a glowing heart worked healingly on my mood. I pulled myself together, and went to get myself photographed. Come, I thought, I'll send it to him. And I came out pretty grim, but still it came out so good that I've never had one like it taken before, nor probably ever will. You have the only copy of its kind, since just after this print, the negative broke, and the second attempt is no good at all.[14]

If Dostoevsky reread this letter two or three months after receiving it, its impact would have become hideously intimate, for his own son Aleksei died unexpectedly on 16 May 1878. Both the Mikhailov letter and *The Brothers Karamazov* as a whole look back to a period thirteen years earlier; two boys are separated by death at the age of four from a loving and unfortunate parent but remain linked to this parent by a lifelong memory. Neither boy completes his education or acquires the nasty concerns and ways of schoolboys, and both retain a child's association with light, love, caresses, and benediction. Both passages involve pictures. In the Mikhailov passage both pictures are real and remarkable: one a portrait so fine that its subject "like a living being. . . stands before me and gazes caressingly," and the other a uniquely excellent picture that is lost except for one surviving print. The Dostoevsky passage ends with the compressed metaphor of a picture (*kartina*) standing for the whole scene with Alesha's mother. It has a real picture, the candle-lit image of the Madonna, at its heart and begins with an extended simile comparing the surviving corner of a vast picture otherwise destroyed to the kind of memory that lets Alesha see his mother "as if she were standing before me alive."

The differences between these sets of pictures follow a pattern. The Mikhailov letter describes an excellent painting of a wonderful child and an excellent photograph of a fine, loving parent. The Dostoevsky passage mentions three pictures. The first picture is excellently done, but the text gives it no subject matter at all since it exists in a novelistic simile, not an elaborated epic one. The second Dostoevsky picture shows an excellent parent and child, Mary and Jesus, but the passage says nothing about its quality of execution; and the third Dostoevsky picture is simply a name for the passage that precedes the word. In short, Mikhailov and Dostoevsky both present excellent subject matter excellently depicted, but Mikhailov assigns one subject figure to each picture and the excellence of depiction to both, while Dostoevsky puts the two excellent figures in one picture and the excellence of depiction in the other, which has no subject matter at all. Mikhailov presents wholes here, pictures with physical substance, a maker whose mastery is described, a subject, and a use (material, effective, formal, and final causes), while the first and last Dostoevsky pictures have none of the four Aristotelian causes, and the second has form and material existence but no execution and no use that is made explicit at this point.

If Dostoevsky transformed Mikhailov's two real pictures into figures of speech, and did the same thing with his benediction, drawing the simile "as if for the Virgin's protection" from the actual benediction "God bless you, my dear, glowing boy," he also reversed the process and incarnated certain figures of speech into real things. This glow about the boy, for example, is a figurative epithet for Mikhailov's son (*Gospod' c toboiu, moi dorogoi, svetlyi mal' chishka*), while in the Dostoevsky passage the light is emitted by a real sun and real lamps. In the same way the word "caressingly" is a suppressed metaphor in Mikhailov, where it modifies the word "gazes," while in Dostoevsky it is the real caress of a real mother. These movements into and out of the figurative have a symmetry comparable to that of the more obvious displacements, dead child and living parent replaced by dead parent and living child, or father separated from child grieves before separate pictures of child and father, while a mother holding a child weeps before the picture of a mother holding a child.

In the natural sciences such a symmetry would suggest the operation of still another conservation law, a conservation of figurativeness, which might be stated as follows: "When a source presents real items and figures of speech, Dostoevsky may realize figures of speech and present real items in similes, but the number of real and the number of figurative items will tend to remain invariant." If one item present in the source is pushed back into a figure of speech, like Mikhailov's picture, another figure of speech is realized, incarnated into a presence in the novel, as Mikhailov's word "glowing" takes shape as Dostoevsky's beloved image of the setting sun.

These conservation laws have led us to relate most of the paragraphs at hand to written sources that have survived. Indeed, we seem to have rather more sources than are necessary. The following comment was written by Anna Grigorievna Dostoevsky on her copy of *The Brothers Karamazov,* at the page this paper has been discussing: "Dostoevsky preserved such a recollection from the age of two, about how his mother took him to communion in their village church, and a pigeon flew through the church from one window to another."[15] The sources already discussed in this paper can be reconciled with this note by invoking deceit, coincidence, or error. Dostoevsky loved to catch the imagination of attractive girls, recounting the fascinating terrors of epilepsy, Siberia, or impending execution, and Anna Grigorievna was very young. To impress her, he may have simply appropriated a detail from *The Raw Youth* that had no biographical sources at all.

On the other hand, Dostoevsky's mother did die when he was young, apparently for nonliterary reasons, and it is rather likely that she took him to a church where he saw a pigeon. Such an experience would have made him more receptive to the literary passages already cited in this paper.

The possibility of error seems even more plausible than that of falsehood or a coincidental parallel between Medardus's experience and Dostoevsky's. The half century since he was two and the four decades since he had first read Hoffmann were quite enough to blur the boundary between fact and fiction, especially since, in either case, he had incorporated the recollection in his own fiction. Dostoevsky claimed to have forgotten two-thirds of *Crime and Punishment* in far less time. If some early personal experience did occur, the distinction between error and coincidence is a quantitative one, depending on the amount of overlap between Dostoevsky's experience and his reading. If this overlap is substantial, the character of the initial experience becomes immaterial, for the neatness of the symbolism, the melodramatic quality of the scene, and its usefulness in catching his wife's attention are simply due to that same exaggerating force that shaped Dostoevsky's memories and his fiction when he recalled Aksakov's mother.

This elaborate overdetermination jeopardizes the theory that the literary matter Dostoevsky borrowed is not destroyed. Even if

Dostoevsky could relegate a substantial part of what he inherited to figures of speech or closely related characters, the multiplicity of sources will oversaturate a given passage unless those sources are related to one another so closely that this relationship itself demands an explanation. And as a matter of fact, all the passages cited are closely related, including the biographical episode, if it is accurate. Directly or indirectly, all these passages derive from a common source—the Bible. Mikhailov, Michael, Myshkin, Medardus, Aksakov, and Aleksei Dostoevsky are all involved in Christian concerns and Christian imagery. Such scenes as Christ's or Mary's presentation in the temple have pagan and Hebrew antecedents, dating to remotest antiquity of course, but for Dostoevsky and his sources these were largely filtered through the New Testament.

The Christ figure not only generates the common features of Alesha's sources but also underlies Alesha directly. Christ, for example, is the only source for Alesha who is physically healthy. Alesha's loving-kindness, his sanctification by his mother, his inner involvement, his reluctance to judge, his freedom from fear and dismay, and his chastity and his capacity to inspire answering love can all be traced directly to the gospel as well as to the various intermediate sources, which were consciously and often nostalgically using the biblical imagery of sunlight, the maternal tears, the embrace and benediction, the presentation in the temple, the paintings, candles, prayer, incense, and ecstasy.

The richness of Dostoevsky's sources (and I know that this study does not exhaust them) is therefore possible because of a common source, the Bible, shaping his intent, literary and polemical. This source reached him through his reading of the text, his experience of the liturgy, through an Orthodox hymn like "Evening Light" (*Vechernyi svet*), and all his other reading in the Christian tradition. At this point it becomes clear that the patterns of change and conservation presented in this book do not operate consciously or unconsciously on independently existing entities but act as criteria for the selection of those materials whose accretion produced the description of Alesha discussed in this chapter. In the paragraph we are studying, Dostoevsky gathered a body of memories, sometimes distorted toward the melodramatic, but always able to be condensed, combined, and incorporated into the novel without inventing new materials, abandoning parts of passages he used, or altering the overall level of figurative expression. In this particular paragraph, Dostoevsky's goals were closely related to the Bible, and so were his sources. It would be interesting to test this formulation on other passages, related to other books. Perhaps if some real life experience of Dostoevsky's could be reconstructed as accurately as can his reading, we could learn whether in general he did record and not create; and whether, as he claimed, he often reached beyond his immediate sources to the truth behind them, as he reached behind his own childhood, and Aksakov's, his son's, and Mikhailov's, behind Medardus and Michael, and all his reworkings of these in his memory and writing to their generating point, which coincided with the point he wished to make here in this novel—the presentation of Jesus in the temple, with all its implications for God, and church, and man.

Chapter Seven

DOSTOEVSKY'S ATTITUDES SHAPE THE ARGUMENTS IVAN KARAMAZOV INHERITS AND USES.

I
CRITICS HAVE FOUND MANY SOURCES FOR IVAN AND THE GRAND INQUISITOR.

The origins of Ivan Karamazov are at least as intricate as those of his brothers, but they provide the clearest examples of certain patterns by which Dostoevsky consciously shaped his materials to reinforce his ideological position. One moment in Ivan's career, the Legend of the Grand Inquisitor, is the most famous passage involving Ivan, and also the passage for which the most sources have been found by the community of scholars.

The word "Legend" emerges not from Dostoevsky's text but from the critical tradition. Ivan Karamazov calls his creation a *poema* or even a *poemka*, but neither of these words is common in the critical treatments of the chapter. Such critical unanimity deserves attention, for there is something Darwinian in our vocabularies; the fittest names for things survive. *Legend* is a word that attracts less attention than *myth* in our century, but it was a favorite of Maupassant, Flaubert, Hugo, Hoffmann, and many other nineteenth-century authors whom Dostoevsky admired and used. The derivation is obvious—that which is to be read—but a definition might draw attention to certain elements or qualities in the text that could otherwise elude us. We can define a legend as a relatively brief and simple narrative, remote in origin, rich in implication, and constituting part of the common heritage of a certain sect or place.

The local color, sectarian associations, and enormous implications of Ivan's tale speak for themselves, but its remoteness is more interesting. Ivan sets his account in the sixteenth century and compares it to accounts from cultures very different from his own, such as medieval France and pre-Petrine Russia. It is also set in Spain, the part of Europe most remote from Russia, culturally and geographically. Narratively, the remoteness is more complex. Dostoevsky tells the legend through Ivan, who speaks largely through the Grand Inquisitor, who in turn devotes much of his speech to points made by the Devil. Ivan is remote from his legend in another sense: it is not a recent work of his: "You know, Alesha, don't laugh, I once composed a *poema*, a year or so ago." The little parenthesis, "don't laugh," adds still another kind of remoteness, the apologetic self-consciousness that inspires his remark a moment later, "It's an absurd thing." Of the same nature but on a larger scale is Ivan's ambivalence about the whole stand he is taking. At the end of the previous chapter he has said, "It may be that I too accept God," and with a smile "like a gentle little boy" added: "You're my kid brother. I don't want to corrupt you and force you from your position; it may be that I would like to heal myself through you." The Grand Inquisitor and the Devil are also repeating positions that they have adopted at a remote period, the Grand Inquisitor as a young man, and the Devil when he tempted Christ.

Dostoevsky had many models for these several kinds of remoteness. Ivan calls the reader's special attention to Victor Hugo's *Notre-Dame de Paris* (1831), which resembles the Legend in certain specific ways: the performance of the mysteries, the reaction of the crowd to the sudden appearance of the playwright, the arrest of Quasimodo, the one-sided conversation between prisoner and judge, and the representation of accumulated human labor as the Tower of Babel, but these elements do not seem to be part of any larger set of correspondences.[1] Indeed, the cardinal in Hugo's book is the diametrical opposite of Dostoevsky's:

> He led a merry cardinal's life...gave alms to pretty girls rather than old ladies, and...was most agreeable to the populace of Paris. He never walked without his entourage of well-born bishops and abbés, dashing, risqué, and roistering at will, and more than once the worthy worshippers of St.-Germain d'Auxerre, passing in the evening under the lighted windows of the Bourbon mansion, had been scandalized to hear the same voices that had chanted vespers by day raised to the sound of glasses with the bacchic proverb of Benedict XII, the pope who had added a third crown to the tiara,

"Bibamus papaliter." . . . Moreover, the Cardinal de Bourbon was a handsome man; he had a beautiful red robe which he wore very well; which meant that he had for him all the women and consequently the better half of the audience. . . . Certainly it would be unjust and in bad taste to boo a cardinal for being late to a show when he is a handsome man and wears his red robe well.

Dostoevsky's cardinal has a face, clothes, companions, and activities that contrast systematically with this description:

An almost ninety-year-old man, tall and straight, with a desiccated face, with sunken eyes, from which there still glowed, like a spark of fire, a flash. Oh, he was not in his magnificent cardinal's vestments, in which he had adorned himself the previous day before the people, when they burned the enemies of the faith. No, at this moment he is simply in his old, coarse monk's cowl. Behind him at a set distance follow his gloomy assistants and slaves in his "holy" guard. (*Pss* 14:227)

This is not the kind of polemic with his sources that Dostoevsky used in making Alesha Karamazov immune to the standardized anticlerical attacks of nineteenth-century Russia. Here we are dealing with a kind of citation Dostoevsky used with sufficient frequency to suggest relish. He could rely on many of his readers knowing *Notre-Dame de Paris*, just as Ivan can talk in shorthand to Alesha, whom he hardly knows, by citing this novel, which forms a part of their common culture. Dostoevsky's readers would not have the details of Hugo's cardinal clear in their minds, but the ironic picture of wordly self-contentment that contrasted so splendidly with the state of the poor and the outcast in Hugo's novel would help to define the Grand Inquisitor by intertextual antithesis. His austere life becomes more austere by contrast with a cited text.

It is easy, of course, to find sources for the Inquisitor's austerity and his sinister fire. Dolinin has suggested Gogol's *Terrible Vengeance*, with an initial transformation into the enigmatic Murin in Dostoevsky's Hoffmannesque short story "The Landlady." E. T. A. Hoffmann himself offers direct examples, too, as Charles Passage suggests. And yet, if this cardinal's appearance in the crowd really is one of the elements underlying the Grand Inquisitor's appearance, it seems to defy the conservation of literary matter as I have described it: there is no character in *The Brothers Karamazov* with the good looks, the well-born elegance, the popularity, the licentious jollity that Dostoevsky had seen in this figure. There is debauchery and drunkenness around old Fedor, and merriment and good cheer at the wedding in Cana, but nothing reminiscent of the life of Hugo's cardinal, whose urbanity is attractive, although the speaker at the end of Hugo's account is obviously ironical about the tension between his behavior and the medieval ideal of Christian self-abnegation. Dostoevsky avoids such obvious ironies, but he does have one repository for the cardinal's sumptuous life. By mentioning the magnificent cardinal's vestments with a minus sign, Dostoevsky dissociates himself from the most common form of clergy bashing, preparing the way for a far more sophisticated attack on the Church of Rome. The Grand Inquisitor has indeed sacrificed his happiness and his youth to his cause, but this appealing fact leaves him as forbidding to his fellow citizens as Hugo's selfish cardinal is attractive to his. The paradox remains intact with the signs changed.

Hugo's readers of course feel the irony of Hugo's attitude toward his cardinal, while Dostoevsky's readers have tended to feel sympathy for the Grand Inquisitor. This sympathy is a heightened and somewhat romanticized version of the emotion inspired by the attractiveness of Ivan, the Inquisitor's creator. Ivan has two particularly attractive traits, the half-desperate, half-apologetic intensity of his affections, and the selfless generosity with which he is prepared to sacrifice his happiness for the sake of others. In a previous scene, Ivan has quoted Schiller to express his feelings for Katerina Ivanovna; here he quotes the returning of the ticket from Schiller's "Resignation" (1784) to express his rejection of God's universe if his personal salvation is inseparable from the suffering of innocent children (*Pss* 14:223, 15:555). Alexandra Lingstadt gives a clear account of Dostoevsky's direct response to Schiller here, and Nina Perlina shows how richly this response was filtered through Alexander Herzen; Ivan Shidlovskii, the mentor whose reading of Schiller Dostoevsky refers to so lyrically in letters to his brother; and Vladimir Pecherin, the romantic Russian émigré who became a fanatical Roman Catholic monk and the subject of some of Herzen's sharpest writings.[2] This quotation of Schiller's poem infects Ivan's second attractive feature with the irony that attends the Schilleresque in *The Brothers Karamazov*; at the same time, it reminds the reader to think about Schiller's Grand Inquisitor in *Don Carlos*. I shall return to Dostoevsky's subversion of Ivan's radical position in a later chapter. At present I am interested in the way Ivan gives this same Schilleresque nobility to his creation, the Grand Inquisitor, who discusses Christ's refusal to turn bread into stones:

> Thou didst promise them the bread of Heaven, but . . . can that compare, in the eyes of the weak, ever transgressing, ever ignoble human race, with that of the earth? And if thou shouldst be followed, in the name of the bread of heaven, by thousands and tens of thousands, what will become of the millions and tens of

millions of beings who have not the might to reject the bread of earth for that of heaven. Or dost thou treasure only the tens of thousands of the great and mighty, while the other millions, numerous as the sands of the sea, weak, but loving Thee, must merely serve as the materials for the great and mighty. No, we treasure the weak too. . . . We will tell them that we are obedient to Thee and govern in Thy name. We shall deceive them again, for we shall not admit Thee to us. In that deceit will be contained our suffering, for we shall have to lie. . . .

There will be thousands of millions of happy children, and a hundred thousand sufferers who have taken upon themselves the accursed knowledge of good and evil. They will die in quiet, in quiet will perish in Thy name, and beyond the grave will encounter only death. But we will preserve the secret and for their happiness will lure them with a heavenly and eternal reward. For if there were something in the other world, of course it would not be for such as they. It is said and prophesied that Thou wilt come and wilt triumph anew, wilt come with Thy elect, with Thy proud and mighty, but we shall say that they have saved only themselves, and we have saved all. It is said that the harlot will be put to shame, sitting on the beast and holding in her hands the *mystery*, that the feeble will rebel anew, that they will tear off her purple and lay naked her "nasty" body. But I shall rise up then and shall show Thee the thousands of millions of happy children who have not known sin. And we who have taken their sin on ourselves for their own happiness will stand before Thee and say "Judge us, if Thou canst and darest." Know that I fear Thee not. Know that I too was in the wilderness, that I lived on locusts and roots, that I blessed the freedom with which Thou hadst blessed mankind, and I was prepared to stand in the number of Thy elect, in the number of the mighty and powerful with the thirst for "filling out that number." But I awoke and did not wish to serve madness. (*Pss* 14:230)

In this passage the Grand Inquisitor carries Ivan's Schilleresque rejection of bliss to its logical extreme, the willingness to accept damnation. In much the same way, he carries Ivan's doubt and ambivalence as to his position to *its* logical extreme. Ivan has said he would reject God's world, "Even though I were not right" (*Khotia by ia byl i neprav*). The Grand Inquisitor has recognized Christ at first sight and has seen him perform a miracle, and has taxed him with not descending from the cross to show his power. In the quoted passage the Grand Inquisitor displays his full belief in the power of Christ but not in his beneficence. He opposes his own beneficence to Christ's power and dares Christ to damn him for doing so. Ivan was not certain that he was right; the Inquisitor is certain that he is wrong; he states, "We shall have to lie," which is about as remote as one can be intellectually from the position one is enunciating.

This special remoteness of the doctrine from its enunciator does not exist in Schiller's poem, and it certainly does not exist in the real legends, the lives of the saints, which reflect the importance of belief in Christianity, for all the Christian use of the *advocatus diaboli* in arriving at decisions on canonization. Moreover, this remoteness is an element Dostoevsky added to a rather standard formula that encompasses Ivan's interview with Alesha and the Inquisitor's with Christ. In this formula the innocent sits in a little room across the table from his tempter, discussing problems that will determine the innocent's whole course of life. Faust sits in such a scene across from Mephistopheles in his study. Jean Valjean, Rastignac, Medardus, Mauprat, and many other of Dostoevsky's favorite characters experience such temptations, but their tempters only occasionally display ambivalence or irony. Mephistopheles and Vautrin may be the tempters most like the Grand Inquisitor, speaking with the fatigue of a life spent outside the community of mankind and raising such great questions as the well-being of the few or the many. They come nearer to Ivan's ambivalent attitude toward his own convictions than any of the other tempters, but they retain an essentially monolithic immoral position.

II
IVAN'S DOUBT ABOUT THE POSITION HE STATES HAS PARALLELS IN PLATO.

But it may be necessary to look entirely outside the Christian tradition to find a passage whose speaker begs with such tentative hope to be proved wrong and then presents such a devastating case against the pieties of his time. In the first book of Plato's *Republic*, Glaucon and Adeimantus display a fond, yet ironic intimacy with Socrates and share his sense of the importance of the subject at hand. "Do you think it is a small matter that you are attempting to determine, and not the entire conduct of life that for each of us would make living most worth while?"[3]

In the second book, Glaucon, like Ivan, plays the devil's advocate: "What I desire is to hear an encomium on justice in and by itself. And I think I am most likely to get that from you. For which reason I will lay myself out in praise of the life of injustice, and in so speaking will give you an example of the manner in which I desire to hear from you in turn the dispraise of injustice and the praise of justice" (2.358E). Ivan's and Glaucon's heartfelt appeals, each disowned by its enunciator, introduce striking catalogs of innocent suffering. Glaucon's hypothetically just man suffers "the lash, the rack, the chains, the branding iron in the eyes," and finally impalement, while Ivan's innocent children are impaled on bayonets by the "artistic" Turks, or else rejected by "Papochka" and "Bozhenka" (nice god), or else torn to pieces by dogs.

In both these dialogues, the devil's advocate is far more eloquent than any answer that is given him, raising one question and reiterating it naggingly: "Is it fair for the innocent to be tortured and their torturers to flourish?" Ivan and Glaucon show only man-inflicted suffering. They consider no earthquakes, as in *Candide*, or plagues of boils, as in Job, but only human torture afflicting the innocent. Both these devil's advocates feel that man causes suffering beyond anything that can be explained as punishment for things past or recompensed by any repayment in the future. Their minds can compass only two conclusions from this fact: either the ultimate is not good, or the good is not ultimate.

Socrates, with facts like Glaucon's in mind, offers the latter alternative: "Neither then could God . . . since He is good, be, as the multitude say, the cause of all things, but for mankind he is the cause of few things, but of many things not the cause. For good things are fewer with us than evil" (2.379C). To Socrates, this simple, observed fact of predominating evil leads back by the logic of causality to the conclusion that God, the ultimate good, cannot also be the ultimate cause. This pessimism is strangely unemotional. Ivan, on the other hand, using Voltaire's inversion of Genesis, appeals to a relationship through analogy, not causality: whether God created Man or man God, the created was analogous to the Creator, in his image and likeness. Ivan can therefore ask, "Is your God good, since man created him in his own image?" and can assert, "I think that if the Devil does not exist . . . [man created him] in his own image and likeness." This more direct and primitive logic leads Ivan's pessimism to the conclusion opposite to Socrates's—that the ultimate is not good.

Originally, perhaps, some similar awareness of human evil gave rise to some of the myths of parricide among the gods, which Socrates feels should be buried, "even if they were true"; and certainly this pessimism leads Ivan to reject God's world, "even though I were not right." In both these statements, when the desirable does not coincide with the true, the speaker opts against the true.

But beyond this split between the desirable and the true, pessimism may take the form of a split within the desirable itself: the useful and the delightful may be at odds with one another at a very high level. This split emerges in rather similar passages in these two dialogues. Socrates describes the joyous welcome of the universal poet in his city, and then his expulsion:

"We should fall down and worship him as a holy and wondrous and delightful creature, but should say to him that there is no man of that kind among us in our city, nor is it lawful for such a man to arise among us, and we should send him away to another city, pouring myrrh down over his head and crowning him with fillets of wool, but we ourselves, for our souls' good, should continue to employ the more austere and less delightful poet." (3.398)

Ivan describes the similar arrival of Christ in Seville: "The populace weeps and kisses the earth on which He goes. Children throw flowers before Him, sing, and cry 'Hosanna!' 'This is He, this is He Himself.'..." In the legend, Christ is taken by the guardian of man's souls and told that though the liberty he offers is attractive, there is no place for it in Seville, so that in the end the Grand Inquisitor says, "Go, and come no more."

In both dialogues, the guardian feels the power of the holy figure but believes that this attractiveness cannot be endured by the vast multitude, who are subject to temptation. The Grand Inquisitor and Plato's guardians have similar backgrounds, too. Both stood out among their fellows as the elect. The guardian, the ablest and most talented of soldiers, might become lost in the bliss of true philosophy or under certain circumstances, which Socrates carefully forestalls for the happiness of the state as a whole, might become a tyrant like Gyges, able to do what he wishes, usurp a kingdom, "and in all things conduct himself among mankind as the equal of a god." In the same way, the Grand Inquisitor had a high destiny; as he tells Christ in the passage quoted, he too "was prepared to stand in the number of Thy elect, in the number of the mighty and powerful" but preferred the well-being of the multitude.

Here, then, are two figures who are willing to sacrifice first truth and then personal happiness to reconcile their pessimism about mankind with their love of mankind. The Grand Inquisitor says specifically, "And this will be our suffering, that we shall have to lie," while Plato's guardians, living in comparable austerity, are to motivate their subjects with the sense that their class and nationhood are inborn by telling them a legend that embodies all the different elements we have ascribed to a typical legend:

"A sort of Phoenician tale, something that has happened ere now in many parts of the world, as the poets aver and have induced men to believe, but that has not happened and perhaps would not be likely to happen in our day, and demanding no little persuasion to make it believable.... All our training and education of them were things that they imagined and that happened to them as it were in a dream; but that in reality at that time they were down within the earth being moulded and fostered themselves while their weapons and the rest of their equipment were being fashioned. And when they were quite finished, the earth as being their mother delivered them, and now as if their land were their mother and their nurse they ought to take thought for her and defend her against any attack and regard the other citizens as their brothers and children of the self-same earth.

".... While all of you in the city are brothers, we will say in our tale, yet God in fashioning those of you who are fitted to hold rule mingled gold in their generation, for which reason they are the most precious—but in the helpers silver, and iron and brass in the farmers and other craftsmen." (3.414D)

The parallels between this legend and the Legend of the Grand Inquisitor lie not so much in coinciding details as in the functions of these legends in the texts they inhabit and the ambivalence that surrounds them. Socrates calls his legend a Phoenician tale and also a lie, while Ivan calls his a *poema* and an absurd thing. And yet for Plato, as for many thinkers and activists today, the centers of that lie, nation and class, are central social truths, and for Ivan, as for many other thinkers and activists today, the guardianship of mankind is the highest moral duty.

No external evidence demonstrates that Dostoevsky had this passage in mind when he wrote the Legend, although it was certainly available to him. If my conservation rule can be used as a criterion, there are many elements in Socrates's legend that find no repository in *The Brothers Karamazov*. Rather than a literary influence, the parallels represent a convergence in the process of creation upon a particular literary form, the dialogue that lapses (or rises) into monologue and then into myth or legend. Dostoevsky could have discovered this pattern in many places. Northrop Frye suggests that Plato evolved it to control the transition from the removal of opposition and doubt to the assertion of his positive position. Plato very probably recognized the form in Homer, where Phoenix, for example, argues hesitantly with Achilles about his obligations to his companions, his father, and his reputation and then shifts to the strange and ancient legend of Meleagros, or where Odysseus is reluctantly brought to dispute with the Phaeacians and then relates his legendary travels, culminating in a voyage to the underworld itself.

Whatever the sources of their literary practice, both authors used this sequence of awarenesses and techniques to deal with issues of primary importance to them and to the interlocutors they had created. For Dostoevsky, this issue was the justice of God; for Plato, it was the justice of men and states. Both these passages emphasize the urgency of their message, and Dostoevsky's letters confirm this sense, as we have seen in discussing his work on the novel. I would suggest therefore, that the two passages are similar in their structure not primarily because of a literary influence, though Dostoevsky's education and outlook would suggest a tie with Plato, but because each author, facing the question of good and evil squarely, a third of the way through his greatest masterpiece, adopted the same set of literary techniques to pose it in its most urgent form, which for Plato was political with religious overtones, and for Dostoevsky was religious with political overtones.

III
BUT THE MAIN SOURCE FOR THE LEGEND IS THE RUSSIAN RADICAL TRADITION.

Although patterns of literary function may obscure those of literary influence as explanations for the form of the Legend, the doctrines, characters, and events are distinctive enough to be traced more specifically. The first striking event in the Legend is the return of Christ to earth. One of the able scholars of the 1920s suggested a source in the Carmina Burana, where the return of Christ is presented with an anticlerical animus on a par with Ivan's.[4] I. I. Lapshin cannot show that Dostoevsky had read the Carmina Burana, and the return of Christ as such does not make this an eminently convincing source. Emil Drougard, on the other hand, has a highly plausible source, a poem called "Christ in the Vatican," ascribed at first to Victor Hugo, whose works Dostoevsky would not have missed, but actually by an insignificant writer of Dostoevsky's time named Cabantous.[5] The most striking difference between the Cabantous poem and Ivan's appears in the mode of Christ's departure. In Cabantous, he departs vertically, like a rocket. This suspension of gravity runs counter to Zosima's doctrine on miracles, but it survives rather neatly in the novel in the desires of the Inquisitor himself, who believes that Christ should have adopted miracle for the benefit of mankind, defying gravity, as the Devil tempted him to do. Here Dostoevsky's relation to his source is again polemical. He retains the miracle, but with a negative sign.

Scholars have advanced a number of other sources for other parts of the Legend, such as Montaigne's "Apology for Raymond Sebond" for the references to the Tower of Babel, and Strauss's *Life of Christ* for the triple temptation by the Devil. Lapshin, who proposes these two sources, points out that Dostoevsky had taken Strauss's work from the library of the Petrashevskii circle, and also discussed it with Vladimir Solovev years later. He cannot demonstrate Dostoevsky's acquaintance with "Sebond," and the issue there is complicated by the presence of a common source for both texts, the Bible. The editors of the *Pss* list such other sources as Goethe, Heine, Jean Paul, and the apocryphal book of Nicodemus, but these and other suggested sources, such as *Paradise Regained*, merge into the whole by mechanisms we have already studied.

Dostoevsky's own publications and notebooks also play much the same role in the genesis of Ivan as they did in that of Alesha and Mitia, especially passages in *The Diary of a Writer* that develop the ideology of the Devil's temptations and the Tower of Babel. One reworking of materials of a rather different sort involved the article by Ivan discussed in the monastery, proposing essentially that civil punishment include excommunication. The idea of an article to characterize the starting point of the hero's doctrine dates back to *Crime and Punishment*, where Raskolnikov had written an article distinguishing the elite, who had the right to murder, from ordinary men, who did not, an idea Dostoevsky connected with Napoleon III and Dmitrii Pisarev. Dostoevsky's important article on the schism among the nihilists illustrates his command of the personal and political dynamics of the movement. It also explores the moral implications of Pisarev's individualistic sense that a few special leaders have an obligation to seize the historical initiative and smash the oppressive past, however much they may regret its beauty. Joseph Frank has persuasively linked this article with the doctrines that lead Raskolnikov to murder,[6] which in turn are related to the ideas of Ivan Karamazov and Smerdiakov. Raskolnikov's article argued for the good that such a privileged elite could do if it stood above the law, and the whole of *Crime and Punishment* argues that a great crime would drive its perpetrator to confession or suicide as surely as a grave disease drives a patient to recovery or death.

Ivan, like Mitia, recapitulates several aspects of Raskolnikov, most especially his intellectual superiority and his serious interest in radical political doctrines. Ivan has never killed anybody, but his creation, the Grand Inquisitor, has killed many for the greater glory of a god whose goodness he questions but whose name he uses for the domination of humanity. The draft materials for Ivan's article contain a great deal of material on the fusion of church and state which was later incorporated into the Inquisitor's doctrines (*Pss* 15:208–9). Ivan the journalist, as opposed to Ivan the *poet* (in Dostoevsky's sense of the word), was working out a theory that Dostoevsky the journalist had already connected with both French Catholicism and French socialism: that qualified humans control the rest of humanity. In action, neither pursues this idea very far, but Ivan's creation, the Grand Inquisitor, devotes his whole life to this effort and claims to improve the destinies of millions. With the clear presentation of his thoughts and feelings on many occasions, Raskolnikov's killings explore the psychological meaning of the theory of the superior man; the Grand Inquisitor's killings explore the social and religious meanings of the same theory in a character whose thoughts and unenunciated ideas Ivan withheld from his listener, so that his psyche, insofar as it exists, remains implicit in his thoughts and actions.

This journalistic background leads to the most important sources for Ivan and his Inquisitor: the Russian radicals whom Dostoevsky knew and read. Dostoevsky saw the Russian radicals of the nineteenth century as a group that increased numerically as it waned morally and intellectually. In the January 1873 *Diary of a Writer*, he refers to Herzen and Belinskii as the old people and compares them nostalgically:

> Herzen was...a product of our lordliness, gentilhomme russe et citoyen du monde....Herzen did not emigrate....no, he simply was born an émigré....[This type of Russian] by seceding from the populace naturally lost God too....This was an artist, a thinker, a brilliant writer, an extraordinarily educated man, witty, a wonderful conversationalist (he spoke even better than he wrote), and magnificent at reflection. Reflection, the capacity to turn his deepest feeling into an object, to set it before him, worship it, even mock it, was developed in him to the highest degree....Belinskii, on the other hand, was not a gentilhomme at all....Belinskii was primarily not a reflective character but rather uncalculatingly ecstatic, always, all his life....
>
> "I adore looking at him," Belinskii suddenly interrupted... pointing at me, "every time I mention Christ like this, his face changes as if he wants to cry....And believe you me, you're a naive man," he fell upon me again, "Believe that your Christ, if he had been born in our time, would have been the most unnoticeable and commonplace man..."
>
> "Why, no—oh!" he was interrupted... "if Christ should appear now, he would join the movement and become its head..."
>
> "Why, yes; why yes!" Belinskii agreed suddenly and with amazing alacrity, "He would precisely have joined the socialists and followed them."
>
> These movers of mankind to whom Christ was destined to adhere were all Frenchmen then; first of all, George Sand, the now quite forgotten Cabet, Pierre Leroux, and Proudhon, who was just beginning his activity then. At that time, as best I remember, Belinskii respected these four most of all. Fourier was no longer respected so much by far. There was also one German, Feuerbach. (Belinskii, who could never in his life learn a single foreign lan-

guage, pronounced it Fierbakh.) Strauss was discussed with approval.

With such warm faith in his idea, this was, of course, the most happiest [camyi shchastliveishii] of people. Oh, people wrote quite pointlessly later on that Belinskii, if he had lived longer, would have joined the slavophiles. Belinskii might have ended up emigrating. (Pss 21:10–12)

Dostoevsky's ironic and conflicting vision of these old radicals, the men of the forties, emerges in this passage. It is full of nostalgia for a youth that was cut short by the years in Siberia, and it is full of respect and affection for two honest, honorable masters of Russian prose and Russian journalism. At the same time, it is ironic about Herzen's wealth and upbringing, and it uses exactly the same word, *primknulsia by*, to describe the joining that the risen Christ and the revived Belinskii might have done. V. L. Komarovich traces the play of utopian socialist thought and imagery in Dostoevsky's writings, as we have seen already;[7] Dolinin traces the shifts in Dostoevsky's attitudes toward Belinskii; and Dryzhakova those toward Herzen.[8] A. Ivanov argues that Dostoevsky's hostility to all radicals casts doubt on the rather flimsy evidence for any real closeness to either of these figures.[9]

For the next generation of Russian radicals, the men of the sixties, Dostoevsky often felt some respect, and as Joseph Frank shows plainly, he also felt considerable agreement with them about what was wrong with Russia and what should be done about it. Even in the early 1860s, however, before Russian journalistic polemics had descended into the bitter and the scurrilous, Dostoevsky gives no sign toward this generation of the warmth that often tempers his ideological rejection of Herzen and Belinskii.[10] Three great figures of this generation—the new people Dobroliubov, Saltykov-Shchedrin, and Pisarev—deserved and received his respect for the brilliance of their prose and the savagery of their polemics. Chernyshevskii's *What Is to Be Done?* may be even more influential, but Dostoevsky reacted angrily and scornfully to its utilitarianism and nagging simplicity. Dostoevsky's most explicit artistic manifesto takes the form of an elaborate attack on a book review by Dobroliubov, "Mr. —— bov and the Question of Art." Here Dostoevsky treats his opponent with ironic distaste for his inability to see the implications of his views on art, but never as a despicable intellect. Dostoevsky's "Schism among the Nihilists" traces the polemic between Shchedrin and Pisarev with a certain amount of glee, but this hostility remains primarily doctrinal.

Only with the third generation of radicals that he knew do Dostoevsky's personal distaste and scorn appear in their full glory.

The imprisonment of Chernyshevskii and the deaths of Dobroliubov and Pisarev left a gap in the radical journals that lesser figures like G. Z. Eliseev and M. A. Antonovich emerged to fill. Dostoevsky treats them as greedy operators who are growing rich by saying what the deracinated intelligentsia desires. Eliseev will appear later in our study as a documented source for Rakitin, but Antonovich is also there in spirit, because Dostoevsky felt so often, as he wrote in one of his notebooks, "What Mr. Antonovich has written was too stupid even for Mr. Antonovich" (*Pss* 20:199), or as he said in print, "Mr. Antonovich...demands that *Time* should educate him and bases his demand on the fact that he is a subscriber to *Time* and paid sixteen rubles for the journal. The editorship hereby notifies him that it in no way took on and likewise cannot in the future take upon itself the difficult obligation of educating *him*" (*Pss* 20:225; emphasis added). Mikhailovskii had an abler mind than Antonovich but was equally consistent in his hostility to Dostoevsky, which was reciprocated.

A mass of other radicals enter Dostoevsky's view, the Petrashevskii circle, the utopian and other socialists they read, the noble Decembrists, the altruistic men of the forties in Russia and in Europe, the lesser men of the sixties, and finally the terrorists, whose advent he had foreseen, carrying the magnificent nastiness of the sixties to its logical conclusion in ideological killers like Karakozov and, at the lowest level, Nechaev. Dostoevsky read and studied this third generation with a journalist's eye, especially if there were court proceedings, and much of *The Diary of a Writer* emerges from that reading, but he also read as a novelist, and *The Possessed* crystallized about what he had read. *The Brothers Karamazov* is set in a period close to Karakozov's shot at the tsar, which traditionally marks the end of the *glasnost'* and restructuring of the 1860s, as well as the break between the second and the third generation of Russian radicals. Herzen survives in the provincial bookcases in the novel, along with Smaragdov, Voltaire, and Schiller, but like them, he is a figure out of the past—like Miusov, the man of the forties out of touch with his own times. The characters discuss, quote, and misquote such figures constantly, as Perlina points out in her rich study of quotation in *The Brothers Karamazov*. Much of the intellectual tension in the novel comes from the encounter of the noble romantic radicalism of Herzen and Belinskii with the tawdry positivistic radicalism of Eliseev and Antonovich, which Dostoevsky saw as its inevitable successor.

The way of thinking that belonged to materialist philosophers and radical journalists penetrated many of the ablest writers of fiction, memoirs, and descriptive prose in the generation usually described as the *Shestidesiatniki*. They published in the *Contemporary*, but Dostoevsky treated them with more respect than he treated the editors and writers of reviews. He mentions Fedor M. Reshetnikov, Aleksander I. Levitov, Nikolai Uspenskii, and other writers of social consciousness more often in his correspondence than in his journalism, and his picture of the Russian intellectual world of the 1860s remained far less polarized than many readers have supposed. In fact, in the March issue of *Time* he blamed some of the hostility to his journal on its position apart from the extremists of the right:

> [There is] such rabidness, such ardor against us that they can't sleep nights because of us, and if they sleep, I'm sure they see us every night in their dreams. . . . And we're bread and butter for all our scribblers in verse, and for their infant children too. And to what end, to what end is all of this? It's because we alone, perhaps, have had enough daring to enunciate sharply the whole truth about the talentlessness, the tawdriness, the laziness, and the fourth-rateness of these radicals. You say that Katkov and Skariatin and Askochenskii do the same. No, it's not the same. They are doing battle in the name of murk, and we in the name of light. People aren't listening to them; they'll listen to us. And don't tell us that we're sitting down between two chairs. Nonsense! That's where we're all headed. (*Pss* 20:94)

This whole radical community of writers and intellectuals, as I shall show, shapes the beliefs of and the attitudes toward Ivan and the Grand Inquisitor.

CHAPTER
EIGHT

DOSTOEVSKY'S ATTITUDES SHAPED THE ATTITUDES OF HIS CHARACTERS AND HIS READERS.

I
READERS HAVE DEBATED DOSTOEVSKY'S ATTITUDE TOWARD IVAN AND HIS INQUISITOR.

Dostoevsky's social and ideological intentions interacted with certain of his sources in ways that have eluded some of the best literary minds that have studied him—at least, those minds differ so sharply that they cannot all be right. Let me quote two typical statements bearing on Dostoevsky's intention. The first is from D. H. Lawrence's introduction to a separate edition of the Grand Inquisitor chapter, translated by S. S. Koteliansky:

> If there is any question: Who is the Grand Inquisitor?—surely we must say it is Ivan himself. And Ivan is the thinking mind of the human being in rebellion, thinking the whole thing out to the bitter end. As such he is, of course, identical with the Russian Revolutionary of the thinking type. He is also, of course, Dostoevsky himself in his thoughtful as apart from his passional and inspirational self. Dostoevsky half-hated Ivan. Yet after all, Ivan is the greatest of the three brothers, pivotal. The passionate Dmitri and the inspired Alesha are, at last, only offsets to Ivan.
>
> And we cannot doubt that the Grand Inquisitor speaks Dostoevsky's own final opinion about Jesus. The opinion is boldly, this: Jesus, you are inadequate. Men must correct you. And Jesus gives the kiss of acquiescence to the Inquisitor, as Alesha does to Ivan.[1]

Lawrence had not read M. M. Bakhtin's remarks about the polyphonic novel, but he knew better than simply to assume that a character is a spokesman for the author. He offers three reasons for identifying Ivan and the Grand Inquisitor with Dostoevsky: Ivan's greatness, his pivotal position in the novel, and the "kiss of acquiescence" he receives. I shall argue later that there was no kiss of acquiescence, and Victor Terras, Nina Perlina, and other excellent readers argue that the text makes Ivan callow, immoral, misguided, and unattractive at every important juncture. Whether Ivan has any real greatness or not, scholars need to reckon with the enormous response he has evoked in many readers who basically agree with Lawrence.

A more impressive body of opinion, however, takes the opposite view of Dostoevsky's intentions. My second statement may also hint at ambivalence on Dostoevsky's part, and certainly agrees that Ivan typifies the "Russian Revolutionary of the thinking type," but it differs from Lawrence's in virtually every other respect. It comes from Dostoevsky's own letter to his editor, Nikolai Liubimov, on 10 May 1879.

> [Ivan's] convictions are precisely what I accept as the synthesis of Russian anarchism in our day: the denial not of God, but of the meaning of his creation. All socialism had its origins and beginnings in the denial of the meaning of historical actuality [*deistvitel' nosti*], and progressed to a program of destruction and anarchism. The original anarchists were in many cases men of sincere convictions. My hero takes up a topic I consider irrefutable [*neotrazimuiu*]: the senselessness of the suffering of children, and deduces from that the absurdness [*absurd*, not *nelopost'*] of all historical actuality. I don't know whether I carried it out well, but I know that the character of my hero is real in the highest degree [*real'noe*]. (In *The Possessed*, there were many characters they attacked me for as fantastic, but later, you believe me, they all were justified by reality, so they must have been imagined correctly.) . . . All that my hero says in the text I sent you is based on reality. All the stories about children occurred, were printed in the papers, and I can show where; nothing was invented by me. . . . As for my character's blasphemy, it will be triumphantly confuted [*oprovergnuto*] in the next (June) issue, on which I am working now with fear and trembling and veneration, considering my task (the crushing of anarchism) a patriotic exploit. Wish me success, my dear Nikolai Alekseevich.[2]

Dostoevsky's statement carries more authority than Lawrence's, but it also raises several questions. The central question for the next several sections can be phrased as a disjunction: either Dostoevsky was lying to his editor or he was an incompetent rhetorician, unable to bring Lawrence and thousands of others to accept his position, or even understand what it was.

This passage is drawn from a good example of a literary genre that has been studied little, although it has been cultivated by many of the masters of European prose: the letter requesting that a deadline be extended. The passage juxtaposes two topics: ideological intent and fidelity to reality. Three of the first four sentences present the concept of the absurd, which was to be so fashionable in Europe three generations later. The first two of these sentences deduce socialism, anarchism, and destruction from this sense of the absurd, and the fourth, with an autobiographical aside, deduces this sense of the absurd from the senselessness of the suffering of children. The third sentence seems to be a puzzling interruption, dealing with the sincerity of the anarchists. In using such phrasing as "synthesis of Russian anarchism in our day," "all socialism had its origins and beginnings in...," "The original anarchists were in many cases...," Dostoevsky is actually claiming that Ivan is the highest artistic achievement under the realist aesthetic of his day, a literary type, an accurate representation of an identifiable segment of society.

The ambitiousness of this claim explains the modest beginning of the next sentence, "I don't know whether I carried it out well," which at first glance conflicts with Dostoevsky's fear at the end of the passage that he had done Ivan too well. Of course, the word "well" means two different things here: I have used it to mean "persuasively, appealingly, powerfully," while Dostoevsky was using it to mean "typically." He even offers a test for the accuracy of a type—predictiveness. The parenthesis in which he claims to have passed this test in *The Possessed* interrupts a rather different argument, which begins with the statement that Ivan is "in the highest degree real" and ends with the claim that "nothing was invented by me." This argument conflicts strikingly with the parenthesis about *The Possessed*. The parenthesis expresses pride in *subsequent* confirmation by reality, while the sentences surrounding it claim that every detail was based on *prior* reality. The implicit paradox is real and important, but for all his love of paradox, Dostoevsky merely voiced the standard doctrine we have already discussed, that artists could perceive reality more sharply than ordinary men, and could select and assemble details whose firm anchor in reality explained their accurate crystallization into a type. This paradoxical dependence of special, even prophetic insight on photographic fidelity to reality rests on metonymic faith in the capacity of the parts of a reality to represent the whole.

Only after asserting his prophetic success and his fashionable fidelity to his sources in reality does Dostoevsky make explicit his intention of triumphantly refuting the blasphemy of his character type, as well as his fear and trembling that this refutation may fail. This fear leads us back to Lawrence's first reason for supposing that Dostoevsky agreed with Ivan: Ivan is the greatest of the brothers. Lawrence's argument can be expanded genetically or rhetorically. Genetically, one can argue that an author cannot create a truly great character without real sympathy for him at some level. Lawrence makes this argument elsewhere with respect to Tolstoi.[3] Rhetorically, one can argue that an author would not select such an attractive mouthpiece for ideas he hopes to crush. To accept these two arguments, one must reject the testimony of Dostoevsky's own letter. As a genre, of course, this kind of letter is characterized by no more authorial candor than novels are. Antianarchism and typicality would have appealed to Liubimov and his chief, Katkov, whose journal, the *Russian Messenger*, was after all the consistently conservative vehicle for an incredible efflorescence of realistic novels. Without denying Dostoevsky's desire to ingratiate himself, I would suggest a more serious reason for his almost compulsive introduction of the question of fidelity to reality before he mentions his ideological intention.

Ivan, as Dostoevsky and Lawrence agree, has his sources in the reality of Russian radicalism. Herzen's *From the Other Shore* and Belinskii's letters to V. P. Botkin and Gogol provided Dostoevsky with much of Ivan's language and ideology. Indeed, these sources offer a simple answer to Lawrence's question about producing a great character without personal involvement with that character. A writer like Lawrence tends to equate greatness with eloquence, and others already have shown that a substantial part of Ivan's eloquence is borrowed from these authors. More important, however, as we have indicated, Dostoevsky had been fond of Belinskii, had participated in the Petrashevskii circle, and had talked with Herzen and possibly with Bakunin enough to feel the magnetism of such figures, sometimes simultaneously with his doubts about their doctrines. At the Petrashevskii interrogations, Dostoevsky said that he read Belinskii's letter to Gogol for its language, not its ideas. He was desperate for excuses, of course, but Apollon Maikov's memoirs suggest that his testimony might have been true. For Dostoevsky in the seventies, Herzen and Belinskii might be wrong, but they were noble in their eloquence, in their willingness to sacrifice their happiness, and in that sincerity of conviction whose relevance seems puzzling at first in the letter to Liubimov. Dostoevsky's fidelity to this nobility of these sources could have made Ivan Karamazov more attractive in his desperate love than seems fitting or strategic in the advocate of a position an author hopes to crush.

This analysis of the letter to Liubimov illustrates a problem that has led some to epistemological despair. The journalistic and epistolary texts we adduce to help interpret *The Brothers Karamazov* require the same sort of interpretation that the novel does. I shall therefore spend the next two sections examining not statements but actions. Since most of these actions are also verbal, my interpretations will be subject to the same theoretical strictures as all readings, but in practice the purposefulness of these actions should remove some of the ambiguity about Dostoevsky's intent.

II
DOSTOEVSKY ASSOCIATES IVAN WITH THE DEVIL.

This formulation of our task suggests an obvious way to test the authenticity of Dostoevsky's fear and trembling. If Ivan's greatness is an accidental side effect of Dostoevsky's fidelity to his sources, we should find in the text a series of efforts to destroy one of the most eloquent and convincing arguments in all literature, an argument whose starting point Dostoevsky himself had called irrefutable.

It has been argued that Dostoevsky showed his disapproval of Ivan by subjecting him to the horrors of brain fever, the indignities of the interviews with Smerdiakov and the courtroom scenes, and the frustrating love for Katerina Ivanovna. Such an argument works for fables, fairy tales, and Western movies, where poetic justice may be built into the genre. It is simply not a part of the nineteenth-century novel. In the last words of *Madame Bovary*, Homais, one of the most despicable characters in all literature, receives the decoration that is the object of his life's desires. *The Idiot* ends with the total destruction of the three main characters, who are not uniformly evil. The children who die in *The Brothers Karamazov* most emphatically do not deserve to do so. The justice of the Dostoevskian universe is infinitely more difficult than that of a fairy tale, and the fate of a character throws no direct light on Dostoevsky's attitude toward that character.

A more sophisticated way of refuting Ivan's position involves not what happens to him but what he does and is. Terras, Perlina, and others argue that Ivan's rhetoric is overblown and his quotations inaccurate enough to undercut his arguments. My own guess is that the audience sophisticated enough to recognize such flaws is tiny today and was vanishingly small in nineteenth-century Russia. Microscopic subtlety, recherché allusiveness, and "buried time bombs" are among the glories of seventeenth- and twentieth-century literature, but Dostoevsky's aesthetic was more robust and brutal, though the tasks it set him were no easier. If Dostoevsky was using such devices to discredit Ivan, they played a relatively minor part in the enterprise.

Valentina Vetlovskaia has cataloged enough unpleasant actions and features of Ivan's to make a convincing case for Dostoevsky's intent to discredit Ivan's argument by discrediting its spokesman.[4] Her study reinforces the problem this novel presents. She shows Dostoevsky using one of the classical rhetorical techniques, the argumentum ad hominem, but leaves us with the evidence of Lawrence and scores of able readers that the technique did not work. I should like to look at one of Vetlovskaia's points more closely, Dostoevsky's effort to discredit Ivan by associating him with the figure of the Devil.

As long as men have talked about sin, they have acknowledged its attractiveness, but in the Middle Ages evil, unlike sin, was presented as unattractive, and its embodiment, the Devil, tended to be represented as repulsive, filthy, stinking, vicious, and subhuman. Dostoevsky needed such a Devil if he intended to discredit Ivan by association with it, but the literature of his day offered a very different figure: as early as Milton, but insistently since Blake, Byron, and Baudelaire, various elements of the diabolic had had a good press. The Grand Inquisitor's Devil is not a stupid and disgusting torturer but a "dire and fearsome" spirit whose very name is taboo. This romantic fascination with the diabolic had weakened a literary resource that Dostoevsky needed—the old Devil who could provide instant hostility. Indeed, within a few years of the creation of the Grand Inquisitor, Swinburne, Strindberg, Raspisardi, Lautréamont, and Bakunin had written major glorifications of the diabolic in five different languages.[5]

To counteract this loss of prefabricated repulsiveness from the consciousness of all but archaizers like Gogol, Dostoevsky has to train his readers to associate scorn or revulsion with the word *devil*. Except for the biblical demons in *The Possessed*, and some ironically conceived ones in *The Diary of a Writer*, devils play little part in Dostoevsky's works. Demonic figures like Murin in "The Landlady" are not connected with any particular supernatural being. But in *The Brothers Karamazov*, a multitude of devils appear. Old Fedor Karamazov introduces these creatures early in the novel, setting the stamp of his own savage weirdness upon them:

You see, it's impossible, I think, that the devils should forget to drag me in with hooks when I die. Well, then I think: hooks? And where do they get them? Made of what? Iron? Forged where? Is there a factory of some sort they've got there? Now, over there in the monastery, the monks probably believe that in Hell, for example, there's a ceiling. But I'm ready to believe in Hell, only without a ceiling: It works out sort of neater, more enlightened, more Lutheran, that is.... Well, if there's no ceiling, therefore, there can't be any hooks, and if there's no hooks and all that's cast aside, that means—implausibly again, who'll drag me in with hooks, because if they don't drag me in, then what will happen, where's there any justice in the world? (*Pss* 14:23)

With or without hooks these devils could not be made grand or attractive. Even where the devil is a larger spirit, Fedor's presence makes him the mocker of mankind:

"Does God exist or not? For the last time!"
"And for the last time, no."
"Then who is laughing at people, Ivan?"
"Must be, the Devil,"—grinned Ivan.
"And the Devil exists?"
"No, the Devil doesn't either." (*Pss* 14:124)

Such talk of the Devil as the mocker and of devils as torturers helps to damp our romantic response to the "dire and fearsome spirit of self-annihilation and non-being" who is the Grand Inquisitor's mentor. Sometimes the torture is explicit and the devils implicit, as in the story of the Virgin's descent into Hell; sometimes the reverse, as with the devils Ferapont encounters; and sometimes both the devils and the torture are explicit, as in the devils Ferapont or Lize or even Alesha vanquishes with a cross. Ferapont and Lize both share the devils' love of pain. Ferapont sees one hiding

behind the door from me, a full-sized one, too, a yard and a half or more tall; its tail was thick and brown and long, and the tip of the tail had slipped into the crack of the door; and I'm nobody's fool, so I suddenly slammed the door to, and caught its tail. And it got to squealing and started slapping around; I took and put the sign of the cross on it; three times I crossed it. And then it died, like a spider that had been crushed. (*Pss* 14:153–54)

Ferapont savors the agonized extinction of this devil just as he takes physical delight in the idea of heroic fasting, and the nastiness of his twisted sensuality becomes linked with that of his imagined victim, so that later, when Ivan is giving his catalog of tortured children, the reader feels the full passion of his comment, "If the Devil does not exist, and it turns out that man created him, then he created him in his own image and likeness." Dostoevsky drew these devils in large part from his readings in old Russian literature, and their antiquity reduces their rhetorical usefulness in dealing with a readership that took pride in its Westernized modernity. Their association with the Devil the Grand Inquisitor quotes remains largely verbal.

The most elaborate picture of an unlovely devil has different sources and a far more intimate relation to Ivan. This is the devil who appears in Ivan's nightmare at the moment of Smerdiakov's suicide. Consider the following passage:

> Ivan felt that he was unwell, but from some dread of telling himself quite clearly that he was sick, he turned from the light and tried to go to sleep. His sleep was heavy and fitful; he was incessantly waking up, tossing restlessly on the bed, and again dozing off for a minute.
>
> Waking up one time, Ivan thought he would not get to sleep anymore. He wanted to get up. His head was leaden; in his arms and legs there was some sort of dull pain. With an effort, he sat up on the bed, leaning with his back in the corner of the room. He sat sometimes with no thought at all, sometimes there awakened in his head a turbulent and hazy consciousness that he felt bad. He would sit, would say: "I feel bad," and again would senselessly focus his eyes on the opposite corner of the room. Suddenly it seemed to him as if something was stirring there. He gazed there. Just so, something was effortfully crawling out of the corner crack, shifted clumsily, and began to grow. It was some sort of a likeness of a human. Ivan rubbed his eyes, and then opened them again; there was no monster there any longer.[6]

This apparition of a very personal demon to a sick man comes from a novel called *The Evil Spirit* (*Likho*), by Dmitrii Vasilevich Averkiev (1836–1905), a writer for Dostoevsky's journals of the 1860s with whom he remained in contact all his life. This passage came out in issue 5 of the weekly the *Flame* (*Ogonek*) five months before Dostoevsky published Ivan's scene with a devil. We have seen that Dostoevsky tended to read as many journals as he could, and he had made a note to himself to look at that issue. Ivan Karamazov's devil appears in much the same way. The following quotation from *The Brothers Karamazov* contains extensive ellipses but no change of order.

> Ivan was sitting on the couch and feeling his head spinning. He felt that he was sick and feeble. He was about to begin going to sleep, but got up restlessly and paced the room to keep the sleep away. At moments he imagined that he must be delirious. But it wasn't his sickness that preoccupied him most: when he sat down

again he began to glance around occasionally, as if he were looking for something. It happened several times. Finally, his gaze was fixed on one point....He sat a long time in his place, firmly supporting his head on both hands and still glancing obliquely at the same point as before, at the couch by the opposite wall. Evidently something was disturbing him, some object, distracting, bothering....

He knew that he was unwell, but detested being sick at that time with revulsion....So he was sitting now, almost conscious of being delirious,...and fixedly staring at some object by the other wall on the couch. Suddenly, someone was sitting there....
(*Pss* 15:70)

Both passages begin with a presentation of sickness and go on to describe restless sleep, weakness, and pain, and then a confusion of mind, to which Dostoevsky gives the label delirium. Finally, both Ivans fix their gaze more and more firmly on a single spot, where an apparition appears. Averkiev's Ivan expresses his incredulity with a gesture, and the creature disappears. Ivan Karamazov's hallucination remains for the entire chapter, and so does his incredulity. In general, Dostoevsky's passage is more extensive, but except for the fear to admit sickness, the parallel elements appear in the same order, as if the Averkiev passage offered a framework upon which Dostoevsky elaborated a very different hallucination. In this passage he has retained none of the qualities of a medieval devil that Averkiev's creature shared with the devils Fedor, Lize, Ferapont, and Grushenka describe. Dostoevsky no longer needs the little, subhuman medieval devils, but a being close enough to Ivan to debase Ivan's arguments, Ivan's rhetoric, and most of all, the "dire and fearsome spirit of self-annihilation and non-being" with whom the Grand Inquisitor had so romantically associated himself. Indeed, as Ivan says repeatedly in this chapter, this devil *is* Ivan, in at least as distinct a way as the Grand Inquisitor, whom Lawrence equates with Ivan, for creation is a somewhat less intimate process than hallucination.

This ideological need works together with the interplay of sources to explain why Dostoevsky preserves so much of Averkiev's apparition scene and so little of his apparition. Averkiev was writing a historical novel and, like Dostoevsky, had plainly been reading folklore and nineteenth-century editions of the Russian lives of the saints, which contain many demonic creatures. He would certainly have been brought up on Faust and E. T. A. Hoffmann, and very probably would have encountered the Nordic tradition of the personal fetish that normally appeared just before one's own death. He had apparently learned what Freud learned from reading Hoffmann, that the sense of the uncanny comes in part from the ontologically ambiguous reintrusion of long-abandoned beliefs. But Averkiev's background and his technique plainly mark another more important source for his apparition scene. He had learned from his old associate Dostoevsky, most specifically from the appearance of a hideous arthropod to the dying radical, Ippolit, in *The Idiot* and the first appearance of Svidrigailov in the room of the delirious Raskolnikov in *Crime and Punishment*. Not only is Svidrigailov mistaken for a hallucination, but he has hallucinations of the three victims of his unpunishable murders, his servant, his wife, and a little girl he raped. Averkiev's apparition scene crystallizes the appealing elements shared by four of Dostoevsky's favorite sources—the lives of the saints, Goethe, Hoffmann, and Dostoevsky.

When Ivan Karamazov, like Svidrigailov, blunders feverishly and beneficently through a storm on his way to his final hallucination, Dostoevsky is returning in his last great novel to the pattern of his first one, to describe the ultimate collision between the rational intellect and the moral imperative. Like Svidrigailov and Raskolnikov, Ivan is conscious of blood guilt that the law cannot touch without his confession. Like those earlier heroes, Ivan has dreams that reflect his victim: in this case, his father, that shrewd, insolent, sophistic, insinuating, provincial mocker and hanger-on who resembles Ivan's devil and, to Ivan's distress, Ivan himself. In short, Ivan Karamazov's embodiment of evil diverges from Averkiev's because Averkiev's sources fitted Dostoevsky's literary taste and ideological purpose better than did Averkiev's text.

In fact, the interesting question is not why Dostoevsky abandoned the Averkiev hallucination as a source, but why he adhered so faithfully to the order of details in a second-rate novel when he had a multitude of sources in better literature. Here, Dostoevsky was really using the same technique he used when he presented the despicable devils of antiquity: the desophistication of a figure whose current identity offered ideological complications. This return to a more primitive, safer kind of Devil was certainly not Dostoevsky's invention; it seems to come from the same source as the Devil's tawdry gentility. Dmitrii S. Likhachev has pointed out that medieval devils can be cruel and dirty, but that this tawdriness (*poshlost'*) can appear only in an age of social mobility and collapsing structures.[7] Mephistopheles has this quality at times, with Martha, for example, but here, as in Averkiev, the richness of the *déjà lu* goes deeper, to a source that Goethe and Dostoevsky both footnoted in their texts by quoting it in extenso—the Book of Job. Many scholars believe the Book of Job was written at the high point of Hebrew culture, perhaps in the reign of David, when urban sophisticates toyed like pastoral poets with the figure of a God whose sons presented themselves subserviently before him as Adam did in Genesis. One of those sons was a hanger-on, who spoke to God when spoken to, but a tempter at the same time, challenging goodness with cynicism, "Doth Job fear God for naught," and prompting the most spectacular display of innocent suffering in literature before Ivan's catalog of tortured children.

The letter to Liubimov explains why Dostoevsky would want to use the Book of Job as a source for the most notable character traits of Ivan's devil, as well as for the technique of desophistication, which led him to such other sources as the Russian lives of the saints and Averkiev's historical novel. According to that letter, Ivan's argument rests on the senselessness of the world, and the task of the novel is to confute Ivan's argument—to justify the ways of God to man. The Book of Job is the greatest and perhaps the oldest theodicy Dostoevsky knew. It begins with the argument Dostoevsky considered unanswerable, the meaninglessness of innocent suffering. Job's children are destroyed, and the full authority of the biblical narrator declares Job innocent before his suffering begins. Bildad the Shuhite and his friends have Ivan's scholarly clear-sightedness, and they enunciate the tempter's argument with the most insistent eloquence the rhetoric of their time affords. In the Book of Job as it stands (many scholars think its sources ended differently), these massively elaborated arguments are destroyed, not by new information or by new ways of using it, but by a theophany. A self-indulgent poetaster like Cabantous may launch his Christ into the empyrean before the eyes of an evil, astonished pope, but Dostoevsky's ideology excluded miracles or theophanies to justify or prove God. As Lia Mikhailovna Rozenblium has so clearly shown, Dostoevsky had very little of the mystic about him.[8] In his notebooks we have seen that he specifically rejected mysticism as a trait for Alesha. Dostoevsky could draw his subservient Devil from the Book of Job, but in an antimystical age, with a nonmystical mind, could not invoke the voice of God after a whirlwind to refute the position argued by the Devil and those associated with him, even though he had told his editor first that it was irrefutable and second that he considered it to be his duty to overthrow it.

III

DOSTOEVSKY INTRODUCES SEVERAL ARGUMENTS AGAINST THE GRAND INQUISITOR'S POSITION.

Perhaps because some of his sources were too eloquent and others conflicted with his ideology on miracles, Dostoevsky resorted to a series of rhetorical maneuvers to carry out the confutation he promised Liubimov. One such maneuver deflates the Grand Inquisitor with a simplicity so transparent as to be invisible.

Ivan Karamazov posits at the start of the Legend that it belongs to a literary genre in which the Son of God can visit earth. The Grand Inquisitor sees him resurrect a little girl, asks him, "Is this Thou, Thou?" and then adds that he does not want an answer. Ivan comments that it would not matter for the account if the Grand Inquisitor were mistaken or delirious, so long as he spoke out. In any case, he addresses Christ as a being who has the power to save or doom mankind, to defy gravity, to turn stones into bread, to rule the kingdoms of the earth, or alternatively to provide for the salvation of an elect. The Inquisitor also says that men are too feeble to obey the commandments of Christ, that in their disobedience men will suffer pangs of guilt, as well as practical misfortunes on earth, and will inevitably earn misfortunes in the hereafter:

> Your great prophet in his vision and his allegory says he saw all the members of the first resurrection, and that there were twelve thousand of them from each tribe. . . . But remember that there were only a few thousand of them in all—and Gods at that—but the remainder? And what are the remaining feeble people to blame for, that they could not endure what the mighty could? (*Pss* 14:234)

By resort to miracle, mystery, and authority, the Inquisitor's church has imposed certain of Christ's laws upon mankind and has concealed from mankind those laws that demand a moral heroism of which mankind is incapable. He says that disobedience to laws that have been suppressed by the church cannot earn damnation for these unknowing sinners:

> We shall tell them that every sin shall be redeemed if it has been committed with our permission. . . . There will be thousands of millions of happy children, and a hundred thousand sufferers who have taken upon themselves the accursed knowledge of good and evil. They will die in quiet, in quiet will perish in Thy name, and beyond the grave will encounter only death. But we will preserve the secret and for their happiness will lure them with a heavenly and eternal reward. For if there were something in the other world, of course it would not be for such as they. It is said and prophesied

that Thou wilt come and wilt triumph anew, wilt come with Thy elect, with Thy proud and mighty, but we shall say that they have saved only themselves, while we have saved all. . . . And we, who have taken their sin on ourselves for their own happiness will stand before Thee and say, "Judge us if Thou canst and darest." (*Pss* 14:230)

This intercession between Man and Christ resembles Christ's intercession between Man and God more than it resembles the Virgin's intercession between Man and Christ in the medieval story Ivan tells about the Virgin's visit to Hell. The Grand Inquisitor feels that he is substituting his own punishment for that which divine justice would otherwise certainly inflict on mankind. Surely he has incurred great sin—not only the suppression of Christ's truth but all the lives in the autos-da-fé. The Grand Inquisitor believes he is doing great good on earth, preventing war and famine and despair, but his supreme exploit is more romantic than anything in Pisarev or Herzen; he has sacrificed not just his life but the happiness of his immortal soul to save mankind from damnation.

Dostoevsky deflates this magnificent gesture with a very simple one. Christ says nothing but kisses the Grand Inquisitor. The kiss burns in the Inquisitor's heart as holy things do in this novel, and his plan changes from execution to banishment for Christ. But if Christ can kiss the Grand Inquisitor, who has imprisoned him, concealed his word, and killed hundreds of his followers, then obviously none of the lesser sinners are cut off from Christ's salvation. The Grand Inquisitor has been unable to sacrifice his immortal soul, because Christ in his mercy kisses him rather than punishing him. Moreover, he has no need to sacrifice his soul, because mankind need not be damned in any case. In a later chapter, indeed, Zosima confirms the argument implicit in this kiss, saying damnation is nothing more than eternal regret at having failed to love actively during the one life that a soul is given in all eternity. Here, in a single kiss, the most absolute and most appealing part of the Grand Inquisitor's exploit becomes an empty and unnecessary gesture. For him the sacrifice retains its nobility, but the reader sees him as deluded by his ignorance of the dimensions of Christ's mercy. He believes that he believes in God and Christ, but he actually believes in a more Euclidean, less merciful being. Christ annuls the romantic acceptance of eternal punishment by refusing to inflict it and vitiates the intercession between humanity and divine justice by displaying his own example of divine mercy.

Only one commentator on this passage has asked, "What are these sins of people taken on one's self? . . . It's really just godlessness; that's the whole secret. Your Inquisitor doesn't believe in God;

that's his whole secret!" Alesha Karamazov says this before he hears about the kiss, and Ivan's answer raises several of the same questions as the kiss: "Even though it were! You've guessed at last. And really it is so, the whole secret is just in this, but really, isn't this suffering?..." Ivan accepts Alesha's deflation of the Grand Inquisitor before offering his own, Christ's kiss. From Dostoevsky's point of view, this willingness to see a magnificent construct vitiated makes sense, if the Liubimov letter expresses a real intention. From Ivan's point of view the Grand Inquisitor might seem to deserve better. But the Legend is not offered as a simple exposition of Ivan's belief. His personal distance from the position he is enunciating makes his destruction of his argument psychologically reasonable, but this affectionate, hesitant candor is one of those features that make him so attractive that among all the commentators on this passage, only Alesha with his own kiss caught the ideological irony embodied in the kiss of Christ. If Dostoevsky intended this kiss to undermine Ivan's argument, he misjudged the vast majority of his readers.

Dostoevsky continues this argument against Ivan in the teachings of Father Zosima and then gives an answer to the problem of evil which is as telling and as devious in its way as Job's theophany. Zosima doubts the reality of Hell as Fedor envisions it, with or without hooks. He agrees with the Grand Inquisitor that the teachings of Christ will fill men with guilt at their failure to fulfill Christ's demands, but he sings a virtual hymn of rejoicing at this guilt. Indeed, as we have seen, he takes one of the central doctrines of the materialists Dostoevsky claimed to be opposing and turns this doctrine to his account. I mean the doctrine of universal causal connections, the belief that all things in the world are interconnected, that no event occurs without its causes and its effects in this world, that if we knew enough we would see the world as a seamless web of causes and effects. I have already mentioned Dostoevsky's detestation of the simplistic, patronizing positivism of Mendeleev, Claude Bernard, and the materialists of his day. Now, with the glee of a combatant trained in the intellectual battles of the 1860s, he puts their central doctrine into the mouth of a holy priest of the Orthodox church. As I quoted Zosima earlier, "Everything is like an ocean...you touch it in one place and it gives at the opposite end of the world" (*Pss* 14:290). In Zosima's doctrine on evil, this universal causal linkage is central. He holds that every one of us at some time in his life has acted out of spite or failed to act in the fullness of goodness. If on introspection no one can deny this, and if the world is really a connected whole, then every one of us is implicated in every sparrow's fall. Ivan had asked, "Why does God permit innocent suffering?" Instead of answering that question, Zosima turns it upon the questioner and asks, "Why do you cause innocent suffering?" He can transform the unanswerable question in this manner because in a totally determined world each of us has a part, directly or indirectly, in every evil thing that happens. In this sense, Zosima proclaims that all men are guilty of all things, but unlike those who try to escape guilt, he rejoices in it and sees it as his bond with the whole of being.

In short, Zosima offers a rhetorical answer to the problem of children's suffering, which Dostoevsky in his letter had considered unanswerable. He does not justify such suffering; he simply calls upon his interlocutor to share the blame, using a variant of the argumentum ad hominem. But even this did not seem to satisfy Dostoevsky. He had still another resource for the destruction of Ivan, the reductio ad absurdum, the carrying of Ivan's doctrines and Ivan's nature to a logical conclusion that discredited them as starting points. This attack upon Ivan's position involved the introduction into the novel of a body of characters whose analogy to Ivan is made distinct, and whose ridiculousness is made more distinct.

IV
RAKITIN IS A PARODY OF IVAN.

Several characters in *The Brothers Karamazov* have closely marked doctrinal, personal, and even verbal ties with Ivan Karamazov. I have already shown how such doubles could be treated as repositories for elements in a character's sources that were not needed for that character but that some conscious or unconscious fidelity to his sources led Dostoevsky to preserve in the novel. In this section and the next, I will show how this collection of genetically related characters evolved into an instrument of Dostoevsky's polemic with the righteousness of Schiller, Herzen, and Belinskii as it emerged in the attractiveness of Ivan and the Grand Inquisitor. I will use Rakitin and Kolia Krasotkin as my examples, although Madame Khokhlakova, Smerdiakov, and others could be used almost as well.

Rakitin, the seminarian on the make, is probably the most repulsive character in *The Brothers Karamazov*, but his full unloveliness emerges only in the chapters after the Legend of the Grand Inquisitor. In his first appearance, only his eyes and his exaggerated humility hint at something distasteful: "A young fellow, apparently about twenty-two, in a layman's frock coat, a seminarian and future theologian, for some reason the protégé of the monastery and its members. He was rather tall, with a fresh face, broad cheekbones, and shrewd, alert, narrow brown eyes. His face expressed utter respectfulness, decent, however, without any evident fawning" (*Pss* 14:36). The narrator hints that Rakitin has some thoughts of a different sort, but a Russian reader would begin to recognize Rakitin only when he starts to talk.

> You're rushing off to the abbot's. I know; he's put on a spread. Since that time he received the archpriest and General Pakhotov, remember it, there hasn't been a spread like that. I'll not be there, but get going, serve the sauces. But tell me one thing, Aleksei: What does this dream mean? That's what I wanted to ask you."
> —"What dream?"
> "Why, prostrating himself before your brother Dmitrii. And he gave his forehead a real bump too."
> "You mean about Father Zosima?"
> "Yes, about Father Zosima."
> "His forehead?"
> "Oh, I expressed myself disrespectfully! Well, all right, it was disrespectful. So, what's the meaning of this dream?"
> "I don't know what it means, Misha."
> "Just as I expected—he wouldn't explain it to you. There's nothing mysterious in this, of course; I guess it's just the usual benignorance [*blagoglupost'*]. But the trick was done on purpose. And now all the devotees in town will get talking and spread it through the district: 'What can be the meaning of this dream?' I think the old boy really was sharp-eyed: he sniffed a crime. Your house stinks with it."
> "What crime?"
> Rakitin plainly wanted to express something.
> "It's going to happen in your fine family, this crime. It'll be between your dear brothers and your Daddy with his bit of a fortune. So Father Zosima banged his forehead just in case. Later, if anything happens—'Oh, the holy elder foretold and prophesied it,' though what's prophetic about banging his forehead on the floor?" (*Pss* 14:72–73)

From this first speech, any of Dostoevsky's original readers would have recognized Rakitin as a type, a certain kind of theological student, the quick, shrewd, observant son of a Russian priest, whose lively language and cynical insight into the establishment led to power, position, and sometimes wealth in the world of the radical journals. The invented word "benignorance" has been connected with Shchedrin,[9] but Dostoevsky certainly intended it to suggest a far more plebian type, like Dobroliubov.

The quick, facile logic, the materialistic or social explanation of the religious, the special awareness of monetary and sexual concerns, the expectation of the criminal, the use of diminutives and of words like "stinks," "sniffed," "devotees" and the short, hard sentences, all call to mind the articles in the *Contemporary* and, after the censor closed it, the *Fatherland Notes* or the satirical journals of the Russian radicals. In short, the style of this first dialogue already implied a tie between Rakitin and Ivan that would later be made explicit. Both were setting out on careers in journalism, but Ivan was starting with the simplicity, sincerity, and intelligence of Belinskii, while Rakitin's style already reflected the tawdry polemics of the writers in the sixties, whom Dostoevsky looked upon as living parodies of Belinskii.

Though in the early part of the novel Rakitin is nothing worse than an ill-natured and somewhat sophomoric gossip, in the pages following the Legend of the Grand Inquisitor, he is quickly established as a vicious parody of Ivan. He finds Alesha crushed by the unjust mockery of Zosima's stinking corpse and adopts the double role of tormentor and tempter, as had Ivan, the Grand Inquisitor, and the Devil, but instead of being tortured himself, he is complacent:

> "Can you really [be in this state] simply because your old boy made a stench? Can you really have seriously believed he'd start throwing miracles. . . . Why, what the hell, why, nowadays a thirteen-year-old schoolboy doesn't believe that. Still, what the hell, . . . So it's God you're mad at now, you've mutinied; they passed him by for a promotion, and didn't give him a medal at the festival. Oh, you people. . . .'
> "I'm not mutinying against my God; I simply 'don't accept His world.'" (*Pss* 14:308)

Alesha's quotation from Ivan's "mutiny" makes explicit the parallel. Rakitin has replaced Ivan as Alesha's tormentor and tempter. Ivan tormented Alesha with stories of cruelty and tempted him to the "absurdity" of advocating vengeance. The Inquisitor tortured Christ with the woes of humanity and dared Christ to destroy him, and the Devil, the chief torturer, tempted Christ in the wilderness. All these tortures are vicarious, and the temptations are toward altruism. Rakitin offers a debased version of these functions; he exacerbates Alesha's personal hurt, and he tempts him with food and drink and sex, the cheap materialist's equivalent of the earthly bread the Grand Inquisitor, the Devil, and the Russian radicals offer.

Having established the parallel with Ivan, Dostoevsky proceeds to the destruction of Rakitin. He uses Rakitin's own denials to suggest the things denied. In two sentences, he indicates not only what two people think of Rakitin but also the petty vengefulness of his reactions: "Your dear brother Ivan once upon a time

proclaimed me a 'talentless liberal bumpkin.' And you too one fine
time couldn't stand it and gave me to understand that I was 'dis-
honorable.' All right! Now I'll have a look at your talent and honor"
(*Pss* 14:309). His destruction continues in the next chapter as we
learn that he brought Alesha to Grushenka not on a whim but
because she had offered him twenty-five pieces of silver to do so.
The reference to Judas is made explicit, and we can say initially
that Dostoevsky's invention took the form of a systematic distortion
of the Judas story in a single direction. Alesha and Rakitin eat
together, not a religious feast, but a snack that breaks the dietary
rules of the monastery. Like Christ, Alesha perceives his treacherous
intent, and tells him to carry it out, but Rakitin is aiming not at
a crucifixion but at a seduction, and this fails instead of succeeding.
The reduction of the sum from thirty to twenty-five pieces of silver
is thus consistent with the lightening of all the other weights in
the fictionalized version. Elsewhere in the novel the same depre-
ciation of currency takes place when Smerdiakov kills his father
and then goes and hangs himself after returning the thirty pieces
of paper—hundred ruble notes—for which he has committed the
crime.

Another piece of nonfiction probably enters the picture here.
Dostoevsky had recently received a letter asking for "thirty rubles
in silver," a normal phrase in a period when a silver ruble would
purchase far more than the inflated paper ruble. The letter came
from a relative he disliked and is dated five months before the
appearance of the book "Alesha" in the *Russian Messenger*. I would
suggest the following chain of associations. The thirty silver rubles
for the disliked relatives suggested the thirty pieces of silver for
Judas. This essentially literary association stimulated a feeling of
distaste, which in turn reminded Dostoevsky of another stimulus
for the same feeling, the radical journalists of his day. That complex—radicals, relatives, revulsion, and Judas, an ideological, a personal, an emotional, and a literary stimulus—suggested a rhetorical
device to Dostoevsky, the use of the familiar element, the Judas
figure, as a means for stimulating in the reader a prefabricated
revulsion for Rakitin. This use of the name of Judas was a commonplace, of course. In Russian literature Dostoevsky could have
found it in writers from Avakkum in the seventeenth century to
his contemporary Saltykov-Shchedrin, whose most famous villain
is nicknamed Little Judas. But the letter is the most plausible core
about which this particular complex of biblical, political, and rhetorical sources crystallized.

The connection with Ivan's promising career in journalism leads
to more elaborate patterns of association for Rakitin, who plans to

marry a rich idiot and grow richer as a radical journalist until he can build himself a stone house on Liteinii Avenue in St. Petersburg. When he takes the witness stand at the trial, he is asked, "Are you that same Mr. Rakitin whose brochure published by the episcopal authorities I recently read with such pleasure, *The Life of the Elder Father Zosima, Who Rests in the Bosom of the Lord,* full of profound and religious thoughts, with a superb and devout dedication to his Eminence? . . . With the sponsorship of his Eminence, your invaluable brochure has circulated and done considerable good" (*Pss* 15:100). Rakitin is embarrassed and claims that he never expected publication, obviously afraid that such a background will affect his reputation in radical circles. That is all. The subject is dropped.

It has been pointed out that Dostoevsky's readers would take this passage as truthful not only because the Russian radicals tended to emerge from theological seminaries—one of the few places they could obtain a free education, and places whose rules and rituals often provoked revolt—but also because one of them, Grigorii Zaxarevich Eliseev, had indeed enriched himself as a radical journalist to the point where he had a large stone house on Liteinii Avenue and a substantial fortune.[10] Eliseev's first book was called "The Biography of the Saintly Grigorii, German, and Varsonofii of Kazan and Sviiaga." The dedication read as follows:

> Your exaltedly eminent Lordship, benevolent Father and Archpastor! From your archpastorial benediction I started upon these labors; with your unceasing attention continued them, and to you I now offer this small item of my making. Your exaltedly eminent Lordship! Accept with your habitual condescension my meager offering and with your condescension the unworthiness of the laborer will take heart for the great work. Your exalted Eminence, benevolent Father, and Archpastor's humblest servant, a student in the Kazan Theological Academy, Grigorii Eliseev.[11]

Since a major Russian author, Nikolai Leskov, had called attention to this passage in a major work (*An Enigmatic Man,* chap. 38) written eight years before *The Brothers Karamazov,* Dostoevsky could count on most of his readership catching the reference, but he was plainly not using the example of Eliseev's sycophancy merely to discredit Rakitin. A direct transcription of his source would have been so much more damning than the sharply abbreviated version he does offer. Rather, he seems to be using Eliseev's life simply as source material to provide that kind of data that will anchor his fiction and give it the treasured capacity to fit even subsequently revealed fact. The episode is there because it happened and because Rakitin's character demanded it. It is brief because the trial was already threatening to overbalance the novel, and the mere discomfiture was enough. In this case, what started as a source became a resource, a literary reference that would characterize Rakitin as a caricature of a radical and contrast him with Ivan, the apotheosis of the radical.

The same presence of a real-life caricature of a Russian radical led Dostoevsky to build into Rakitin parodies of one of the greatest parodists of his time, Dmitrii Minaev. Rakitin's poem about Madame Khokhlakova's foot would have reminded contemporary readers of Minaev's poems about provincial women, but the pointlessness Minaev found in their lives becomes simple self-expression for Rakitin. Here, as V. S. Dorovatovskaia-Liubimova has shown, the polemic cuts both ways. Because the reference to Minaev's parodies would have been recognizable in his time, Dostoevsky was essentially using this recognition as a way of saying Rakitin was a Minaev, at the same time he was saying that Minaev was a Rakitin. Since he had already linked Rakitin with Ivan, he is creating a careerist parody for the independence and ambition with which Ivan is arranging his career.

Like any respectable Russian radical of his day, including Ivan, who had named one of his works the "Geological Revolution," Rakitin was much involved with the natural sciences, especially with the materialist claim that science could explain everything. Mitia Karamazov reports on Rakitin's beliefs:

> You see, there in the nerves, in the head, that is, there in the brain these nerves—(to hell with them!) there are these little tails; the nerves have these little tails, now as soon as they wiggle there, that is, you see, I look at something with my eyes, like this, and they wiggle, these little tails, and as they wiggle there appears an image and it doesn't appear immediately but a certain moment a second goes by there, and something like a moment appears, that is, a moment, damn the moment, not a moment but an image, that is an object, or an event, now then, damn it, that's why I observe, and then I think—because of the tails. (*Pss* 15:28)

With the care he frequently displays, Dostoevsky footnoted this passage with references to Claude Bernard, the French neurologist, materialist, and proponent of the scientific method of discovery who had been made a literary symbol in a book Dostoevsky had parodied fifteen years earlier, *What Is to Be Done?* by Chernyshevskii. Here I would suggest that the articles on physiology and neurology in many journals of Dostoevsky's time provide more than adequate sources for Rakitin's teachings as Mitia recounts them.

One element, however, is missing. The articles in the journals were sometimes pedantic, sometimes superficial, often arrogant, but they were not stupid. Dostoevsky's ideological enemies, especially the scientific ones, tended to have good minds, and he knew it.

Can we find a source for the sarcastic scorn that Mitia heaps upon Rakitin in this passage? Dostoevsky's correspondence may provide a clue, for he received letters from readers of every persuasion and every level of intellect. Let me cite a letter that can serve as an example of a genre. It came late in December 1876 from a Kharkov businessman named Ballin, whose letterhead proclaims that he was a dealer in sewing machines, materials, aids, incidentals for writing, educational games, scales, and disinfectant substances. S. V. Belov, who is probably the greatest storehouse of Dostoevskiana alive, informs me that these dealerships were the cover for an illegal printing press. Dostoevsky would have had no way of knowing the level of his correspondent's commitment to radical causes, but he would have felt it in his passionate and fuzzy materialism. Ballin's letter begins with praise for Dostoevsky's short story "The Gentle Creature" and goes on to the admission that he has not read the second half, adding, "Oh well, you don't get everything read." Now, of all Dostoevsky's works, "The Gentle Creature" depends most on the climactic realization that is presented on the very last page. Without that, it is a totally different work of art. Dostoevsky could only have responded to this opening with annoyance. The letter goes on to elucidate certain of Ballin's theories about consciousness:

> As concerns spiritualism, I am fully convinced of the realness of ideas. Thought and feeling I cannot conceive otherwise than as an aggregate of organized molecules appearing in our brain as a result of external influences, and these external influences I consider to be the external expression of the life around us. I cannot conceive an individual otherwise than humanly, and therefore accept as individuals also such beings as the Earthly sphere and the sun. By consciousness I mean such a complicated interaction of the parts of the individualized substance in various places and at various times. Understanding consciousness in this way, it appears incontrovertible to me that consciousness develops proportionally with the cooperation of the mass. Hence I deduce a vicious conclusion— that the consciousness of the sun, for example, must exceed human consciousness by a million times, the more so because the individual psychic activity is in specific relation to the size of the surface of the individual and the surface of the sun is also very great. It's plain that in saying the consciousness of the sun, I have in mind something altogether uncomprehended by me, and not a human consciousness made great.[12]

This portentous and disconnected fabric of fashionable phrases would have become linked in Dostoevsky's mind with the self-satisfaction in the beginning of the letter, and with the materialism that underlies this quotation, to form a real-life parody of radical style and doctrine, one of the early centers about which the figure of Rakitin appears.

Dostoevsky sees Rakitin related to Ivan in much the same way that he sees Eliseev and Minaev and Ballin related to Herzen and Belinskii. The greedy, vicious, foolish epigones become the sources for the lesser figure, just as the great figures become the sources for Ivan.

V
KOLIA KRASOTKIN IS A PARODY OF IVAN AND THE GRAND INQUISITOR.

The finest parody of Ivan and his Inquisitor is Kolia Krasotkin, the thirteen-year-old schoolboy who can strike terror into the hearts of his mother, his teachers, and his classmates. Like Ivan, Kolia is very intelligent, is "incessantly tortured with self-consciousness," reads Voltaire, and has a breadth of reading that astonishes those around him. But his intelligence is a schoolboy's smartness, amusing to watch, and his self-doubt and self-consciousness involve his appearance and his wits, not his moral position. He quotes Voltaire but from trivial school compendia, without understanding him.

In the third chapter of book 5, when Ivan meets Alesha he says he wants to see him "very much; I want to get acquainted with you once and for all, and to get you to know me. . . . I've finally learned to respect you. It's plain this man stands firm. . . . I love these firm ones, whatever they may stand for, even if they're little galoots like you." The intensity of the affection overrides the patronizing words, and Alesha responds in kind, "You're just the same sort of young man as all the other twenty-three-year-olds, the same young, youthful, fresh and wondrous boy, a weanling, and to sum it up, a boy. Tell me, did I hurt your feelings badly?"

When Kolia summons Alesha, in book 9, chapter 4, he also "very, very much wanted to get acquainted," and says so (*Pss* 14:478–79). Later, he says, "I'm glad to know you, Karamazov. I've wanted to know you for a long time. . . . I learned long ago to respect you as a rare being. . . I have heard that you are a mystic and were in the monastery. I know you are a mystic, but . . . that didn't stop me. Contact with reality will cure you" (*Pss* 14:499). Kolia here constitutes the realization of Ivan's characterization of himself and Alesha as "Russian boys." He is a real, not a figurative boy, and at the simplest level he believes the patronizing words he is using. At the same time, his respect and affection for Alesha emerge in close parallel to Ivan's, and the intensity of his feelings overrides the self-consciousness of his mannerisms. Ivan's claim to be an immature Russian youth made him seem sophisticated. Kolia's realization of that claim carries the reader back to actual implications of what Ivan said.

One puzzling moment in the novel is Kolia's long account of the goose (*Pss* 14:495–96). Kolia tells a lame story of a piece of boyish cruelty. He had asked a stupid peasant whether a cart wheel would decapitate a goose that was pecking under it. He watched from the side where the goose was pecking, winked at the right moment, and the peasant made the cart move, cutting the goose's neck in two. "You did that on purpose," people cry. "No, not on purpose," Kolia answers, but the stupid peasant says, "It wasn't me, that's the one that got me to do it." Kolia's answer has the hauteur of his intellectual superiority: "I hadn't taught him at all; I had simply expressed the basic idea and only spoke hypothetically." This guiltily rationalized account seems overly expanded in the novel until it takes its place with Ivan's struggle to avoid admitting that his basic idea has seduced Smerdiakov into killing, and with Smerdiakov's teaching, which leads little Iliusha to torture dogs by feeding them bread with pins in it. These two vicarious assaults remind readers of Ivan's role in the murder, at the same time robbing him of any sympathy that might attach to him as a misconstrued manipulator.

Kolia's behavior trivializes the ideas of the Grand Inquisitor and the Devil, as well as those Ivan expresses himself. He trains the dog Zhuchka to play dead and resurrect itself and then stages the child's equivalent of a miracle for Iliusha. He exploits the mysterious secret of who founded Troy and crushes the boy who learns it. He performs an exploit that is the modern child's equivalent of Christ's second temptation in the wilderness, casting himself between the tracks of an oncoming train. And he uses authority, deception, and force for the good of the little group of schoolboys who are his equivalent of the Grand Inquisitor's humanity. The Grand Inquisitor said,

> Oh we shall finally persuade them not to be proud; we shall show them they are feeble, they are only pitiable children, but that the happiness of children is the sweetest thing of all. They will grow timid and will start to look up to us and squeeze against us in fear, like fledglings to their mother. They will feel wonder and

terror at us. . . . Yes, we will make them work, but in the hours free from work, we will arrange their life like children's play . . . and they will worship us as their benefactors. (*Pss* 14:236)

Kolia realizes some of these metaphors, actually arranging childish games and the obedience of the boys, "as to a god." He even says,

> Yes, in general I love the small fry. I have two fledglings on my hands at home right now; even today, they delayed me. So [the boys] stopped beating Iliusha, and I took him under my protection. I can see that he's a proud boy. I tell you that; he's proud, but in the end, he has entrusted himself to me like a slave, fulfills my slightest commands, obeys me like a God, and tries to imitate me. So now you too, Karamazov, have gotten together with all these fledglings? (*Pss* 14:479)

Everything here echoes Ivan and cheapens Ivan; the pride of sinful humanity becomes the stubbornness of a pathetic child. The whole of humanity whom the Inquisitor loves and serves shrinks to two little groups of children who reinforce Kolia's ego. The Inquisitor's dominion becomes a child's bossiness when both compare themselves to gods. And Kolia's resurrection of the dog becomes a comment on Ivan's dreams of resurrecting the dead and all the talk of miracles, because we can see the effect of this miracle: "If the unsuspecting Krasotkin had understood how torturingly and murderously such a moment could influence the health of the sick boy, he would not have thought of playing a trick like the one he played." The word "murderously" here removes Kolia from the world of mere mockery, making him an involuntary killer in his blind superiority.

Radicalism in Dostoevsky's day was almost a club in which membership required certain attitudes. Certain novels and journalistic pieces, friendly, hostile, and ambivalent, ranging from Turgenev's *Fathers and Children* to Chernyshevskii's *What Is to Be Done?* had canonized the list of prescribed beliefs: materialism, scientism, positivism, atheism, socialism, internationalism, realism, feminism, and in the 1870s populism, all coupled with hostility to sentiment, tradition, prejudice, manners, the aesthetic, the establishment, and the government. Except for feminism and internationalism, Kolia manages to take every pose demanded of a radical. In the chapter "A Schoolboy," he begins: "They're scum. . . . Doctors and the whole medical filth, speaking in general, and of course, in detail. I reject medicine. It's a useless establishment." This remark might seem anti-scientistic, but in the tradition of Russian radicalism, the deliverers of medical care received none of the honor received by the investigators of medical truth.

Kolia goes on to attack Alesha and the boys for sentimentalizing in their visits to Iliusha, and later, after "an impressive silence," he makes an excursion into scientism and utopian political positivism:

"I love to observe realism, Smurov. Have you observed how dogs meet and sniff each other. There's some general law of nature there."

"Yes, it is sort of funny."

"No, it's not funny. You're wrong about that. In nature there's nothing funny, however it might seem to a man with his prejudices. . . . That's a thought of Rakitin's, a remarkable thought. I'm a socialist, Smurov."

"And what's a socialist? . . ."

"That's if all are equal and own common property, and there are no marriages, and religion and all the laws are the way each person wants, and, well, and so on. You're still young for that; it's early for you. It's chilly, though. . .

"Have you noticed, Smurov, the way in winter, if it's fifteen or eighteen degrees, it doesn't seem so cold as now, for example, at the beginning of winter. . . . With people it's all a matter of habit, in everything, even in governmental and political relationships."
(*Pss* 14:472)

After this excursion Kolia pauses, as we saw above in chapter 3, section 1, to tease a benign peasant he passes, concluding, "I love to talk with the people, and am always prepared to give it its due. . . . With the people, you have to know how to talk." The picture of the young radical pontificating to a devotedly receptive follower had become ironic at least as early as *Fathers and Children*, and savage in Leskov's *Enigmatic Man*.

The catalog of shibboleths recurs two chapters later in another setting, also as old in this tradition as Turgenev, with the young man patronizingly enlightening the older about radical doctrine. This indoctrination of Alesha also starts with the statement that medicine is a villainy, but it is interrupted by the concerns involving Iliusha and returns to a schoolboy cynicism about history that parodies Ivan's sense of the meaninglessness of history as Dostoevsky described it to Liubimov.

"I don't ascribe much importance to all those schoolboy stories, and in general haven't much respect for world history. . . . It's the study of a series of human stupidities, and that's all. I respect only mathematics and science. . . . Again, these classical languages. . . .

"Classical languages, if you want my opinion about them, are a police measure. . . they're cultivated because they're boring and therefore stultify our aptitudes. . . . It was pointless, so how could it be made more pointless?—and that's when they thought up the classical languages. . . . "

"And he's the top student in Latin," one boy shouted out of the group. (*Pss* 14:498)

In enunciating one of the standard doctrines of the practical and scientific radicals, Kolia displays his magnanimous disinterestedness. This rejection of what he elsewhere labels "baseness" (*podlost'*) offers the child's equivalent of the nobility with which the Grand Inquisitor rejects the salvation he has the ability to earn. The gesture is the same, and the love for the oppressed is the same, but the schoolboy's showing off infects the reader's recollection of the Inquisitor's magnificent self-sacrifice.

Dostoevsky's central quarrel with the radicals may well have involved their attitude to religion. Kolia follows his splendid thirteen-year-old's statement that contact with reality would cure Alesha's mysticism with a definition of mysticism, "Well, God and all." He elaborates his ideas about God, which turn out to be a travesty of Ivan's ambivalent abstention from denial:

"I don't have anything against God. Of course, God is only a hypothesis. . . but. . . I admit that He is necessary for order. . . for the order of the world and so on. . . and if He did not exist, it would be necessary to invent Him," added Kolia, starting to blush. . . . "Even without believing in God, it's possible to love mankind. . . Voltaire didn't believe in God, but loved mankind. . . . I've read *Candide*, in a Russian translation. . . . I'm a socialist, Karamazov, an incorrigible socialist. . . . The Christian faith has served only the rich and noble to hold the lower class in slavery, isn't that true?. . . I am not against Christ. That is a fully human figure, and if He lived in our time, He would have joined the revolutionists and maybe played a prominent role—that's certain, even."

The talk about hypotheses, the order of things, the necessity for God, the possibility of love without God all plainly remind the reader of Ivan. The talk about socialism, the sin of Christianity, and Christ's need to join the revolutionists all recall the Grand Inquisitor. To readers in 1880 they would also recall the passage from *The Diary of a Writer* where Dostoevsky had shown Belinskii's reaction to the idea that Christ would have been a socialist. Ivan had observed "that everything that in Europe is a hypothesis is immediately an axiom for the Russian boy." His frequent repetition of the word "boy" (*mal'chik*) prepares the reader for the repetition of these doctrines by a real boy, culminating in the word-for-word repetition of Voltaire's aphorism about the invention of God. But this aphorism is the highest reach of Kolia's sophistication, whereas for Ivan, it is the starting point for two passionate statements about a single vision of humanity. We have already discussed the first: (1) "I think that if the Devil does not exist, and it turns out that man created him, then he created him in his own image and likeness." The second is so powerful that it needed Kolia's parody. (2) "And indeed, man did invent God. It would be nothing strange and nothing wondrous for God to really exist but the wondrous thing is that such a thought, the thought of the necessity of God, could creep into the head of such a savage and evil animal as man, it is so holy, so touching, so wise, and does such honor to man."

Through this entire catalog of shibboleths, Ivan's doctrines become associated with the conceit and embarrassed self-consciousness that are the most visible traits of Kolia. This rhetorical function of Kolia's conceit is curiously related to the best-known source for Kolia. Georgii Chulkov has shown how many of Kolia's doctrines coincide closely with statements made by Belinskii.[13] And we know that in the early seventies Dostoevsky found conceit to be a central feature in Belinskii's character. Arkadii Dolinin has summed up Dostoevsky's attitude to Belinskii in the early seventies by using a series of quotations from Dostoevsky's letters:

"Belinskii, most rotten, dull, and shameful phenomenon of Russian life." "A stink bug, Belinskii was just an impotent and feeble little talent." "Belinskii cursed Russia and knowingly brought upon her so much woe." "In Belinskii there was so much petty conceit, viciousness, impatience, exacerbation, baseness, but most of all, conceit. It never occurred to him that he himself was disgusting. He was pleased with himself in the highest degree, and that was already a stinking, shameful, personal stupidity." "He related to Gogol's characters superficially to the point of meaninglessness....He scolded Pushkin when Pushkin cast off his false pose....He rejected the end of Eugene Onegin...." "He didn't even understand his own people. He didn't even understand Turgenev." Etc.[14]

Here, there could be a source for some of the conceit in Kolia, and some of Kolia's littleness and incomprehension may have had their origins in the vision of Belinskii these letters reflect. Of course, the nastiness that is such a conspicuous part of these letters has disappeared. Kolia can be cruel, arrogant, conceited, and destructive, but there is nothing stinking, shameful, talentless in him. These qualities seem to survive in two places. One is Kolia's vision of himself: "Tell me, Karamazov," he asks, "Do you despise me terribly?" The other repository for these unpleasant qualities is Rakitin, who embodies them superbly.

Dolinin argues, however, that Dostoevesky's view of Belinskii, and his political attitude as a whole, underwent a revolution in 1876, and that by the time *The Brothers Karamazov* began to emerge, he expressed himself with some of the old ardor he had felt for the Belinskii who honored and befriended him in 1846. He refers to him as "the most honorable and noble Belinskii" and writes the article on Belinskii and Herzen that I have already quoted at length in chapter 7, section 3.

The chronological lines are not so neat as Dolinin makes them, but Dostoevsky certainly responded ambivalently to Belinskii. If the vile and nasty part of the vision finds its repository in Rakitin and in Kolia's image of himself, what about the honorable and noble vision, which coincides more closely in time with the writing of *The Brothers Karamazov?* Here, the most obvious repository is Ivan himself, and indeed, an excellent critic of Dostoevsky, Alfred Rammelmeyer, has made Belinskii a chief source for the Grand Inquisitor, documenting his case primarily by referring to Belinskii's letter to Botkin, which A. N. Pypin had published not long before.

Ivan and Kolia resemble both visions of Belinskii, one primarily the noble vision, one primarily the petty, conceited vision, with Rakitin as the repository for all the vile traits associated with either vision. Kolia might, of course, resemble Belinskii because Ivan contains much Belinskian material and Kolia is a parody of Ivan. According to this pattern, Dostoevsky, like many others, found Belinskii a noble and attractive figure who had done enormous harm to Russia and its literature. He incorporated this ambivalence in the attractive and noble figures of Ivan and the Inquisitor, who both cause tremendous harm in the world, and then parodies these two in the loving and lovable figure of Kolia, who does so much harm to Iliusha and the others in his little world.

On the basis of the notebooks for *The Brothers Karamazov,* I would suggest another pattern of development. For years, Dostoevsky had been working on several projects, including *The Life of a Great Sinner,* a novel about children, *Atheism,* and "The Russian Candide." After an auspicious childhood the great sinner was to fall into radicalism and eventually be saved. This career coincides possibly with Ivan's, or Alesha's, but plainly with Kolia's as it has already begun and as it develops into the great unhappiness that Alesha foresees. If this formulation is right, in the mid-1870s the common features of these four projected works converged upon the figure of little Kolia Krasotkin. The earliest surviving notes for the novel relate to him; the figure of Ivan emerges only later. Ivan, then, like Rakitin, would have come into existence as the repository for traits that could not be incorporated in a child.

Once the character of Ivan had been spun off, it assumed the residual loveliness of Belinskii and Herzen. Indeed, it might perhaps be argued that the ideological revolution in Dostoevsky's thinking which Dolinin dates to 1876 was the result and not the cause of the emergence of Ivan in the mass of materials that were to become the novel. Just as life can imitate art, the creative process can generate ideology. About the figure of Ivan would gather the noble doubts, the mighty pity, and the love of life, of humanity, of family which were later to make Ivan so dangerous to the ideological intentions Dostoevsky described in his letter to Liubimov. In this case, I would suggest that the child is the father of the man.

VI
Dostoevsky Led His Readers into Russian Radicalism in Order to Show Them the Way Out.

We no longer need Dostoevsky's letter to Liubimov or any other statement as evidence in our evaluation of Lawrence's argument that Dostoevsky agreed with Ivan and the Grand Inquisitor. We have been looking at what Dostoevsky did, not what he said. We have ascribed his eloquence not to his sincerity but to his borrowings. We have ascribed the kiss of Christ not to acquiescence but to ideological irony, since his pardon not only vitiates the greatest reason for the Inquisitor's sacrifice but also demolishes the romantic sacrifice itself. We have ascribed the pivotal position of Ivan in part to the parodic figures clustering around him. And we have offered the rhetorical energy expended on the deprecation of Ivan as evidence of Dostoevsky's good faith in his promise to confute Ivan's doctrines.

In this final section on Ivan, we must return to the disjunction we started with and ask why Dostoevsky's rhetoric failed to convince Lawrence and so many others. Lawrence, of course, was writing an introduction to that dubious enterprise, a separate edition of the Legend of the Grand Inquisitor. The isolation of the passage could explain Lawrence's misreading but not the widespread prevalence of his view. One could say that many readers read badly or read with preestablished conclusions, because certain early errors had been immortalized. But major writers should have a rhetoric that will preclude such errors on the central issues of a work. The final explanation for Dostoevsky's failure to communicate his intent may involve a technical trick that Dostoevsky had mastered early in his career.

I have mentioned a number of connections between *The Brothers Karamazov* and *Crime and Punishment*. Let us consider the passage in *Crime and Punishment* where Raskolnikov has just committed the double murder and stands poised for his getaway. He opens the door and listens at the head of the stairs. Someone goes out of the building. He is about to leave, when he hears someone entering the building and grows convinced that they are coming to visit his victims. At the last minute, he slips back and silently bolts the door, then listens, holding his breath, while this visitor and another discuss how to get in. And at some point in these three pages, readers suddenly realize that they too are holding their breath, that the descriptions of Raskolnikov have been contagious, and that without willing it or even knowing it at first, the readers have concentrated their entire poised attentiveness and desire upon the escape of this hatchet murderer. In short, Dostoevsky manipulates the reader into the experience of having just committed a murder.

He uses this device many times in *Crime and Punishment*. It is not original with him, for it is a common trick in the picaresque to involve the reader's attention in the escape of a first person narrator he deplores. Stanley Fish suggests that Milton implicates the reader in *Paradise Lost*, inspiring sympathy with Satan as a way of letting men experience Adam's fall and then destroying this sympathy step by step, until all the fallen angels turn to snakes; thus Blake's belief that Milton favored Satan rests on the beginning of the work and not on the whole.[15] Dostoevsky later abandons this technique; in the novels after *Crime and Punishment*, he never shows us the mind of a murderer from the inside. But in *The Brothers Karamazov*, he brings us inside the mind of Ivan, whose "all is lawful" stimulates or liberates Smerdiakov's murderous proclivities, or who at best lacks the moral acumen to withstand Smerdiakov's imputation of evil.

By carrying his reader through a genuine experience of what it means to be a Russian radical—and a compassionate, noble, generous, tortured, loving one—Dostoevsky implicates his reader in the feelings of guilt, self-consciousness, stupidity, or savagery to which he makes radicalism lead Ivan, Kolia, Rakitin, and several other characters. We have discussed the epigraph of the novel, from the Gospel according to St. John: "Except a corn of wheat fall upon the ground and die, it abideth alone, but if it die, it bringeth forth much fruit." The seed here is the grace of God, and John says that it will bear fruit only if it dies. By this reckoning, the Grand Inquisitor's effort to isolate mankind from evil is actually making grace sterile by not letting it die. Dostoevsky prefers to tempt his readers, as Rakitin and Ivan tempted Alesha, and as the Devil tempted Christ. He tries to carry his readers through a death of grace as dangerous as Zosima's in his youth, or Alesha's when his faith is shaken, hoping he can bring them out beyond to the point where they become fertile disseminators of grace. Dostoevsky thus is engaging not in communication but in manipulation. Instead of the semiotic model, which assumes that literature communicates preexisting materials, we need a cybernetic one, which assumes that literature guides its readers by making them respond and by integrating their responses into the continuing literary experience.

This use of a novel for the propagation of active grace entails the danger that the process may stop at the first step, and the less grave but more likely danger that readers may interpret the author's intention as stopping at the first step. Dostoevsky took this risk, and a substantial, but I think decreasing, number of his readers have justified his fear and trembling.

CHAPTER NINE

CONCLUSION

I
MUCH OF WHAT DOSTOEVSKY DID TO HIS MATERIALS IS UNIVERSAL, BUT HE READ MORE, REHEARSED HIS EXPERIENCE MORE, AND KEPT TRYING NEW COMBINATIONS.

I am finally ready to present a coherent narrative of the processes by which Dostoevsky generated a powerful novel, not ex nihilo, but out of a body of experience of which the most nearly knowable part was his reading. One large question remains: which of the processes described here are peculiar to Dostoevsky, and which are common to many authors, or perhaps to all humanity? We know that Dostoevsky read less systematically than Tolstoi, that his reading lists were thematic, associative, even dialogic, so that before he read a book it already had ties to other materials in his mind, and these ties already had something novelistic about them.

I have described how much of Dostoevsky's creation took place as a part of cognition, memory, and recall, using the same processes we all use, at the most basic level. Partly because of the anatomy of the brain, and partly because of the sociology of the psychological community, recent studies of memory and cognition tend to focus on the verbal, the visual, or the emotional, but rarely on all three at once. In the study of creation, these distinctions, like the much debated boundary between cognition and memory, lose their importance, and we face one central fact: we remember things that are organized.[1]

Verbally, we remember unrelated items, even half a dozen of them, with great difficulty. Fortunately, items are almost always related, if only because we encounter them together. More often, they sound alike, signify parts of a single whole, or signify things that have features in common. Sometimes, we simply put them together to form a whole. College students find it hard to memorize lists of arbitrary pairs of nonsense syllables so as to answer "wak," for example, when prompted by the syllable "kos"; but they find it easy to remember the same number of nonsense words like "koswak," and even easier to learn the same number of syllables in nonsense sentences like "Koswak plongord ugwich." We seem to have an almost unlimited memory for items that can be incorporated into chunks of data that in turn form larger chunks, and so on.[2]

Dostoevsky's chunks, I suspect, would cluster more heavily than most peoples' around moral and emotional values. Goodness or love, anger or evil, would often be the common feature linking the elements in a chunk. Once a chunk had such an emotional loading, it would tend to gather new and old experiences about it by assonance, metonymy, metaphor, and all the other patterns of association. At a certain point, certain morally and emotionally loaded chunks of chunks of verbal material would become large and intricate enough to be organized as an argument, by the patterns of rhetoric rather than by those of association. Once such a chunk of chunks became an argument, the accretion process became more orderly. Dostoevsky's reading lists would emerge from such an argument, and in his memory he would file the materials he read as potential evidence for or against some position. At this point, he would begin making his often passionate notes for *The Diary of a Writer*, or whatever other journalistic enterprise he was working on at the time. Some of the ideological transformations described in the chapter on Ivan were probably achieved no more consciously than those described for Alesha under the heading of the unconscious. *The Diary of a Writer* article on Herzen and Belinskii, for example, already contains much of the moral and emotional ambivalence that would later shape the identity of Ivan.

Visually, at the most basic level, Dostoevsky's perceptions and memory also operated according to patterns neurologists and psychologists may be beginning to understand. Unlike the ear, the eye has receptors that record many millions of changing stimuli. Compared to the transistors in most computers, the nerve cells that turn this flood of data into usable information are complex, slow, and sometimes perverse living things. Transistors react a thousand times faster and are far less likely to send random signals. But unlike most transistors, a nerve cell may have direct connections with up to a thousand others, may react only when the number of incoming stimuli reaches a certain sum, may grow either more or less sensitive to repeated or continuing stimuli, and probably may strengthen or weaken certain of its interconnections in response to its experience.

These simple properties do much to turn the unreliable signals our receptors transmit into the beautiful clarity of the world we know. If a given receptor fails to send a signal when stimulated, the many neighboring receptors will take its place, since receptors have many direct connections overlapping in the next layer. In the same way, when a receptor cell performs a gratuitous act, as Dostoevsky's characters sometimes do, and sends a signal for no external reason, summing cells in the next layer will not transmit the isolated signal, so that our picture of the world has fewer random irregularities than the primary receptors transmit.[3]

Each of the many millions of receptors in the eye sends a signal when stimulated but stops sending signals when stimulated continuously for several seconds. This fading turns eye nerves into motion detectors, which has obvious Darwinian value for recognizing threats or prey. But the eye shifts slightly every second, so that the edges of forms send signals because they are shifted to different stimuli, while the central areas do not, because they receive the same stimuli. Thus the motion of the eye makes the motion detector into an edge detector. In nature, most sharp edges mark the outlines of objects; exceptions like the markings on a zebra confirm this rule, since they evolved by confusing the outline detectors of canines and cats.

In the diagram we see the decagon on the left as a decagon rather than as ten lines because a more elaborate simplifying mechanism prompts us to see things we can name or at least imagine as entities, just as it is easier to remember a nonsense word than two nonsense syllables. By adding two more lines, in the middle diagram, I make it hard to see this form as a decagon; it becomes a convex hexagon and two squares, which the Gestalt psychologists incurred unfair opprobrium for calling "better" figures.[4] But when I bend the two added lines, as in the diagram on the right,

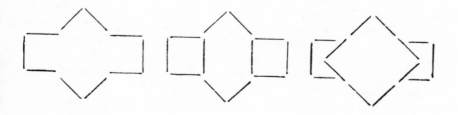

something interesting occurs. We see a square on top of an oblong, much as Dostoevsky saw certain chunks of verbal material as an argument. Adding a dimension sometimes makes figures "better," and it is hard not to add on-topness when we see these strokes. In much the same way, when we receive similar signals from a series of points in our visual field, one after the other, in a certain order, we add a sense of motion in time to our perception, because this picture is "better" than the discontinuous existence of an entity. By reducing our world to outlines and then reconstituting forms in space and time, we create a world that is "better" than what our eyes can give us, and that enables us to function better than a blur would. In this sense, "better" is a Darwinian word. Whether within our lifetime or in the lifetime of our genes hardly matters; simple outlines, regular outlines, convex outlines, and moving outlines have represented objects often enough for us to survive by treating them as objects.

The perception of forms in three dimensions does not, of course, depend on line intersection alone. Size, position in the visual field, sharpness of outline, recession of perspective lines, atmospheric perspective, and most of all binocular parallax also produce this awareness. When and only when both eyes lock onto an object, certain summing nerves receive enough stimulus from its outline to send a signal to those nerves that record what muscle tension on the eyes permitted that lock. That muscle tension gives a reading of the third dimension which has to be correlated with other data. Most people can look cross-eyed at these letters and see them at the wrong distance.

A	A	A	A	A	A	A	A	A	A	A
B	B	B	B	B	B	B	B	B	B	B
C	C	C	C	C	C	C	C	C	C	C
D	D	D	D	D	D	D	D	D	D	D
E	E	E	E	E	E	E	E	E	E	E

A finger pointed at the page encounters an imaginary transparent surface or passes through an imaginary surface that supports the letters above the page; but the presence of that finger requires us to use physical effort upon the eye muscles to keep them focused wrong. This effort is a measure of a physical drive that might be called Occam's meat ax, a physical aversion to adding explanatory entities like the transparent surface. It returns the eye to its more or less random hunt for a fit. As soon as the eye muscles and the hand muscles send signals similar enough in the distance they suggest to activate a summing nerve that needs their combined, or at least noncontradictory, signals, that nerve will feed a particular location for the page into our schema of the space around us.

These materials suggest that the simplest cognition is a creative process, a process of innumerable trials and errors by large numbers of slow and not very reliable nerves whose simple properties operate in a structure that first abstracts and then reconstitutes a world. The world we see is the artifact of summing nerves that cannot react to unconfirmed signals and can react to nonexistent signals when they make the outline sharper and the picture "better." This world is "better" than what the receptors report in terms of simplicity, memorability, manipulability, survival value, and probably resemblance to that world that feeds its data to the receptors in the first place. When a picture suddenly becomes "better," something resembling a summing nerve rewards us with an "Aha!" the sudden realization that bodies of disorganized data can form a whole. I would argue that closely analogous processes shape our more elaborate cognition of form in space and of motion in time, and that special variants of these processes shape Dostoevsky's creation of his novelistic worlds. We do not know enough to study the neurology of artistic creation, and Dostoevsky would have reacted to such a study with monumental rage, but we do know that the genes that shape our brain, like the authors who furnish it, tend to reuse existing formulas as much as possible. The particularly Dostoevskian transformations that took place at this cognitive level most probably included the tendencies to exaggerate, to Russify, and to redistribute the emotional elements in a text.

As Dostoevsky read of objects and events, he had the kind of mind that saw them and reacted to them emotionally. He constructed worlds in three dimensions to contain them and set these worlds in motion in their own time scheme. If we are to function at all, we all carry in our memories the "script" of certain repeated experiences.[5] We remember going to a restaurant as a sequence of standardized actions and file the personal or literary experience of a particular visit under the generalized heading along with its special qualities, the pretty waitress, the greasy menu, and so on. As Dostoevsky read of people, places, objects, and events, he filed them in his memory under various "scripts." These scripts in turn would cluster in his memory, linked by the emotions they stimulated or presented; by parallel actors, motivations, events; or by their fitting together as parts of a whole in space and time, much as the square on the oblong formed a whole in three dimensions. This reverse metonymy, the part entering into the whole, would form an entity out of scripts that were themselves epitomes of individual experiences, literary or other. To paraphrase Belinskii, Dostoevsky did his reading in images. "Better" for him meant not only neater, more symmetrical, more convex, and so on, but also more vivid and emotionally coherent, so that he misquotes Aksakov about the weeping mother because she was already a part of the script and "belonged" in the passage when he read it.

At a certain point in the genesis of a work, Dostoevsky would have that experience which he compared to the birth of a diamond in his somewhat ecstatic letter to Maikov. As Dostoevsky describes it, this event has the same mysterious "aha" quality that Gestalt psychologists find in those moments when two or more isolated and often puzzling stimuli suddenly cohere into an intelligible whole, perhaps by activating a summing nerve cell that can only transmit that insight when it receives signals from the right combination of nerves. Whatever the mechanism, I would suggest that at this moment Dostoevsky had discovered a correspondence between an argument that had been evolving in the sequential, verbal areas of his brain and a vision of people, places, and events that had been coalescing in the pattern-making areas of his brain. The link in Dostoevsky's case will usually be his own emotions. Certain arguments and certain stories made him angry. Anger sometimes made him laugh, and just as the almost identical signals flashing from the right eye and the left eye set a summing signal flashing in our brain that shifts our vision into three dimensions, so with Dostoevsky, the memories of events and arguments would suddenly lock, and each would feed its material into a whole where it would find its matching slot.

This whole was still not complete. It would be reworked, as he told Maikov, in many notebook sketches, in drafts, at the moment of dictation, and in corrections, and it might never become a novel at all, returning to the stockpile in his memory as elements for some other synthesis. In fact the unwritten novels provide the best picture of this "Aha!"; *Atheism,* "the Russian Candide," *The Life of a Great Sinner,* and even the novel about children, all show the moment when ideological argument merged with character and action in time and space. The projected play about Il'inskii in Tobolsk may not have reached that point; perhaps Dostoevsky's distrust of romanticism aborted the project before the ideological component had matured enough to match the melodrama. In the notebooks for *The Raw Youth,* Dostoevsky gave a prosaic summary of the process I have just described:

> To write a novel, it is necessary to supply oneself first of all with one or several strong impressions actually experienced by the au-

thor's soul. In this is the job of the poet. Out of this impression develops the theme, the plan, the structured whole [*tema, plan, stroinoe tseloe*]. This is already the work of the artist, although the artist and the poet help each other in both the former and the latter—in both cases. (*Pss* 16:10)

A month or two after Dostoevsky wrote this note, his wife underlined the importance of this second step, in which the plan develops out of the generating impression.

My kind and dear Fedochka, here's what I'll tell you about your work: I beg you not to hurry to begin work; rather if some time passes, the plan will appear of itself; haste only hinders it. I remember how it was with *The Idiot* and *The Possessed*. You tortured yourself a long time over the plan for the novel, and when it had come together, the work went very fast. You have lots of time ahead of you. If you should only start work in September in Petersburg, you still would have time to work through a lot. Otherwise, with haste you can spoil the whole business and have to rework the plan, and that hinders the artistry. Forgive me, my darling, for giving you advice, but I'm doing this openheartedly and as your greatest admirer who would be pained if the novel didn't succeed.[6]

This "plan" does not mean the chapter outline, for that would always go on developing long after Dostoevsky started sending text to his publishers. It is plainly distinct from that "diamond" or "impression" which brought the central elements of the novel together in the presence of strong emotions. It is centrally the work of the "artist" and not the "poet," but the unconscious continues to play a part as the plan appears of itself. In short, it is the solution to a problem, as Poincaré understood it, and not that higher achievement of a mathematician, the discovery of a problem. The problem Dostoevsky had to solve before he could begin "working," as his wife put it, seems to have usually involved the narrative technique, the simple question of first person or third person in *Crime and Punishment* and *The Raw Youth*; but in all the novels Dostoevsky came late and with intense anxiety to the intricate relationship among the author, the narrator, and the reader.

His solutions to this problem are as numerous as his novels. Sometimes they are relatively simple, as in *Crime and Punishment*, where he restricts his anonymous and almost invisible narrator's consciousness to what Raskolnikov saw and did and felt, except for very brief excursions into the minds of Svidrigailov and Razumikhin, whose careers form the chief alternatives to Raskolnikov's. Sometimes they are brilliantly intricate, as in the *Notes from*

Underground, where the first person narrator infuriates the reader with his rhetorical inconsistencies and emotional vacillation between extremes. Sometimes the intricacies get out of hand, leading to Dostoevsky's own dissatisfaction with *The Idiot.*[7] This last stage in the prehistory of *The Brothers Karamazov,* far more than the stages usually associated with personal inspiration, shows Dostoevsky at his most Russian and his most Dostoevskian: at this period in the history of the novel, as is well known, the Western Europeans had moved from the novel that tells what is happening to the novel that shows what is happening and were in the process of developing narrators whose consistency and integrity of identity (whether mad or sane, wise or foolish) would guarantee the verisimilitude of the account; but the Russians, with Gogol, Tolstoi, and Dostoevsky at their head, where exploring a new kind of novel, the manipulative novel, which may tell, and show, but which gains its power by carrying the reader through the same experiences that the characters are having. To achieve this goal, they were inventing a whole range of new narrative techniques. The emotional groundwork for the Grand Inquisitor passage had been in place in Dostoevsky's mind for years, but the real achievement as I have described it in these pages took shape as Dostoevsky labored on his plan and engaged his reader in the experience of being a Russian radical. As his wife's letter suggests, this last moment in the prehistory of the novel was painfully difficult for Dostoevsky because no tradition and no body of critical understanding existed to give names to the enterprise in which he was engaged.

At the end of *Crime and Punishment* and the beginning of *The Brothers Karamazov,* Dostoevsky mentions a sequel that would carry his story to its proper conclusion. The sequel to my book already exists. The community of scholars over several decades culminating in the *Pss* carry Dostoevsky's creative process from the point where I have left it, through his notes and drafts, to the text as he completed it. I have tried to amplify the work they have already done on the central moment of creation in such a way as to demystify that moment without diminishing the excitement that attaches to it.

NOTES

CHAPTER ONE

1. Harold Bloom, *A Map of Misreading* (New York: Oxford University Press, 1975), 9.

2. Michael Riffaterre, *The Semiotics of Poetry* (Bloomington: Indiana University Press, 1978), 115.

3. In V. L. Komarovich, *Die Urgestalt der Brueder Karamasoffs* (Munich: Piper, 1928), xiii.

4. Stanley Edgar Hyman, *The Tangled Bank* (New York: Atheneum, 1962), 313.

5. Plato, *Meno*, 85, trans. Paul Shorey (London: Loeb Classical Library, 1978), 317.

6. Brewster Ghiselin, ed., *The Creative Process, a Symposium* (New York: New American Library, 1963), 39.

7. George Steiner, *Tolstoi or Dostoevsky: An Essay in the Old Criticism* (New York: Alfred A. Knopf, 1959), 3.

8. Lucretius, *De rerum natura*, 5.8, trans. W. H. D. Rouse (London: Loeb Classical Library, 1965).

9. Homer, *Odyssey*, 8.487, trans. Robert Fitzgerald (Garden City, N.Y.: Doubleday-Anchor, 1961), 400.

10. N. K. Piksanov, ed., *Iz arkhiva Dostoevskogo, pis'ma russkikh pisatelei* (Moscow and Petrograd: Gosudarstvennoe Izdatel'stvo, 1923), 15–22.

11. Homer, *Odyssey*, 22.346.

12. Homer, *Iliad*, 6.128, trans. Richmond Lattimore (Chicago: University of Chicago Press, 1959).

13. John Milton, *Paradise Lost*, 1.16, in *Poetical Works* (London: Oxford University Press, 1946), 182.

14. Horace, *Carmina*, 3.1.2, in *The Odes and Epodes*, trans. C. E. Bennett (London: Loeb Classical Library, 1978), 169.

15. Blaise Pascal, *Pensées*, 65–66, in *Oeuvres complètes* (Paris: Gallimard, 1954), 1101. Unless otherwise stated, all translations into English are mine.

16. Gustave Lanson, "Le centenaire des Méditations," *Revue des deux mondes* 56 (1 Mar. 1920): 75–98; rpt. in Lanson, *Essais de méthode, de critique, et d'histoire littéraire* (Paris: Hachette, 1965), 425.

17. John Livingston Lowes, *The Road to Xanadu* (Boston and New York: Houghton Mifflin, 1927).

18. Donald Stauffer, "Genesis, or the Poet as Maker," in *Poets at Work*, ed. Charles D. Abbott (New York: Harcourt Brace, 1948), 41.

19. Matt. 5:18.

20. E. N. Opochinin, "Besedy c Dostoevskim," *Zven'ia* 6 (1936): 471.

21. Donald Fanger, *Dostoevsky and Romantic Realism* (Cambridge, Mass.: Harvard University Press, 1965).

22. Viktor V. Vinogradov, *Problema avtorstva i teoriia stilei* (Moscow: Gozlitizdat, 1961), 506.

23. 15 May 1869, in F. M. Dostoevskii, *Polnoe sobraniie sochinenii* (Leningrad: Nauka, 1972), vol. 29 (part 1), p. 39 (hereafter cited as *Pss*). Subsequent short references to this work are in the text.

24. *G-n. -bov i vopros ob iskusstve*, *Pss* 18:101.

25. 10 May 1879, in F. M. Dostoevskii, *Pis'ma*, 4:53, ed. A. S. Dolinin (Moscow: Gosudarstvennoe Izdatel'stvo, 1928–56) (hereafter cited as *Pis'ma*). Cf. also A. F. Koni, *Vospominaniia o pisateliakh* (Leningrad: Lenizdat, 1965), 230.

26. Leonid P. Grossman, *Seminarii po Dostoevskomu* (Moscow: Gosudarstvennoe Izdatel'stvo, 1922), 67.

CHAPTER TWO

1. Compton Mackenzie, *Literature in My Time* (Freeport, N.Y.: Books for Libraries Press, 1967), 185.

2. Henry James, *Letters*, ed. Percy Lubbock (New York: Octagon Books, 1970), 2:236.

3. Eugène-Melchior de Vogüé, *Le roman russe* (Paris: Plon, 1886), 203.

4. Ibid., 259.

5. Ibid., 267.

6. K. G. Seeley, "Dostoevsky and the French Criticism from the Beginning to 1960" (Ph.D. diss., Columbia University, 1960).

7. A. L. Bem, "Dostoevskii, genial'nyi chitatel'," in *O Dostoevskom, sbornik statei*, 3 vols., ed. Bem (Prague: F. Svoboda, 1929, 1933, 1936), 2:7–24.

8. 22 Feb. 1854, *Pss* 28, pt. 1: 172.

9. Grossman, *Seminarii po Dostoevskomu*, 7. G. M. Fridlender and L. P. Desiatkina have added more than two hundred books from a second

list and other sources: "Biblioteka Dostoevskogo (novye materialy)," in *Dostoevskii, materialy i issledovaniia*, ed. Fridlender et al., vol. 4 (Leningrad: Nauka, 1980).

10. Akademiia Nauk, Institut Istorii, *Delo Petrashevtsev* (Moscow and Leningrad: Izdatel'stvo Akademii Nauk SSSR, 1937), 2:558ff.

11. *Pss*, 27:111. For further lists see Vera Stepanovna Nechaeva, *Opisanie rukopisei F. M. Dostoevskogo* (Moscow: Biblioteka Imeni Lenina, 1957), 143–44.

12. Grossman, *Seminarii po Dostoevskomu*, 9.

13. Cf. Konrad Onasch, "Dostoevskij's Kinderglaube," *Canadian-American Slavic Studies* 3 (Fall 1978): 377–81.

14. Grossman, *Seminarii po Dostoevskomu*, 68.

15. Geir Kjetsaa had made these markings available to the scholarly community. See Kjetsaa, *Dostoevsky and His New Testament* (Atlantic Highlands, N.J.: Humanities Press, 1984).

16. 19 Dec. 1880, *Pis'ma*, 4:222.

17. 30 Apr. 1854, *Pss* 28, pt. 1: 170.

18. Grossman, *Seminarii po Dostoevskomu*, 43–45.

19. Valentina E. Vetlovskaia, "Ob odnom iz istochnikov *Brat'ev Karamazovykh*," in *Izvestiia Akademii Nauk*, seriia literatury i iazyka, vol. 40, 1981, 436–45.

20. Sergei Hakel, "Zosima's Discourse in *The Brothers Karamazov*," in *New Essays on Dostoevsky*, ed. Malcolm Jones and Garth Terry (Cambridge: Cambridge University Press, 1983), 145ff.; and Sven Linner, *Starets Zosima in "The Brothers Karamazov": A Study in the Mimesis of Virtue* (Stockholm: Almqvist & Wiksell, 1975), 57ff.

21. Zdenek V. David, "The Formation of the Religious and Social System of Vladimir S. Soloviev" (Ph.D. diss., Harvard University, 1960).

22. 1 Jan. 1840, *Pss* 27, pt. 1: 68–70.

23. 27 Mar. 1854, *Pss* 27, pt. 1: 179.

24. Leonid P. Grossman, "Dostoevskii i Evropa," in *Dostoevskij: Put', poetika, tvorchestvo* (Moscow: N. A. Stolliar, 1928), 151–213.

25. Ibid.; see also Ludmilla B. Turkevich, *Cervantes in Russia* (Princeton, N.J.: Princeton University Press, 1950).

26. Iurii D. Levin, "Dostoevskii i Shekspir," in *Dostoevskii, materialy i issledovaniia*, ed. Fridlender et al., vol. 1 (1974), 108–35; and K. I. Rovda, "Pod znakom realizma," in *Skekspir i russkaia kul'tura*, ed. M. P. Alekseev (Moscow: Nauka, 1965), 590ff.

27. William Brumfield, "Thérèse Philosophe and Dostoevsky," *Comparative Literature* 32 (1980): 238–52.

28. A. S. Dolinin, ed., *F. M. Dostoevskii v vospominaniiakh sovremennikov* (Moscow: Khudozhestvennaia Literatura, 1964), 195.

29. Leonid P. Grossman, "Russkii Kandid," *Vestnik Evropy* 5 (1914): 193–203.

30. Linner, *Starets Zosima*, 112–41.

31. For an outline of the polemic with Rousseau see Barbara Howard, "The Rhetoric of Confession: Dostoevskij's *Notes from Underground* and Rousseau's *Confessions*," *Slavic and East European Journal* 25 (1981): 16–32.

32. Dolinin, *Dostoevskii v vospominaniiakh*, 79–80.

33. M. P. Alekseev, "O vliianii na Dostoevskogo tvorchestva Shillera, Mol'era, Pushkina," in *Tvorchestvo Dostoevskogo, sbornik statei i materialov*, ed. Grossman (Odessa: Vseukrainskoe Gosudarstvennoe Izdatel'stvo, 1921), 41–62.

34. B. G. Reizov, "K istorii zamysla *Brat'ev Karamazovykh*," *Zven'ia* 6 (1936): 545–73; and Alexandra Lyngstad, *Dostoevskij and Schiller* (The Hague: Mouton, 1975).

35. A. L. Bem, "Slovar' lichnykh imen u Dostoevskogo," in *O Dostoevskom*, 2:1–81.

36. *Pis'ma*, 1, 466.

37. 18 Apr. 1880, *Pis'ma*, 4, 194.

38. Charles Passage, *Dostoevski the Adapter* (Chapel Hill, N.C.: University of North Carolina Press, 1954).

39. Robin Miller, "The Metaphysical Novel and the Evocation of Anxiety: *Melmoth the Wanderer* and *The Brothers Karamozov*," in *Russianness: Studies in Memory of Rufus Mathewson* (Ann Arbor, Mich.: Ardis, 1988), 94ff.

40. 31 July 1861, *Pss*, 28, pt. 2: 19.

41. Joan D. Grossman, *Edgar Allan Poe in Russia: A Study in Legend and Literary Influence* (Würzburg: Jal-Verlag, 1973); and Leon Burnett, "Dostoevsky, Poe, and the Discovery of Fantastic Realism," in *F. M. Dostoevsky (1821–1881): A Centenary Collection*, ed. Burnett (Oxford: Holdan Books, 1981).

42. Tsvetan Todorov, *The Fantastic*, trans. Richard Howard (Middletown, N.Y.: University Press Books, 1973).

43. A. L. Bem, "Dostoevskii, genial'nyi chitatel'," in *O Dostoevskom*, 2:14–19.

44. Ia. E. Golosovker, *Dostoevskii i Kant* (Moscow: Izdatel'stvo Akademii Nauk, 1963); G. Belzer, *Hegel en Dostoievsky* (Leiden: E. J. Brill, 1953).

45. Leonid P. Grossman, "Dostoevskii i Bakunin," in *Dostoevskij: Put', poetika, tvorchestvo* (1928).

46. Alexander Vucinich, *Darwin in Russian Thought* (Berkeley and Los Angeles: University of California Press, 1988).

47. Fanger, *Dostoevsky and Romantic Realism.*

48. Nikolai Gogol, *Polnoe sobraniie sochinenii* (Leningrad: Izdatel'stvo Akademii Nauk, 1951), 6:20.

49. S. A. Reiser, "K istorii formuly 'Vse my vyshli iz gogolevskoi 'Shineli,'" in *Poetika i stilistika russkoi literatury: Pamiati Akademika Viktora Vladimirovicha Vinogradova*, ed. M. P. Alekseev (Leningrad: Nauka, 1971), 187–88.

50. I. M. Katarskii, *Dikkens v Rossii* (Moscow: Nauka, 1966), 361ff.

51. 17 Apr. 1877; *Pss* 29, pt. 2: 151–52.

52. 15 July 1876; *Pss* 29, pt. 2: 100.

53. Reisov, "K istorii zamysla *Brat'ev Karamazovykh.*"

54. Emile Zola, *Les Rougon-Macquart*, vol. 1 (Paris: Gallimard, 1960), 41.

55. Reizov, "K istorii zamysla *Brat'ev Karamozovykh.*" E. H. Kiiko reviews much of the more recent work on Sand and Dostoevsky in "Dostoevskii i Zhorzh Sand," *Acta Litteraria Academiae Scientiarum Hungaricae* 24 (1982): 65–85.

56. June 1876, 1.2, *Pss* 23:33–36.

57. Regis Messac, "Bulwer-Lytton et Dostoievski: De Paul Clifford à Raskolnikof," *Revue de littérature comparée* 4 (1926): 638–53.

58. July–Aug. 1877, 2, 3, *Pss* 25:200.

59. D. S. Merezhkovskii, *Tolstoi i Dostoevskii* (St. Petersburg, 1901). Sergei Belov's bibliography lists over two hundred items involving Tolstoi and Dostoevsky between 1917 and 1965, within the Soviet Union: *F. M. Dostoevskii, bibliografiia proizvedenii F. M. Dostoevskogo i literatury o nem, 1917–1965* (Moscow: Kniga, 1968), 400.

60. A. N. Batiuto, "Idei i obrazy," *Russkaia literatura* 1 (1982): 76–96.

61. Nathalie Babel Brown, *Hugo and Dostoevsky* (Ann Arbor, Mich.: Ardis, 1978), 69–101.

62. Dec. 1877, *Pss* 26:111.

63. V. A. Kotel'nikov, "Dostoevskii i Ivan Kireevskii," *Russkaia literatura* 4 (1981): 57–76.

64. Charles Moser, *Antinihilism in the Russian Novel of the 1800s* (The Hague: Mouton, 1964).

65. Grossman, "Dostoevskii i Evropa"; and Malcolm Jones, "Dostoevsky and Europe: Travels in the Mind," *Renaissance and Modern Studies* 24 (1980): 38–57.

CHAPTER THREE

1. Komarovich, *Die Urgestalt der Brueder Karamasoffs*; A. S. Dolinin, F. M. *Dostoevskii, materialy i issledovaniia* (Leningrad: Akademiia Nauk SSSR, 1928); *Pss*, 15.

2. V. L. Komarovich, "Fel'etony Dostoevskogo," in *Fel'etony sorokovykh godov*, ed. Iu. G. Oksman (Moscow: "Akademia," 1930), 112.

3. F. M. Dostoevsky, *Materialy i issledovaniia*, ed. A. S. Dolinin (Leningrad: Izdatel'stvo Akademii Nauk, 1935), 16.

4. E.g., 7 Jan. 1876, *Pss* 29:71; 10 Mar. 1876, *Pss* 29:76.

5. Grossman, "Russkii Kandid."

6. Gary Saul Morson describes the relation between these elements in *The Boundaries of Genre: Dostoevsky's "Diary of a Writer" and the Traditions of Literary Utopia* (Austin: University of Texas Press, 1981; rpt. Evanston, Ill.: Northwestern University Press, 1988).

7. Dostoevsky, *Materialy*, ed. Dolinin, 14.

8. *Pis'ma*, 4:7.

9. *Pis'ma*, 4:118.

10. *Pis'ma*, 4:212.

CHAPTER FOUR

1. Reizov, "K istorii zamysla *Brat'ev Karamazovykh*," 552ff.

2. *Pss* 4:284, quoting TsGBIA, Fond 801, opisanie 79/20, #37, 1–37.

3. The dispute about what happened to Mikhail Dostoevsky continues. The only sure facts seem to be that he died suddenly on his country estate and that the family revealed no other information. This silence has been taken to suggest that if it was homicide, it was justifiable homicide, an argument supported by Mikhail's drinking, his temper, and the subjection of peasant women to their master. Joseph Frank argues that there was less to the issue in fact than meets the eye, although Dostoevsky probably believed in the murder, with all its psychological implications. See Frank, *Dostoevsky: The Seeds of Revolt* (Princeton, N.J.: Princeton University Press, 1976), 85–88.

4. P. K. Marti'ianov, "Na perelome veka," *Istoricheskii vestnik* 11 (1895): 450.

5. TsGBIA, Fond 801, opisaniie 79/20, #37, unnumbered pages, 2 Aug. 1844, Question 7.

6. I will not study quotation at length because Nina Perlina has written an excellent book covering Dostoevsky's uses of quotation, misquotation,

reference, and other kinds of intertextuality in *The Brothers Karamazov: Varieties of Poetic Utterance* (Lanham, Md.: University Press of America, 1985).

7. Komarovich, *Die Urgestalt der Brueder Karamasoffs*, 167ff.; George Sand, *Mauprat* (Paris, 1883), 58–75.

CHAPTER FIVE

1. Denis Diderot, "Entretien avec d'Alembert," in *Oeuvres* (Paris: Bibliothêque de la Pléiade, 1951), 879.

2. Hippolyte Taine, "Cerebral Vibrations and Thought," *Journal of Mental Science* 101 (April 1877): 879; trans. from *Revue philosophique de la France et de l'étranger*.

3. 10 Aug. 1880, *Pis'ma*, 190.

4. Jules Liegeois, *De la suggestion et du somnambulisme* (Paris: O. Doin, 1899), 89.

5. Karl Ludwig Von Reichenbach, *Der sensitive Mensch*, vol. 2 (Stuttgart: Cotta, 1855), 593–94.

6. Hippolyte Bernheim, *Automatisme et suggestion* (Paris: Alcan, 1917), 61.

7. 27 Mar. 1878, *Pis'ma*, 4:14.

8. Vsevolod Solov'ev, *Vospominaniia o Dostoevskom* (St. Petersburg, 1881), 10; cited in *Literaturnoe nasledstvo* 83:357.

9. 24 Mar. 1878, *Pis'ma*, 4:10.

CHAPTER SIX

1. S. V. Kovalevskaia, *Vospominaniia i pis'ma* (Moscow: Izdatel'stvo Adakemii Nauk SSSR, 1961), 96.

2. *Epokha* 9 (Sept. 1864): 26.

3. Ibid., 13, 21.

4. E. N. Konshina, *Zapisnye tetradi F. M. Dostoevskogo* (Moscow and Leningrad: Akademiia, 1935), 47; and L. M. Rozenblium, "F. M. Dostoevskii v rabote nad romanom *Podrostok*," *Literaturnoe nasledstvo* 58 (1965): 59.

5. Grossman, *Seminarii po Dostoevskomu*, 22.

6. S. T. Aksakov, *Sobranie sochinenii*, 4 vols. (Moscow: Gosizdat, Khudozhestvennaia Literatura, 1955–56), 2:36–37.

7. Ibid., 1:127.

8. S. N. Durylin, "Ob odnom simvole u Dostoevskogo," in Gosudarstvennaia Akademiia Nauk, *Dostoevskii, sbornik statei* (Moscow, 1928),

163–99; and V. L. Komarovich, "Mirovaia garmoniia Dostoevskogo," *Atenei* 1–2 (1924): 112–42.

9. Passage, *Dostoevsky the Adapter*, 178.

10. E. T. A. Hoffmann, *The Devil's Elixirs*, trans. Ronald Taylor (London: Calder, 1963), 4–10.

11. *Epokha 9* (Sept. 1864): 7.

12. Lucretius, *De rerum natura*, 1.150; William Shakespeare, *King Lear*, 1.1.90; Lowes, *Road to Xanadu*.

13. *Pis'ma*, 3:225.

14. Vladimir Mikhailov, letter to Dostoevsky, 2 Apr. 1878, 13. The manuscript is in the Lenin Library, Fond 93, II, 6/102.

15. Grossman, *Seminarii po Dostoevskomu*, 66.

CHAPTER SEVEN

1. Victor Hugo, *Notre-Dame de Paris* (Paris: Imprimerie Nationale, 1904), 12, 55, 161, 369ff, 153.

2. Perlina, *Varieties of Poetic Utterance*, 117ff.

3. Plato, *The Republic*, trans. Paul Shorey (London: Loeb Classical Library, 1978), 1:344E. Further references to *The Republic* are in the text.

4. I. I. Lapshin, "Kak slozhilas' Legenda o Velikom Inkvizitore," in *O Dostoevskom*, ed. Bem, 1:129ff.

5. Emil Drougard, "La Legende du Grand Inquisiteur et Le Christ au Vatican," *Revue des études slaves* 14 (1934): 224.

6. Joseph Frank, "The Genesis of *Crime and Punishment*," in *Russianness: Studies in Memory of Rufus Mathewson* (Ann Arbor, Mich.: Ardis, 1988): 124–43.

7. V. L. Komarovich, "Iunost' Dostoevskogo," *Byloe* 28 (1924): 3–43, and "Mirovaia garmoniia Dostoevskogo," both rpt. in Donald Fanger, ed., *O Dostoevskom, stat'i* (Providence, R.I.: Brown University Press, 1966).

8. A. S. Dolinin, *Poslednie romany Dostoevskogo . . .* (Moscow: Sovetskii Pisatel', 1963); and Elena N. Dryzhakova, "Dostoevskii i Gertsen," in *Dostoevskii, materialy i issledovaniia*, ed. Fridlender et al., 1:219–39.

9. A. Ivanov, "O traditsionnoi oshibke v otsenke vstrech Dostoevskogo s Gertsenom," *Novyi zhurnal* 141 (Dec. 1980): 234–52.

10. The best description of the tone of this journalism, and Dostoevsky's place in it, may be in V. S. Dorovatovskaia-Liubimova, "Dostoevskii i shestidesiatniki," in Gosudarstvennaia Akademiia Nauk, *Dostoevskii, sbornik statei*, 5–61.

CHAPTER EIGHT

1. D. H. Lawrence, "Introduction" to *The Grand Inquisitor*, trans. S. S. Koteliansky (London: Elkin Matthews & Marrot, 1930), iv.

2. 10 May 1879, *Pis'ma*, 53.

3. E.g., D. H. Lawrence, *Selected Literary Criticism*, ed. Anthony Beal (New York: Viking, 1956), 189.

4. Valentina Vetlovskaia, "Ritorika i poetika," in *Issledovaniia po poesii i stilistike* (Leningrad: Nauka, 1972), 163–84.

5. Maximilian Rudwin, *The Devil in Legend and Literature* (Chicago: Open Court, 1931), 15ff.

6. Dmitrii V. Averkiev, a passage from *Likho*, in *Ogonek* 5 (1880): 97.

7. D. S. Likhachev, "Predislovnyi rasskaz Dostoevskogo," in *Poetika i stilistika russkoi literatury*, ed. M. P. Alekseev (Leningrad: Nauka, 1971).

8. L. M. Rozenblium, "Tvorcheskaia laboratoriia Dostoevskogo romanista," *Literaturnoe nasledstvo* 77 (1965): 39ff.

9. S. S. Borshchevskii, *Shchedrin i Dostoevskii, istoriia ikh ideinoi bor'by* (Moscow: Gosudarstvennoe Izdatel'stvo Khudozhestvennoi Literatury, 1956).

10. Dorovatovskaia-Liubimova, "Dostoevskii i shestidesiatniki."

11. Nikolai Leskov, *Polnoe sobranie sochinenii*, vol. 3 (Moscow: Gosizdat Khudozhostvennoi Literatury, 1957), 363.

12. Letter from Ballin to Dostoevsky, 19 Dec. 1876. In Institut Russkoi Literatury (Pushkinskii Dom, Leningrad), Fond 100, 24693, CCXI b 2.

13. G. I. Chulkov, *Kak rabotal Dostoevskii* (Moscow: Sovetskii Pisatel', 1939).

14. Dolinin, *Poslednie romany Dostoevskogo*, 26.

15. Stanley Fish, *Surprised by Sin* (New York: St. Martin's Press, 1967).

CHAPTER NINE

1. Gregory W. Jones, "Tests of a Structural Theory of the Memory Trace," *British Journal of Psychology* 69 (1978): 351–67.

2. Gordon H. Bower, "Organizational Factors in Memory," *Cognitive Psychology* 1 (1970): 18–46.

3. David E. Rumelhart et al., *Parallel Distributed Processing* (Cambridge, Mass.: MIT Press, 1987): Laird Cermak and Fergus Craik, *Levels of Processing in Human Memory* (New York: Wiley, 1979); John R. Anderson, *The Architecture of Cognition* (Cambridge, Mass.: Harvard University Press, 1983).

4. Wolfgang Koehler, *Gestalt Psychology* (New York: Liveright, 1934).

5. Gordon H. Bower et al., "Scripts in Memory for Text," *Cognitive Psychology* 11 (1979): 177–220.

6. S. V. Belov and V. A. Tunimanov, *F. M. Dostoevskii, A. G. Dostoevskaia, Perepiska* (Leningrad: Nauka, 1976), 111.

7. Robin Miller, *Dostoevsky and "The Idiot": Author, Narrator, and Reader* (Cambridge, Mass.: Harvard University Press, 1981).

BIBLIOGRAPHY

An exhaustive bibliography of Dostoevsky's creative process would demand a book in itself, but a list of the chief bibliographies and the chief collections of scholarly articles that I consulted, followed by a list of the materials I actually cite, will offer a good starting point for research in this area.

BIBLIOGRAPHIES (IN CHRONOLOGICAL ORDER)

Dostoevskaia, Anna Grigorievna. *Muzei Pamiati F. M. Dostoevskogo*. St. Petersburg: Pantaleeva, 1906.

Sokolov, N. A. *Materialy dlia bibliografii F. M. Dostoevskogo*. In *Dostoevskii, stat'i i materialy*, ed. Dolinin, vol. 2.

Tomashevskii, Boris. "Bibliografiia." In *F. M. Dostoevskii, Polnoe sobranie sochinenii*, vol. 13. Moscow: Gosudarstvennnoe Izdatel'stvo, 1929.

Belov, Sergei. *F. M. Dostoevskii, bibliografiia proizvedenii F. M. Dostoevskogo i literatury o nem, 1917–1965*. Moscow: Kniga, 1968.

——— . *1966–69* in *Dostoevskii i ego vremia*, ed. G. M. Fridlender et al. Leningrad: Nauka, 1971.

——— . *1969–74* in *Dostoevskii, materialy i issledovaniia*, ed. Fridlender et al., vol. 1.

Dostoevskii Studies and its predecessor, *The Bulletin of the International Dostoevskii Society*, have published an annual Dostoevsky bibliography since 1970.

COLLECTIONS (IN CHRONOLOGICAL ORDER)

Miller, Orest, ed., *F. M. Dostoevskii, Polnoe sobraniie sochinenii*. Vol. 1. St. Petersburg: Suvorin, 1883.

Zelinskii, Vasilii Apollonovich, ed. *Kriticheskii komentarii k sochineniiam F. M. Dostoevskogo, sbornik statei*. 4 vols. 4th ed. Moscow: Balandin, 1901–6.

Zamotin, I. I., ed. *F. M. Dostoevskii v russkoi kritike*. Warsaw: Tipografiia Okruzhnogo Shtaba, 1913.

BIBLIOGRAPHY

Grossman, Leonid P., ed., *Biblioteka Dostoevskogo*. Odessa: Ivasenko, 1919.

———, ed. *Tvorchestvo Dostoevskogo, sbornik statei i materialov*. Odessa: Vseukrainskoe Gosudarstvennoe Izdatel'stvo, 1921.

Russkoe Bibliologicheskoe Obshchestvo. *Dostoevskii, odnodnevnaia gazeta*, Petrograd, 30 Oct. (12 Nov.) 1921.

Dolinin, Arkadii Semenovich [A. S. Iskoz], ed. *Dostoevskii, stat'i i materialy*. 2 vols. Petrograd: Mysl', 1922, 1925.

Grossman, Leonid P. *Seminarii po Dostoevskomu*. Moscow and Petrograd: Gosudarstvennoe Izdatel'stvo, 1922.

Brodskii, N. L., ed. *Tvorcheskii put' Dostoevskogo, sbornik statei*. Leningrad: Seiatel', 1924.

Komarovich, Vasilii Leonidovich, ed. *Die Urgestalt der Brueder Karamasoffs*. Munich: Piper Verlag, 1928.

Gosudarstvennaia Akademiia Nauk, Literaturnaia Sektsiia, 4. *Dostoevskii, sbornik statei*. Moscow: Trudy, Gosudarstvennaia Akademiia Nauk, 1928.

Bem, Alfred Ludvigovich, ed. *O Dostoevskom, sbornik statei*. 3 vols. Prague: F. Svoboda, 1929, 1933, 1936.

———, ed. *Psikhoanaliticheskiie etiudi*. Prague: Petropolis, 1938.

Dolinin, A. S., ed. *F. M. Dostoevskii, materialy i issledovaniia*. Leningrad: Akademiia Nauk SSSR, 1935.

Zven'ia 6 (1936): 413–600.

Modern Fiction Studies 4, no. 3 (Autumn 1958).

Stepanov, N. L., et al., ed. *Tvorchestvo F. M. Dostoevskogo*. Moscow: Izdatel'stvo Akademii Nauk SSSR, 1959.

Wellek, René, ed. *Dostoevsky*. New York: Twentieth Century Views, 1961.

Wasiolek, Edward, ed. *"Crime and Punishment" and the Critics*. San Francisco: Wadsworth, 1961.

Literaturnoe Rasledstvo 77, 83, 86 (1965, 1971, 1973).

Canadian-American Slavic Studies 6, 8, 12, 17 (1970–78).

Fridlender, Georgii Mikhailovich, et al., eds. *Dostoevskii, materialy i issledovaniia*. Vols. 1–. Leningrad: Nauka, 1974–.

Rice, Martin, and Rudolf Neuheuser, eds. *Bulletin of the International Dostoevsky Society*. After 1978, *Dostoevsky Studies*.

Burnett, Leon, ed. *Dostoevsky (1821–1881): A Centenary Collection*. Oxford: Holdan Books, 1981.

Kauchtschischwili, Nina, ed. *Actualité de Dostoevskij*. Bergamo: La Quercia, 1982.

Jones, Malcolm V., and Garth M. Terry, eds. *New Essays on Dostoevsky*. Cambridge: Cambridge University Press, 1983.

Jackson, Robert Louis, ed. *Dostoevsky: New Perspectives*. Englewood Cliffs, N.J.: Prentice-Hall, 1984.

Miller, Robin Feuer, ed. *Critical Essays on Dostoevsky*. Boston: G. K. Hall, 1986.

ADDITIONAL WORKS

Akademiia Nauk, Institut Istorii. *Delo Petrashevtsev*. Moscow and Leningrad: Izdatel'stvo Akademii Nauk SSSR, 1937–51.

Aksakov, Sergei Timofeevich. *Sobranie sochinenii*. 4 vols. Moscow: Gosizdat, Khudozhestvennaia Literatura, 1955–56.

Alekseev, Mikhail Pavlovich. "O vliianii na Dostoevskogo tvorchestva Schillera, Mol'era, Pushkina." In *Tvorchestvo Dostoevskogo*, edited by Grossman, 41–62.

Anderson, John R. *The Architecture of Cognition*. Cambridge, Mass.: Harvard University Press, 1983.

Averkiev, Dmitrii V. *Likho*. Ogonek 5 (1880).

Batiuto, A. N. "Idei i obrazy." *Russkaia literatura* 1 (1982): 76–96.

Belov, Sergei Vladimirovich, and Vladimir Artemovich Tunimanov. *F. M. Dostoevskii, A. G. Dostoevskaia, Perepiska*. Leningrad: Nauka, 1976.

Belzer, G. *Hegel en Dostoievsky*. Leiden: E. J. Brill, 1953.

Bem, Alfred Liudvigovich. "Dostoevskii genial'nyi chitatel'." In *O Dostoevskom*, edited by Bem, 2:14–19.

———. "Slovar' lichnykh imen u Dostoevskogo." In *O Dostoevskom*, edited by Bem, 2:1–81.

Bernheim, Hippolyte. *Automatisme et suggestion*. Paris: Alcan, 1917.

Bloom, Harold. *A Map of Misreading*. New York: Oxford University Press, 1975.

Borshchevskii, Solomon Samoilovich. *Shchedrin i Dostoevskii, istoriia ikh ideinoi bor'by*. Moscow: Gosudarstvennoe Izdatel'stvo Khudozhesvennoi Literatury, 1956.

Bower, Gordon H. "Organizational Factors in Memory." *Cognitive Psychology* 1 (1970): 18–46.

———, et al. "Scripts in Memory for Text." *Cognitive Psychology* 11 (1979): 177–220.

Brown, Nathalie Babel. *Hugo and Dostoevsky*. Ann Arbor, Mich.: Ardis, 1978.

Brumfield, William. "Térèse Philosophe and Dostoevsky." *Comparative Literature* 32 (1980): 238–52.

Burnett, Leon. "Dostoevsky, Poe, and the Discovery of Fantastic Realism." In *F. M. Dostoevsky (1821–1881): A Centenary Collection*, edited by Burnett. Oxford: Holdan Books, 1981.

Cermak, Laird, and Fergus Craik. *Levels of Processing in Human Memory.* New York: Wiley, 1979.

Chulkov, Georgii Ivanovich. *Kak rabotal Dostoevskii.* Moscow: Sovetskii Pisatel', 1939.

David, Zdenek V. "The Formation of the Religious and Social System of Vladimir S. Soloviev." Ph.D. diss., Harvard University, 1960.

de Vogüé, Eugène-Melchior. *Le roman russe.* Paris: Plon, 1886.

Diderot, Denis. "Entretien avec d'Alembert." In *Oeuvres.* Paris: Bibliotêque de la Pléiade, 1951.

Dolinin, Arkadii Semenovich [A. S. Iskoz], ed. *F. M. Dostoevskii v vospominaniiakh sovremennikov.* Moscow: Khudozhestvennaia Literatura, 1964.

———. *Poslednie romany Dostoevskogo, kak sozdavalis' "Podrostok" i "Brat'ia Karamazovy."* Moscow and Leningrad: Sovetskii Pisatel', 1963.

Dorovatovskaia-Liubimova, V. S. "Dostoevskii i shestidesiatniki." In Gosudarstvennaia Akademiia Nauk, *Dostoevskii, sbornik statei.*

Dostoevskii, Fedor M. *Materialy i issledovaniia.* Edited by A. S. Dolinin. Leningrad: Izdatel'stvo Akademii Nauk, 1935.

———. *Pis'ma.* Edited by A. S. Dolinin. Moscow: Gosudarstvennoe Izdatel'stvo, 1928–56.

———. *Polnoe sobraniie sochinenii.* Edited by G. M. Fridlender et al. Leningrad: Nauka, 1972–.

Drougard, Emil. "La Legende du Grand Inquisiteur et Le Christ au Vatican." *Revue des études slaves* 14 (1934): 224–25.

Dryzhakova, Elena N. "Dostoevskii i Gertsen." In *Dostoevskii, materialy i issledovaniia*, edited by Fridlender et al., 1:219–39.

Durylin, Sergei Nikolaevich. "Ob odnom simvole u Dostoevskogo." In Gosudarstvennaia Akademiia Nauk, *Dostoevskii, sbornik statei*, 1963–99.

Fanger, Donald. *Dostoevsky and Romantic Realism.* Cambridge, Mass.: Harvard University Press, 1965.

———, ed. *O Dostoevskom, stat'i.* Providence, R.I.: Brown University Press, 1966.

Fish, Stanley. *Surprised by Sin.* New York: St. Martin's Press, 1967.

Frank, Joseph. *Dostoevsky: The Seeds of Revolt.* Princeton, N.J.: Princeton University Press, 1976.

———. "The Genesis of *Crime and Punishment.*" In *Russianness: Studies in Memory of Rufus Mathewson.* Ann Arbor, Mich.: Ardis, 1988.

Fridlender, G. M., and L. P. Desiatkina, "Biblioteka Dostoevskogo (novye materialy)." In *Dostoevskii, materialy i issledovaniia*, ed. Fridlender et al.

Ghiselin, Brewster, ed. *The Creative Process, a Symposium.* New York: New American Library, 1963.

Gogol, Nikolai. *Polnoe sobraniie sochinenii.* Leningrad: Izdatel'stvo Akademii Nauk, 1951.

Golosovker, Iakov Emmanuilovich. *Dostoevskii i Kant.* Moscow: Izdatel'stvo Akademii Nauk, 1963.

Grossman, Joan D. *Edgar Allen Poe in Russia: A Study in Legend and Literary Influence.* Würzburg: Jal-Verlag, 1973.

Grossman, Leonid P. "Dostoevskii i Bakunin." In *Dostoevskii: Put', poetika, tvorchestvo.* Moscow: N. A. Stolliar, 1928.

———. "Dostoevskii i Evropa." In *Dostoevskij: Put', poetika, tvorchestvo,* 151–213. Moscow: N. A. Stolliar, 1928.

———. *Poetika Dostoevskogo.* Istoriia i Teoriia Iskusstv, 4. Moscow: Gosudarstvennaia Akademiia Khodozhestvennykh Nauk, 1925.

———. "Russkii Kandid." *Vestnik Evropy* 5 (1914): 193–203.

Hakel, Sergei. "Zosima's Discourse in *The Brothers Karamazov."* In *New Essays on Dostoevsky,* edited by Jones and Terry.

Hoffmann, E. T. A. *The Devil's Elixirs.* Translated by Ronald Taylor. London: Calder, 1963.

Homer. *Iliad.* Translated by Richmond Lattimore. Chicago: University of Chicago Press, 1959.

———. *Odyssey.* Translated by Robert Fitzgerald. Garden City, N.Y.: Doubleday, 1961.

Horace. *The Odes and Epodes.* Translated by C. E. Bennett. London: Loeb Classical Library, 1978.

Howard, Barbara. "The Rhetoric of Confession: Dostoevskij's *Notes from Underground* and Rousseau's *Confessions." Slavic and East European Journal* 25 (1981): 16–32.

Hugo, Victor. *Notre-Dame de Paris.* Paris: Imprimerie Nationale, 1904.

Hyman, Stanley Edgar. *The Tangled Bank.* New York: Atheneum, 1962.

Ivanov, A. "O traditsionnoi oshibke v otsenke vstrech Dostoevskogo c Gertsenom." *Novyi zhurnal* 141 (Dec. 1980): 234–52.

James, Henry. *Letters.* Edited by Percy Lubbock. New York: Octagon Books, 1970.

Jones, Gregory W. "Tests of a Structural Theory of the Memory Trace." *British Journal of Psychology* 69 (1978): 351–67.

Jones, Malcolm V. "Dostoevsky and Europe: Travels in the Mind." *Renaissance and Modern Studies* 24 (1980): 38–57.

Katarskii, Igor' Maksimilianovich. *Dikkens v Rossii.* Moscow: Nauka, 1966.

Kiiko, E. H. "Dostoevskii i Zhorzh Sand." *Acta Litteraria Academiae Scientiarum Hungaricae* 24 (1982): 65–85.

Kirai [Kiraly] D. [Julia]. "Raskolnikov i Gamlet." In *Problemy poetiki russkogo realizma XIX veka.* Leningrad: Izdatel'stvo Leningradskogo Universiteta, 1984.

Kirpichnikov, Alexsandr Ivanovich. *Dostoevskii i Pisemskii.* Odessa: Shtab Odesskogo Voennogo Okruga, 1894.

Kirpotkin, Valerii IAkovlevich. *Dostoevskii i Belinskii.* Moscow: Sovetskii Pisatel', 1960.

Kjetsaa, Geir. *Dostoevsky and His New Testament.* Atlantic Highlands, N.J.: Humanities Press, 1984.

Koehler, Wolfgang. *Gestalt Psychology.* New York: Liveright, 1934.

Komarovich, Vasilii Leonidovich. *Dostoevskii.* Leningrad: Obrazovanie, 1925.

———. "Fel'etony Dostoevskogo." In *Fel'etony sorokovykh godov,* edited by Iu. G. Oksman. Moscow: "Akademia," 1930.

———. "Inost' Dostoevskogo." *Byloe* 28 (1924): 3–43.

———. "Mirovaia garmoniia Dostoevskogo." *Atenei* 1–2 (1924): 112–42.

———. *Die Urgestalt der Brueder Karamasoffs.* Munich: Piper, 1928.

Koni, Anatolii Fedorovich. *Vospominaniia o pisateliakh.* Leningrad: Lenizdat, 1965.

Konshina, E. N. *Zapisnye tetradi F. M. Dostoevskogo.* Moscow and Leningrad: Akademiia, 1935.

Kotel'nikov, V. A. "Dostoevskii i Ivan Kireevskii." *Russkaia literatura* 4 (1981): 57–76.

Kovalevskaia, Sofia Vasilevna. *Vospominaniia i pis'ma.* Moscow: Izdatel'stvo Akademii Nauk SSSR, 1961.

Lanson, Gustave. *Essais de méthode, de critique, and d'histoire littéraire.* Paris: Hachette, 1965.

Lapshin, Ivan Ivanovich. "Estetika Dostoevskogo." In *Dostoevskii, stat'i i materialy,* edited by Dolinin, 1:95–152.

———. "Kak slozhilas' Legenda o Velikom Inkvizitore." In *O Dostoevskom,* edited by Bem, vol. 1.

Lawrence, D. H. "Introduction" to *The Grand Inquisitor,* trans. S. S. Koteliansky. London: Elkin Matthews & Marrot, 1930.

———. *Selected Literary Criticism.* Edited by Anthony Beal. New York: Viking, 1956.

Leskov, Nikolai. *Polnoe sobranie sochinenii.* Vol. 3. Moscow: Gosizdat Khudozhestvennoi Literatury, 1957.

Levin, Iurii D. "Dostoevskii i Shekspir." In *Dostoevskii, materialy i issledovaniia,* edited by Fridlender et al., 1:108–35.

Liegeois, Jules. *De la suggestion et du somnambulisme.* Paris: O. Doin, 1899.

Likhachev, Dmitrii Sergeevich. "Predislovnyi rasskaz Dostoevskogo." In *Poetika i stilistika russkoi literatury: Pamiati Akademika Viktora Vladimirovich Vinogradova,* edited by M. P. Alekseev. Leningrad: Nauka, 1971.

Linner, Sven. *Starets Zosima in "The Brothers Karamozov": A Study in the Mimesis of Virtue.* Stockholm: Almqvist & Wiksell, 1975.

Lowes, John Livingston. *The Road to Xanadu.* Boston and New York: Houghton Mifflin, 1927.

Lucretius. *De rerum natura.* Translated by W. H. D. Rouse. London: Loeb Classical Library, 1965.

Lyngstad, Alexandra. *Dostoevskij and Schiller.* The Hague: Mouton, 1975.

MacKenzie, Compton. *Literature in My Time.* Freeport, N.Y.: Books for Libraries Press, 1967.

MacPike, Loralee. "Dickens and Dostoevsky: The Technique of Reverse Influence." In *The Changing World of Charles Dickens,* edited by Robert Giddings. Totowa, N.J.: Vision; Barnes & Noble, 1983.

———. *Dostoevsky's Dickens.* Totowa, N.J.: Barnes & Noble, 1981.

Markovitch, Milan. "La volonté de puissance chez Balzac et Dostoievski." In *Festgabe für Paul Diels,* edited by Erwin Koschmieder and Alois Schmaus, 252–59. Munich: Isar Verlag, 1953.

Mart'ianov, P. K. "Na perelome veka." *Istoricheskii vestnik* 11 (1895): 450.

Merezhkovskii, Dmitrii Sergeevich. *Tolstoi i Dostoevskii.* St. Petersburg, 1901.

Messac, Regis. "Bulwer-Lytton et Dostoievski: De Paul Clifford à Raskolnikof." *Revue de littérature comparée* 4 (1926): 638–53.

Miller, Robin. *Dostoevsky and "The Idiot": Author, Narrator, and Reader.* Cambridge, Mass.: Harvard University Press, 1981.

———. "The Metaphysical Novel and the Evocation of Anxiety: *Melmoth the Wanderer* and *The Brothers Karamazov.*" In *Russianness: Studies in Memory of Rufus Mathewson.* Ann Arbor, Mich.: Ardis, 1988.

Milton, John. *Poetical Works.* London: Oxford University Press, 1946.

Morson, Gary Saul. *The Boundaries of Genre: Dostoevsky's "Diary of a Writer" and the Traditions of Literary Utopia.* Austin: University of Texas Press, 1981. Reprint. Evanston, Ill.: Northwestern University Press, 1988.

Moser, Charles. *Antinihilism in the Russian Novel of the 1880s.* The Hague: Mouton, 1964.

Nechaeva, Vera Stepanovna. *Opisaniie rukopisei F. M. Dostoevskogo.* Moscow: Biblioteka Imeni Lenina, 1957.

Onasch, Konrad. "Dostoevskij's Kinderglaube." *Canadian-American Slavic Studies* 3 (Fall 1978): 377–81.

Opochinin, E. N. "Besedy c Dostoevskim." *Zven'ia* 6 (1936): 457–84.

Pascal, Blaise. *Oeuvres complètes*. Paris: Gallimard, 1954.

Passage, Charles. *Dostoevski the Adapter*. Chapel Hill: University of North Carolina Press, 1954.

Perlina, Nina. *The Brothers Karamazov: Varieties of Poetic Utterance*. Lanham, Md.: University Press of America, 1985.

Piksanov, Nikolai Kiriakovich, ed. *Iz arkhiva Dostoevskogo, pis'ma russkikh pisatelei*. Moscow and Petrograd: Gosudarstvennoe Izdatel'stvo, 1923.

Plato. *Meno*. Translated by Paul Shorey. London: Loeb Classical Library, 1978.

Plato. *The Republic*. Translated by Paul Shorey. London: Loeb Classical Library, 1978.

Reiser, Solomon Abramovich. "K istorii formuly 'Vse my vyshli iz gogolevskoi 'Shineli.'" In *Poetika i stilistika russkoi literatury: Pamiati Akademika Viktora Vladimirovicha Vinogradova*, edited by M. P. Alekseev, 187–88. Leningrad: Nauka, 1971.

Reizov, Boris Georgievich. "K istorii zamysla *Brat'ev Karamazovykh*." *Zven'ia* 6 (1936): 545–73. Reprinted in *Iz istorii evropeiskikh literatur*, 129–38. Leningrad: Izdatel'stvo Leningradskogo Universiteta, 1970.

Riffaterre, Michael. *The Semiotics of Poetry*. Bloomington: Indiana University Press, 1978.

Rovda, K. I. "Pod znakom realizma." In *Shekspir i russkaia kul'tura*, edited by M. P. Alekseev. Moscow: Nauka, 1965.

Rozenblium, Lia Mikhailovna. "F. M. Dostoevskii v rabote nad romanom *Podrostok*," *Literaturnoe nasledstvo* 58 (1965): 59.

———. "Tvorcheskaia laboratoriia Dostoevskogo romanista." *Literaturnoe nasledstvo* 77 (1965): 7–56.

———. *Tvorcheskie dnevniki Dostoevskogo*. Moscow: Nauka, 1981.

Rudwin, Maximilian. *The Devil in Legend and Literature*. Chicago: Open Court, 1931.

Rumelhart, David E., et al. *Parallel Distributed Processing*. Cambridge, Mass: MIT Press, 1987.

Sand, George. *Mauprat*. Paris, 1983.

Seeley, K. G. "Dostoevsky and the French Criticism from the Beginning to 1960." Ph.D. diss., Columbia University, 1960.

Solov'ev, Vsevolod. *Vospominaniia o Dostoevskom*. St. Petersburg, 1881.

Stauffer, Donald. "Genesis, or the Poet as Maker." In *Poets at Work*, edited by Charles D. Abbott. New York: Harcourt Brace, 1948.

Steiner, George. *Tolstoi or Dostoevsky: An Essay in the Old Criticism*. New York: Alfred A. Knopf, 1959.

Taine, Hippolyte. "Cerebral Vibrations and Thought." *Journal of Mental Sciences* 101 (April 1877): 879. Translated from *Revue philosophique de la France et de l'étranger.*

Terras, Victor. *A Karamazov Companion: Commentary on the Genesis, Language, and Style of Dostoevsky's Novel.* Madison: University of Wisconsin Press, 1981.

Tiukhova, Elena Vasil'evna. *Dostoevskii i Turgenev.* Kursk: Kurskii Gosudarstvennyi Pedagogicheskii Institut, 1981.

Todd, William Mills. *Literature and Society in Imperial Russia.* Stanford, Calif.: Stanford University Press, 1978.

Todorov, Tzvetan. *The Fantastic.* Translated by Richard Howard. Middletown, N.Y.: University Press Books, 1973.

Turkevich, Ludmilla B. *Cervantes in Russia.* Princeton, N.J.: Princeton University Press, 1950.

Tynianov, Iurii. *Dostoevskii i Gogol'.* Petrograd: Opoiaz, 1921.

Vetlovskaia, Valentina E. "Ob odnom iz istochnikov *Brat'ev Karamazovykh.*" In *Izvestiia Akademeii Nauk,* seriia literatury i iazyka, vol. 40, 1981, pp. 436–45.

———. "Ritorika i poetika." In *Issledovaniia po poesii i stilistike.* Leningrad: Nauka, 1972, pp. 163–84.

Vil'mont, Nikolai. *Dostoevskii i Shiller.* Moscow: Sovetskii Pisatel', 1984.

Vinogradov, Viktor Vladimirovich. *Evoliutsiia russkogo naturalizma, Gogol' i Dostoevskii.* Leningrad: Akademia, 1929.

———. *Problema avtorstva i teoriia stilei.* Moscow: Gozlitizdat, 1961.

Von Reichenbach, Karl Ludwig. *Der sensitive Mensch.* Vol. 2. Stuttgart: Cotta, 1855.

Vucinich, Alexander. *Darwin in Russian Thought.* Berkeley and Los Angeles: University of California Press, 1988.

Zola, Emile. *Les Rougon-Macquart.* Vol. 1. Paris: Gallimard, 1960.

Studies of the Harriman Institute

Soviet National Income in 1937 by Abram Bergson, Columbia University Press, 1953.

Through the Glass of Soviet Literature: Views of Russian Society, Ernest Simmons Jr., ed., Columbia University Press, 1953.

Polish Postwar Economy by Thad Paul Alton, Columbia University Press, 1954.

Management of the Industrial Firm in the USSR: A Study in Soviet Economic Planning by David Granick, Columbia University Press, 1954.

Soviet Policies in China, 1917–1924 by Allen S. Whiting, Columbia University Press, 1954; paperback, Stanford University Press, 1968.

Literary Politics in the Soviet Ukraine, 1917–1934 by George S. N. Luckyj, Columbia University Press, 1956.

The Emergence of Russian Panslavism, 1856–1870 by Michael Boro Petrovich, Columbia University Press, 1956.

Lenin on Trade Unions and Revolution, 1893–1917 by Thomas Taylor Hammon, Columbia University Press, 1956.

The Last Years of the Georgian Monarchy, 1658–1832 by David Marshall Lang, Columbia University Press, 1957.

The Japanese Thrust into Siberia, 1918 by James William Morley, Columbia University Press, 1957.

Bolshevism in Turkestan, 1917–1927 by Alexander G. Park, Columbia University Press, 1957.

Soviet Marxism: A Critical Analysis by Herbert Marcuse, Columbia University Press, 1958; paperback, Columbia University Press, 1985.

Soviet Policy and the Chinese Communists, 1931–1946 by Charles B. McLane, Columbia University Press, 1958.

The Agrarian Foes of Bolshevism: Promise and Defeat of the Russian Socialist Revolutionaries, February to October 1917 by Oliver H. Radkey, Columbia University Press, 1958.

Pattern for Soviet Youth: A Study of the Congresses of the Komsomol, 1918–1954 by Ralph Talcott Fisher, Jr., Columbia University Press, 1959.

The Emergence of Modern Lithuania by Alfred Erich Senn, Columbia University Press, 1959.

The Soviet Design for a World State by Elliot R. Goodman, Columbia University Press, 1960.

Settling Disputes in Soviet Society: The Formative Years of Legal Institutions by John N. Hazard, Columbia University Press, 1960.

Soviet Marxism and Natural Science, 1917–1932 by David Joravsky, Columbia University Press, 1961.

Russian Classics in Soviet Jackets by Maurice Friedberg, Columbia University Press, 1962.

Stalin and the French Communist Party, 1941–1947 by Alfred J. Rieber, Columbia University Press, 1962.

Sergei Witte and the Industrialization of Russia by Theodore K. Von Laue, Columbia University Press, 1962.

Ukrainian Nationalism by John H. Armstrong, Columbia University Press, 1963.

The Sickle under the Hammer: The Russian Socialist Revolutionaries in the Early Months of Soviet Rule by Oliver H. Radkey, Columbia University Press, 1963.

Comintern and World Revolution, 1928–1943: The Shaping of Doctrine by Kermit E. McKenzie, Columbia University Press, 1964.

Weimar Germany and Soviet Russia, 1926–1933: A Study in Diplomatic Instability by Harvey L. Dyck, Columbia University Press, 1966.

Financing Soviet Schools by Harold J. Noah, Teachers College Press, 1966.

Russia, Bolshevism, and the Versailles Peace by John M. Thompson, Princeton University Press, 1966.

The Russian Anarchists by Paul Avrich, Princeton University Press, 1967.

The Soviet Academy of Sciences and the Communist Party, 1927–1932 by Loren R. Graham, Princeton University Press, 1967.

Red Virgin Soil: Soviet Literature in the 1920's by Robert A. Maguire, Princeton University Press, 1968; paperback, Cornell University Press, 1987.

Communist Party Membership in the U.S.S.R., 1917–1967 by T. H. Rigby, Princeton University Press, 1968.

Soviet Ethics and Morality by Richard T. De George, University of Michigan Press, 1969; paperback, Ann Arbor Paperbacks, 1969.

Vladimir Akimov on the Dilemmas of Russian Marxism, 1895–1903 by Jonathan Frankel, Cambridge University Press, 1969.

Soviet Perspectives on International Relations, 1956–1967 by William Zimmerman, Princeton University Press, 1969.

Kronstadt, 1921 by Paul Avrich, Princeton University Press, 1970.

Class Struggle in the Pale: The Formative Years of the Jewish Workers' Movement in Tsarist Russia by Ezra Mendelsohn, Cambridge University Press, 1970.

The Proletarian Episode in Russian Literature by Edward J. Brown, Columbia University Press, 1971.

Labor and Society in Tsarist Russia: The Factory Workers of St. Petersburg, 1855–1870 by Reginald E. Zelnik, Stanford University Press, 1971.

Archives and Manuscript Repositories in the U.S.S.R.: Moscow and Leningrad by Patricia K. Grimsted, Princeton University Press, 1972.

The Baku Commune, 1917–1918 by Ronald G. Suny, Princeton University Press, 1972.

Mayakovsky: A Poet in the Revolution by Edward J. Brown, Princeton University Press, 1973.

Oblomov and His Creator: The Life and Art of Ivan Goncharov by Milton Ehre, Princeton University Press, 1973.

German Politics under Soviet Occupation by Henry Krisch, Columbia University Press, 1974.

Soviet Politics and Society in the 1970's, Henry W. Morton and Rudolph L. Tokes, eds., Free Press, 1974.

Liberals in the Russian Revolution by William G. Rosenberg, Princeton University Press, 1974.

Famine in Russia, 1891–1892 by Richard G. Robbins, Jr., Columbia University Press, 1975.

In Stalin's Time: Middleclass Values in Soviet Fiction by Vera Dunham, Cambridge University Press, 1976.

The Road to Bloody Sunday by Walter Sablinsky, Princeton University Press, 1976; paperback, Princeton University Press, 1986.

The Familiar Letter as a Literary Genre in the Age of Pushkin by William Mills Todd III, Princeton University Press, 1976.

Russian Realist Art. The State and Society: The Peredvizhniki and Their Tradition by Elizabeth Valkenier, Ardis Publishers, 1977; paperback, Columbia University Press, 1989.

The Soviet Agrarian Debate by Susan Solomon, Westview Press, 1978.

Cultural Revolution in Russia, 1928–1931, Sheila Fitzpatrick, ed., Indiana University Press, 1978; paperback, Midland Books, 1984.

Soviet Criminologists and Criminal Policy: Specialists in Policy-Making by Peter Solomon, Columbia University Press, 1978.

Technology and Society under Lenin and Stalin: Origins of the Soviet Technical Intelligentsia by Kendall E. Bailes, Princeton University Press, 1978.

The Politics of Rural Russia, 1905–1914, Leopold H. Haimson, ed., Indiana University Press, 1979.

Political Participation in the U.S.S.R. by Theodore H. Friedgut, Princeton University Press, 1979; paperback, Princeton University Press, 1982.

Education and Social Mobility in the Soviet Union, 1921–1934 by Sheila Fitzpatrick, Cambridge University Press, 1979.

The Soviet Marriage Market: Mate Selection in Russia and the USSR by Wesley Andrew Fisher, Praeger Publishers, 1980.

Prophecy and Politics: Socialism, Nationalism, and the Russian Jews, 1862–1917 by Jonathan Frankel, Cambridge University Press, 1981.

Dostoevsky and "The Idiot": Author, Narrator, and Reader by Robin Feuer Miller, Harvard University Press, 1981.

Moscow Workers and the 1917 Revolution by Diane Koenker, Princeton University Press, 1981; paperback, Princeton University Press, 1986.

Archives and Manuscript Repositories in the USSR: Estonia, Latvia, Lithuania, and Belorussia by Patricia K. Grimsted, Princeton University Press, 1981.

Zionism in Poland: The Formative Years, 1915–1926 by Ezra Mendelsohn, Yale University Press, 1982.

Soviet Risk-Taking and Crisis Behavior by Hannes Adomeit, George Allen & Unwin Publishers, 1982.

Russia at the Crossroads: The 26th Congress of the CPSU, Seweryn Bialer and Thane Gustafson, eds., George Allen & Unwin Publishers, 1982.

The Crisis of the Old Order in Russia: Gentry and Government by Roberta Thompson Manning, Princeton University Press, 1983; paperback, Princeton University Press, 1986.

Sergei Aksakov and Russian Pastoral by Andrew A. Durkin, Rutgers University Press, 1983.

Politics and Technology in the Soviet Union by Bruce Parrott, MIT Press, 1983.

The Soviet Union and the Third World: An Economic Bind by Elizabeth Kridl Valkenier, Praeger Publishers, 1983.

Russian Metaphysical Romanticism: The Poetry of Tiutchev and Boratynskii by Sarah Pratt, Stanford University Press, 1984.

Ruling Russia: Politics and Administration in the Age of Absolutism, 1762–1796 by John LeDonne, Princeton University Press, 1984.

Insidious Intent: A Structural Analysis of Fedor Sologub's Petty Demon by Diana Greene, Slavica Publishers, 1986.

Leo Tolstoy: Resident and Stranger by Richard Gustafson, Princeton University Press, 1986.

Workers, Society, and the State: Labor and Life in Moscow, 1918–1929 by William Chase, University of Illinois Press, 1987.

Andrey Bely: Spirit of Symbolism, John Malmstad, ed., Cornell University Press, 1987.

Government and Peasant in Russia, 1861–1906: The Prehistory of the Stolypin Reforms by David A. J. Macey, Northern Illinois University Press, 1987.

The Making of Three Russian Revolutionaries: Voices from the Menshevik Past, Leopold H. Haimson, ed., in collaboration with Ziva Galili y Garcia and Richard Wortman, Cambridge University Press, 1988.

Revolution and Culture: The Bogdanov-Lenin Controversy by Zenovia A. Sochor, Cornell University Press, 1988.

A Handbook of Russian Verbs by Frank Miller, Ardis Publishers, 1989.

1905 in St. Petersburg: Labor, Society, and Revolution by Gerald D. Surh, Stanford University Press, 1989.

INDEX

Absurdity, 128–29
Aesthetic, classical, 6; realistic, 6–7; romantic, 7
Affect, chief displacements of, 6
Aglaia Epanchina: parallel with Lize Xoxlakova, 94
Aksakov, Sergei, 97–98, 101
Alesha Karamazov, 80–81, 83, 86, 89–109, 137, 140, 143, 148, 151, 156, 160; encounter with the Devil, 133; link to unwritten works, 48–49; parallels in *Père Goriot*, 37; and the place of history in life, 36–37; remembering his brother, 82
—Sources of: Alesha Dostoevsky, 54, 101; Christa, 108; Medardus, 103; Myshkin, 51, 95–96, 103; in unwritten works, 50
Alesha (peasant's son), 103
Alternatives as sequence, 70
Amnesia: personal experience of, 78–79; as theme, 77–78
Anatomy of seeing: analogy to creating, 161
Antonovich, M. A., 21, 124
"Apology for Raymond Sebond" (Montaigne), 120
Argumentum ad hominem, 132
Arkadii (*The Raw Youth*), 98–99, 101
Aristotle, 7
Atheism (unwritten work), 49, 164
Automatism and Suggestion (Bernheim), 77
Averkiev, Dmitrii Vasilevich, 134–36

Bakhtin, M. M., 128
Ballin: relation to Herzen, 147–48
Balzac, Honoré de, 16
Bazarov, 47
Belinskii, Vissarion G., 23, 81, 122–23, 130, 154, 164; as source for Kolia, 153
Belot, Adolphe, 18
Belov, Sergei V., 23, 147
Bem, A. L., 17
Benignorance, 142
Beranger, Pierre-Jean de, 32

Bernard, Claude, 75, 140; attacks on, 34
Bernard Mauprat, 69; parallel with Mitia, 67
Bernheim, Henri, 77, 78
Bible, the, 19–21, 156; Book of Job, 137; as literary source, 121; Esau story, 65; Genesis, 117; as source for Alesha, 108
Bloom, Harold, 2
Böhme, Jakob, 21
Botkin, V. P., 130, 154
Braid, James, 76
Byron, Lord George Gordon, 32

"Carmina Burana," 120
"Cerebral Vibrations and Thought" (Taine), 75
Charcot, Jean-Martin, 76
Chernyshevskii, N. G., 75, 150
Children: as center of a novel, 95; suffering of, 114, 117, 128–29
Christ: and the Grand Inquisitor, 115–16, 138–39; as source for Alesha, 108
"Christ in the Vatican" (Cabantous), 120
Chudak, Alesha as, 92–93
Chulkov, Georgii, 153
Citizen (periodical), 52
Classical aesthetic, 6–7
Classical philology, 2
Classics, 22–25
Coleridge, Samuel Taylor, 5
Condensation: in character of Alesha, 101
Confession d'une jeune fille (Sand), 18
Confession d'un enfant du siècle (Musset), 18, 27
Confessions (Rousseau), 27
Conservation laws: of figurativeness, 106–7; of literary matter, 65, 113, 119; of sources, 103. *See also* Laws, literary
Contemporary (periodical), 143
Contrast: between desirable and true, 117; between ideological intent and